COMMUNICATION IN *IT* AGE

COMMUNICATION IN *IT* AGE

DHIRAJ SHARMA
Sr. Lecturer
Regional Institute of Management & Technology,
Mandi Gobindgarh (Punjab)

Himalaya Publishing House
MUMBAI • NEW DELHI • NAGPUR • BENGALURU • HYDERABAD • CHENNAI • PUNE
LUCKNOW • AHMEDABAD • ERNAKULAM • BHUBANESWAR • INDORE • KOLKATA

First Edition : 2004
Reprint : 2010

Published by : Mrs. Meena Pandey
for **HIMALAYA PUBLISHING HOUSE PVT. LTD.,**
"Ramdoot", Dr. Bhalerao Marg, Girgaon, **Mumbai - 400 004.**
Phones: 2386 01 70/2386 38 63, Fax: 022-2387 71 78
Email: himpub@vsnl.com
Website: www.himpub.com

Branch Offices:

New Delhi : "Pooja Apartments", 4-B, Murari Lal Street, Ansari Road, Darya Ganj, **New Delhi - 110 002.** Phone: 23270392, 23278631 Fax: 011-23256286

Nagpur : Kundanlal Chandak Industrial Estate, Ghat Road, **Nagpur - 440 018.** Phone: 2738731, 3296733 Telefax : 0712-2721215

Bengaluru : No. 16/1 (Old 12/1), 1st Floor, Next to Hotel Highlands, Madhava Nagar, Race Course Road, **Bengaluru - 560 001.** Phone : 22281541, 22385461, Telefax: 080-22286611

Hyderabad : No. 3-4-184, Lingampally, Besides Raghavendra Swamy Matham,Kachiguda, **Hyderabad - 500 027.** Phone: 040-27560041, 27550139, Mobile:- 09848130433 Telefax: 040-27560041

Chennai : No. 85/50, Bazullah Road, T. Nagar, **Chennai - 600 017.** Phone: 044-28344020, 32463737, 42124860

Pune : No. 527, "Laksha" Apartment, First Floor, Mehunpura, Shaniwarpeth, (Near Prabhat Theatre), **Pune - 411 030.** Phone: 020-24496323/24496333/32326733

Lucknow : C-43, Sector - C, Ali Gunj, **Lucknow - 226 024.** Phone: 0522-2339329, 4068914

Ahmedabad : No. 114, "SHAIL", 1st Floor, Opp. Madhu Sudan House, C.G.Road, Navrang Pura, **Ahmedabad – 380 009.** Phone: 079-26560126, Mobiles: 09327324149,09314679413

Ernakulam : No. 39/104 A, Lakshmi Apartment, Karikkamuri Cross Rd., Ernakulam, **Cochin – 682011**, Kerala. Phone: 0484-2378012, 2378016, Mob.: 09344199799

Bhubaneswar : 5 Station Square, **Bhubaneswar (Orissa) - 751 001.** Mobile: 9861046007, E-mail:- orissa@himpub.com

Indore : Kesardeep Avenue Extension, 73, Narayan Bagh.Flat No. 302, IIIrd Floor, Near Humpty Dumpty School, Narayan Bagh, **Indore (M.P.) 452 007** Mobile: 09301386468

Kolkata : 108/4, Beliaghata, Main Road, Near ID Hospital, Opp. SBI Bank **Kolkata - 700 010.** Mobile: 09910440956, E-mail:- nkmitra@himpub.com

Printed by : Shri Krishna offset Press Delhi-93

DEDICATION

This small piece of work is dedicated to :
my father ***Shri R.L. Sharma,***
a Mentor, a Guru, and a Friend in true sense.
What I am today is due to Him.

PREFACE

There is no doubt that technology is an important aspect of the communication environment. Today's Communication Age centres on the technical evolution of electronic Information Technology (IT). The invention of telegraph brought a revolution in communications by transmitting information in electrical form instantly to distant locations. This new phenomenon of instant information was later expanded by the telephone, radio and television. Then the digital electronic computer revolutionised the generation and processing of information. Business transactions that were formerly recorded, compiled, and sorted laboriously by hand are now processed by the computer in the twinkling of an eye. As the computer developed and matured, communication and processing technologies were joined into networks that now stretch around the world, affecting all areas of global society. Now people have their own personal workstations and powerful home computers. The average computer a person might have in his home is more powerful by several orders of magnitude than an old super computer like ENIAC. The computer revolution has been proved to be the fastest growing technology in man's history. Although the marriage of Communication and IT is built around this technical theme, its emphasis is equally relevant on social change. The transformations in information technology came in the context of social forces such as business, politics, culture etc. The present text highlights the interaction between human communication and the development of information technology. To gain proficiency in communication today, without a sound knowledge of IT and familiarization with its tools and techniques, would be much difficult, if not impossible.

Communication in IT age is written to help Business Communication and IT students in understanding the basic theories and postulates concerning these two diverse fields. Present text focuses on the technological changes that are revolutionizing business communication. The efforts have been made to integrate our conventional understanding of Business Communication with the growing knowledge of Information Technology. The field of information technology is also extensively discussed in the present book. It is worth mentioning here that no formal qualification in Communication or IT is required to understand the contents of this book. Starting with an introductory chapter, the book goes on to cover all the basic and technical details of Communication and IT. Simple-to-understand and user-friendly approach has been followed throughout the text.

This book can be used by students of business management, commerce, computer science, engineering and in general as well. The present text also serves as a course book for many degree and diploma courses being run by various colleges and universities. In a nutshell, present book is useful for everyone who is curious about Business Communication or Information Technology.

A book of this type naturally gained a number of ideas from the previous books, magazines, and articles on these two subjects. I express my gratitude to all these authors, too numerous to acknowledge individually. I am indebted to Mr. D. P. Pandey of Himalaya Publishing House without whose efforts and special interest in this project, the book would not have been possible in its present shape. I owe special thanks to my brother Mr. Neeraj Sharma, Faculty – Computer Science, Punjabi University, Patiala, who continues to provide a sounding board for new ideas and technical support.

Although every effort has been made to make this book simple and understandable, it is still no novel. There would be mistakes that have inadvertently crept in and I owe up to them. Suggestions, criticism, and views of the readers are welcome in this regard.

Dhiraj Sharma

dhiraj2001@indiatimes.com

CONTENTS

PART A

INTRODUCTION

1

Communication In IT Age

INTRODUCTION

To some, this is the atomic age; for some it is the computer age; to others, the information age and if it is to be information age then it can better be called Communication Age as information has no meaning in itself if it is not to be communicated. Today, we are all deeply involved in the Communication Age. In fact, it will be more accurate to say that we are in a communication revolution. Every day we are, not surprisingly, witnessing innovations and technological advancements pacing up the developments in communication and its methods.

The human history, can be seen to fit patterns. The pattern takes the shape of three great advances or waves. The first wave of transformation began when some prescient person about 10,000 years ago planted a seed and nurtured its growth. The age of agriculture began, and its significance was that people moved away from wandering and hunting and began to cluster into villages and develop culture. The second wave came in the shape of machines, the Industrial Revolution began in the 18th century, and people began to leave the peasant culture of farming to come to work in the urban factories. It culminated in the Second World War and the explosion of the atomic bombs. Just after this, we began to receive intimations of a gathering third wave, based not on 'machine power' but on 'mind power.' It is what we variously call the communication or the information or the knowledge age, and it is powerfully driven by information technology.

Technological changes in the area of communication significantly increased in the nineteenth century but even before that telegraph connected through wires provided the biggest channel for written communication. After that, with the invention of various writing machines there was a vast improvement in the quality, quantity and speed of written communication. With the advancement of printing techniques, communication among the literate masses became a simple matter. Great revolutions and struggles for freedom in all over the world could involve the masses because of speedy and efficient communication.

All this we can say started with the invention of printing, which can be termed as the First Phase of technological advancements in the area of communication. In the early 19th century, with the power press printing, the daily newspaper took birth. The Second Phase brought the inventions of the telegraph, the telephone and photography and that also in the 19th century. Along with this followed phonograph, movie camera and projector, all the contributions by the Great Thomas Edison. With this now it was possible to store sound and moving pictures.

In 1907, with the invention of the triode vacuum tube by DeForest, radio and television changed the scenario. The pace of development sharply increased with the invention and later on wide use of Radio, Television, and Electronic Typewriter. All these technological advancements led to the Third Phase of revolution in communication. Radio was considered as the extension of the ear as the print media as the extension of human eye. So, altogether a new world was taking shape with the inventions of first printing media then phonograph, camera, movies and later on launching of television — all this was a big turning point in communication.

These improvements in the area of communication gave birth to the Conventional Office i.e. office run by an executive with the help of a secretary using most recent technology taking care of all the office work like typing, filing, storing information, generating reports, attending customers, telephone calls and other routine work. The major characteristic of the conventional office was that all the data and information processing was, in fact, paper processing which is just opposite of our present IT based office which can be termed as a Paperless Office. (This concept was widely predicted to arrive in the 1980s but never materialized. The prospects are better in the present decade).

The Third Phase of modern communication climaxed only in the 20th century. Computers brought tremendous changes in the way we use information and communicate. The development of intelligent information systems and decision support systems attempt to endow machines with the intelligence found in human beings. Expert Systems help the decision maker in taking right and logical decisions but now the efforts are being made to replace the decision maker (Artificial Intelligence) with an intelligent machine where the chances of wrong decisions are negligible. We can say all this is the dawn of the Fourth Phase.

In this 21st century, where the world has become a small globe — multi-media, paging, cellular telephony, Internet, Satellite communication, cable media, DTH (Direct to Home promising hundred of channels on TV) etc. have changed the pattern of our thinking and our style of living. Miracles of communication technology! Although to McLuhan, a great sociologist, all the media are 'the extensions of man' for him the world is now a small village — a global village. He says[1]. "The speed of information in the global village means that every human action or event involves everybody in the village in the consequences of every event." It means a very small world as all are closely knit together with the strong media of communication and technology.

Today, a business executive in his technologically equipped office is privileged with the strongest means of communication and the latest information. The conventional office served as the basis for the origin and development of today's, what we can name it, perhaps, most suitably is the, **IT office** and that in turn has given the biggest boom to improved communication in organisations. IT office i.e. office supported by the latest information and communication technology, knows no boundaries national or international, an executive sitting in the IT office is

1. McLuhan, M; (1967), Understanding Media: The Extensions of Man. London: Sphere.

connected through the latest IT means with the entire world and has access to all types of data and information whether written, verbal or in some visual format. Not only accessing or retrieving information rather the whole gamut of today's business can be managed promptly sitting on the executive chair in the office. Facsimile Transmission, Electronic mail, Teleconferencing, Video conferencing, Multimedia, Collaborative computing, LAN/WAN, Voice recognition devices, Virtual reality and such other numerous channels have empowered today's executive to communicate in the best manner in this IT age.

NATURE OF INFORMATION TECHNOLOGY

Information technology has become a strategic decision as it requires a huge outlay of funds that is critical to many organisations. It affects all the levels of management and overall functioning of the organisation and could mean a revolution for various information systems. The other side of implementing IT can also not be ignored, that is the danger of too much automation in the concern may pose threat to many jobs. In a survey to judge the impact of IT on organisations, following are the main concerns for business executives:

- Managing the Information System and its development
- Justifying the cost of new systems
- Getting substantial benefits from IT
- Transformation of data into useful information for management
- Staff resistance
- Involvement of senior managers and political factors
- Backing up vital information for reliability and integration of databases
- Keeping information about the latest trends and developments in IT
- Planning technology upgradation
- Availability and attitude of IT professionals
- Taking care of legal, audit and other regulatory requirements

INFORMATION TECHNOLOGY IN INDIA

India has emerged as a global power in the Information Technology (IT) as one of the largest generators and exporters of software in the world. In India, the software industry is, perhaps, the fastest growing sector with a growth rate exceeding 50% over the last five years and with a turnover of US $8.2 billion and exports of US$ 6.2 billion during the year 2000-2001. The government has targeted an export of US$ 50 billion by the year 2008 for the software industry[2]. This would require focused initiatives to accelerate the Internet revolution in India, emphasizing the creation of useful contents in Indian languages, IT enabled services, IT education, electronics and computer hardware manufacturing, and exports, E-commerce and Internet based E-Business. The Indian software professionals have already created their brand image in the global market. Today, more than 260 of the Fortune 1000 companies, i.e. , almost

---

2. Data used here is taken from the Annual Report 2000-01, issued by Ministry of Information Technology, Govt. of India.

one out of every four global giants, outsource their software requirements to India. India has a distinct standing in the world market for providing excellent quality. A large number of Indian software companies have acquired international quality certification. It is important to note that 20 out of 37 companies in the world, who have acquired the highest quality standard for software practices are located in India. Majority of the multi-national companies operating in the area of IT have either Software Development Centre or Research Development Centre in India. Today, one of the biggest Indian economy's natural resources is it's abundant technically skilled manpower. India has the second largest pool of English-speaking scientific professionals in the world today, second only to the US. As on 31 December 2000, the software industry in India employed about 4,10,000 professionals.

In order to give a concerted and focused approach to developing this sector further, the Government set up a new Ministry of Information Technology on 15 October 1999 to be the nodal institutional mechanism for facilitating all the initiatives in the central government, the state governments, academia and the private sector for all round growth of IT. The ministry seeks to play the role of a pro-active facilitator, motivator and promoter and launch initiatives to ensure the spread of IT to the masses for enabling speedy IT-led development. Government policy is to encourage both software development and hardware manufacturing in the country by creating an appropriate environment. The government has also recommended that each ministry must allocate 2-3 per cent of its budget for IT promotion. This is a step for the development of domestic software industry and a move towards integrating IT with government functioning and e-governance.

A Long Way To Go

India does have built-in advantages: a thriving private sector, an impressive technology track-record, a high-skilled managerial manpower pool, a robust (though a little unwieldy) legal system and a highly comfortable comprehensibility in the English language. But India's disadvantages can be glaring too, as brought out by the Booz-Allen study of 2001. Although the telecom networks are among the country's fastest growing infrastructure, they are neither well developed nor dependable yet. India's Internet usage continues to be sluggish, at less than 1 million. India's PC population is 4.5 million, making it only 4 per 1,000 people.

If India is to be both a driver and a beneficiary in the IT outsourcing world, it is time to get aggressive: by launching new IT education programmes, making a paradigm shift in technology, and using its skilled work force in a cost-effective manner.

INFORMATION TECHNOLOGY IN BUSINESS COMMUNICATION

(1) Role of Computers in Business Correspondence

Computers are widely used for drafting business letters. Software provides numerous functions for editing, printing and storing of documents. Computer software has been developed that checks writing for corrections as well as for certain principles of style. Computers, word processing provides following different functions for the user and it also provides analyses of work with suggestions for improvement.

(a) **Spelling checkers**: Spelling checkers are word-processing programs which are very useful in finding and correcting spelling mistakes in a document. Earlier they used to come separately but nowadays they are an integral part of a word-processing program. Spelling checkers contain dictionary words so whenever the user uses a word which is not present in its database, it indicates an error, and user can decide whether to change the word according to given options by the computer program or to leave the word unchanged.

(b) Language checkers: Not only the spellings or words of a document can be checked but the language of the document can also be corrected. Today, several programs have been developed for checking the errors of punctuation, grammar, comma etc. These programs can also check a variety of other errors, for example wrong use of abbreviations and quotation marks, space before or after punctuation marks, capitalization, repeated words, and incorrectly expressed numbers (such as Rs.10, 80.75).

It is quite obvious that a computer program cannot detect all the errors and moreover, it cannot be 100 per cent accurate, as the developers cannot codify all the rules of language. Even then these programs are very useful as they point out possible errors in a document and the user can decide the action from given options.

(c) Variety of business letters databases: Although not common in India, a variety of model business letters are available for use with computers. These come in the shape of CDs (Compact Disks) or in floppy disks. These databases cover almost every type of business letters which are required in routine for example sales letters, collection letters, reminders for dues, promotion letters etc. The user can call up the letter for the situation he is facing and then adapt the letter to the specific situation.

Such letters save time and they are professionally designed using appropriate words justifying the situation. Even if a letter does not contain the exact wording required by the user, it gives some idea about the format and presentability. These databases are not easily available and most of them are poor in quality, although this limitation will be overcome in time. The biggest drawback of these ready-made letters is that they lack individuality and originality.

(2) Computer Networks

Through communication links, computer systems at different locations can be connected together, which enables free flow of information and data. Computer networks or Wide area networks are used by large corporations having operations at many distant locations; different business organisations forming trading partners; and universities or government institutions — to exchange data, share hardware, software and data resources. Electronic Data Interchange (EDI) is the name given to the exchange of structured data between the computer systems of trading partners. It is predicted that this method of 'paperless' trading will revolutionise the way companies do business. EDI covers trade data interchange (invoices, purchase orders, acknowledgements, delivery instructions, etc), product data interchange (CAD/CAM, engineering design, etc), interactive enquiry/confirmation messages, and electronic funds transfer. EDI is now being implemented, nationally and internationally, for organisations of every size in many different business sectors, including retail, manufacturing, commerce, transport and shipping.

EDI speeds up the trading cycle, enabling a faster response to customer orders and requests. In addition, by using agreed message (or data exchange) standards, EDI simplifies the customer's data processing task by accurately supplying only that minimum amount of data that is required by the customer. In addition to document printing and mailing cost savings, the effort required for verifying and keying outgoing and particularly incoming documentation, such as invoices, is unnecessary. Shorter order, delivery and payment cycles imply lower stock levels, the release of valuable capital and improved cash flow. 'Just-in-time' manufacturing relies on a close link between the manufacturer, the supplier and the customer. EDI forges this link by providing the timely and accurate information required on a daily basis, whilst promoting the trust and commitment required on a long-term basis. EDI software packages are now available for handling incoming and outgoing data and for linking to internal company applications.

(3) Facsimile Transmission

FAX transmission allows exact copies of the text as well as pictures to be sent in a few seconds from one machine to another anywhere in the world- via telephone lines or satellite. The quality of duplication has improved greatly in the last few years and will likely continue to get better. A FAX copy of a document is as legally binding as the original.

The time advantage of sending something by FAX rather than through the mail is obvious, but FAX transmission is also replacing the older telex transmission, which can send only words. It is costlier than the mail, but since saved time usually means saved money, the increase in FAX use has been dramatic and will no doubt continue. This facility is becoming very popular commercially with more than two million machines sold worldwide. In certain business sectors the facsimile machine is as indispensable as the photocopier.

(4) Teletex

Teletex is a recent text transmission facility which offers transmission speeds up to thirty times faster than Telex. Users operate Teletex over public communication networks. Teletex offers point-to-point communication between terminals such as electronic typewriters, word processors and suitably equipped PCs. It offers document transfer with a high degree of accuracy and speed (one A4 page can be sent in about 20 seconds), and 24- hour service with unattended receipt of messages (as with Telex).

(5) Photocopiers

In addition to electronic typewriters, word processors, and personal computers, other technological developments have affected business communication practices in the IT office.

Since 1960s, photocopiers applying the technique of xerography (a process for copying printed material) have become one of the most widespread reproduction technologies. Almost in every big/medium business house we can see a photocopier. A photocopier or copy machine reproduces the original document without changing or deteriorating the contents of the original document. Photocopiers are also preferred for mass duplications. Modern copying machines differ in size and capacity. Some are small enough to be hand carried. The larger ones are immobile but may reduce or expand original pages and documents, edit them, duplicate both sides automatically, and produce multiple copies with great speed.

(6) Telephones

The telephone was one of the early revolutionary technological developments that influenced the nature of human communication. Today's telephone equipment contains re-dialling, number storing, call-waiting, and other features for the electronic office. Moreover, the idea of combining voice (analog) and data (digital) transmission capability using telephone technology has significant potential for business communication. The development of mobile telephone-the cellular telephone- has been an especially significant achievement. This was developed by AT&T in 1946, cellular telephones allow the mobility to the users to communicate from wherever they are instantly, at any time of the day or night. The mobile telephone carries messages via regular telephone lines. Large city areas are divided into smaller geographical sub-areas called 'cells'. These cells are connected to one another through sub-area antennas, transmitters, and individually assigned frequencies. As vehicles move from one cell to another, a computer transfers a call automatically to successively adjacent cells without the caller's or receiver's awareness. Because the calls originate and end in cells, the transfers among cells can be accomplished through telephone rather than radio transmission. Voice quality is maintained throughout each conversation.

Mobile telephone has changed the business communication environment as this allows instantaneous communication with improved quality and quantity of information. In India, still the equipment and operating costs are high compared to conventional calling.

(7) Microfilm

Today, for various types of business presentations or conferences microfilms are used widely. A microfilm is a narrow photographic film (usually 35mm or 16 mm wide) on which various types of data and information can be stored and retrieved. The typical procedure with microfilming involves photographing only one or two pages of a book, journal article or other document on a single frame. As for newspapers, one page can be photographed on a single frame.

Official documents, production plans, sales charts, equipment and machine details, important events, graphs and pictures can be stored on microfilm. It is very convenient for the user as the contents of a fairly long document can be stored on a small film. The contents can be read by, or shown to, participants in a group conference through the microfilm reader. The images are directly projected on the reader-screen and photocopies can be produced as paper prints or projectable transparencies.

(8) Viewdata

Viewdata has become a familiar public information service as well as finding use in the travel, motor, insurance and banking trades. The attraction of Viewdata is its ease of use, particularly where users have minimal computer or technical literacy. Use is made of colour displays and graphics. A domestic colour television set fitted with a suitable adaptor can be used to provide a low-cost terminal into the service. Alternatively the facility can be used as a dedicated Videotex terminal or as a PC with Viewdata software. In a Viewdata system the vast amounts of data are stored on the host computer as pages. Users follow a routing from one index page (menu) to another until the required page of information is reached. On the Viewdata terminal, information is presented in character frames divided into a number of rows and columns; e.g. Prestel, developed by British Telecom, uses 24 rows and 40 columns. Each character position can be occupied by either an alphabetic or numeric character or by a graphic mosaic cell used to construct chunky graphics.

(9) CDs, DVDs, Floppy Disks and Zip Disks

In addition to or in place of traditional methods of storing of information and data today several new devices have emerged which not only store a large amount of data on a very small media but ensure the security and safety of data. Audiotapes and videotapes were commonly used but they are being replaced by CDs (Compact Disks), DVDs (Digital Video Disks), Floppy Disks and Zip disks. These devices, however, are very expensive in India.

(10) Teleconferencing and Videoconferencing

This technology ranges from simple text based communication through audio conferencing, through still pictures to full motion video. This acts as a substitute for face-to-face meetings by providing simultaneous video images of meeting participants, along with a two-way voice transmission. Besides transmitting their images and voices, the participants may also present charts, graphs or other material. Teleconferencing or Videoconferencing or any other form, all the variants of this technology make use of wide area communications networks, each using progressively more capacity from the wide area network with correspondingly higher costs:

Computer Teleconferencing or also known as Text-based Teleconferencing as it uses a personal computer together with a modem, telephone line, and appropriate software.

Audio or Voice based Teleconferencing uses telephone facilities similar to those used for the common conference call (often likewise called a conference call).

Autographic Teleconferencing uses audio exchanges and limited video or graphic visual support (conference call plus still pictures).

Video-based Teleconferencing uses equipment that allows participants to see as well as speak to one another.

(11) E-mail

With the internet coming into existence, it is now extremely simple and convenient to communicate across the globe and world wide, by sitting at home, anywhere in the world, any time of the day or night and the name of this Inter-active communication facility across computers is known as E-mail or Electronic Mail. Therefore, e-mail proposes nothing less than almost instant written communication between computer terminals. The term *E-mail* usually refers to internal mail sent from computer to computer by linked networks. E-mail is becoming increasingly popular day by day. It has been estimated that 40 million people use e-mail in the US but unfortunately this number is negligible in the case of India.

Electronic mail services (e-mail) can be set up over wide area networks for use in providing a private (within one organisation) or public messaging service. The user of this service is able to prepare messages locally and send the resultant messages via a network of other users. Equally the user is able to receive messages. Messages are stored in a user's mailbox which is simply an allocated area of storage on the host computer where the mail software resides. Each user has password control over access to his mailbox. Messages can be read or updated by the mailbox holder and transmitted to other users if required. The basic ingredients typically required to access an electronic mail service comprise a terminal, modem, telephone line and relevant access authority.

It's benefits are many

- Without any delay or time lag, the transmission of the message is instant.
- Facilitates frequent communication between the sender and the receiver, messages can go back and forth quickly, reducing the need for meetings and telephoning.

- It has the ability to deliver information fast to an enormous amount of people.
- Substantially cuts the costs of internal mail.
- It is a form of written communication so it is more reliable and can serve as a legal or binding document.
- E-mails can be sent anytime, without any problem and costs of differing time zones.

E-mail suffers from some demerits also

- Both the parties communicating must have the access to computers.
- Small firms cannot afford computers, their installation and maintenance so not cost effective.
- After sending an e-mail we are no longer in control of the effects of the message and can only wait in suspense.
- Receivers have to wade through a lot of junk and undesirable mails, since it's so easy to send messages everywhere.
- Reading off a screen is more difficult and slower than reading printouts.
- Long messages that go beyond a single screen (still less than a page) pose particular difficulty.
- It requires frequent access of Internet.
- Senders many times send off unnecessary or damaging messages, without thinking their impact on the reader.
- E-mails may contain viruses.

(12) Message Handling Service

One of the limitations of current electronic mail services is that mailboxes can only be reached by users of the same service. The CCITT X.400 Message Handling Service is currently being introduced by the majority of PTTs in Western Europe and the United States, will provide a link between public and private electronic mail services. It will provide worldwide, vendor-independent, open systems interconnection for millions of users of messaging services, stand-alone terminals and personal computers.

(13) Voice Mail

Sometimes called voice processing, voice mail is a telephone answering system, in which the caller leaves a message in a 'mailbox,' rather than having to speak directly to the receiver. It's advantages are:

The same message can be routed to several people at once; the service is readily available and unlike e-mail receivers do not need a computer, but only a touch-tone phone. It reduces the time and effort needed to send brief routine messages.

As with E-mail, the receiver may delay or forget to review the messages, and the sender will never know. Voice mail has some disadvantages also:

Listening to a message is much slower than reading it. Callers are more likely to be unfocused or unclear if the message is long. Many people ramble or do not enunciate clearly.

(14) E-commerce

Thanks to the Internet for the electronification of commerce and business. E-commerce can be defined as business or commercial interaction via computers using the Internet. It is also defined as shopping via the Internet. Actually, it is much more than mere interaction or shopping. From a communications, perspective, electronic commerce is the delivery of information, products/services, or payments via telephone lines, computer networks, or any other means. E-commerce or Electronic Commerce is a generic term that refers to the combinations of all commercial or business transactions executed over the network of computers for the exchange of money, commodity or service between the buyers and the sellers. It covers national and international funds and data transfer for commercial transactions. E-commerce provides the facility to the buyer to buy a commodity or service via the Internet and pay through a bank that is electronically linked to the buyer and which informs either side with debit/credit information through the computer. E-commerce facilitates business not only in one's area but also nationally and internationally. E-commerce has a wider scope; it is not mere buying or selling through Internet. It involves online transaction of information, money and monetary instruments for international banking and financial institutions. It is helpful to modern corporations in several ways. The needs of international banks and bank consortiums are met through global networks.

BUSINESS COMMUNICATION THROUGH THE INTERNET

These days Internet has become an effective medium for business communication. The Internet is a collection of networks—a network of networks—that communicates with each other by using the same standards (protocols) of communication. Users access the Internet by contacting a computer that connects to the Net. It is a set of some 50,000 interconnected networks supporting over five million computers in over 80 countries. Currently, the number of users is around 20 million, yet the growth rate continues at 10-15 per cent per month.

Internet being an invaluable source of information plays a vital role in E-commerce and business negotiations. It is also true that in a country like India this source is underutilized and due to unawareness its use is not very common and easy. But those who are blessed to use this facility are making their business smooth and easy. Now, sitting in the office, saving time, money and avoiding botheration of travelling, negotiations can be made through the Internet. Choice of a mutual place is no more a headache. Negotiations can be more realistic now as the executive has complete access to office, secretary, files and any other material required for discussion. (However, benefits of face-to-face negotiations are there, personal and direct contact with the people is always appreciated and beneficial for business.) The Internet provides business executives with up-to-date information on competition, buyer's changing demands, technological changes and a lot of market updates.

	Industrial Age	IT Age
Business firms	Narrow Approach	Broader Vision
Buyers	Limited Access to manufacturer	Direct and all time access to manufacturer
Markets	'Narrow Size and Limited Customer Base	Global market and International Customer Base
Suppliers	Relationship based on Proximity	Digital Relationship
Inter-mediaries	Separate organisations	Closely Linked Sub-systems
Employees	Formal and Rigid Managerial Control	Functionally diversed and Result oriented teams

Fig. 1.1 : Information Technology Business Model

Other benefits through 'Net-Negotiations' to the communicating parties are all those possible advantages which we think of the written communication (other than chatting or conversation through PC phone). One considerable benefit through the Internet is that the receiver of the e-mail views the message as legal or binding document. That implies written statements will be taken more seriously and thoroughly especially if they contain some sensitive issue.

The promptness in making quick decisions is always considered as a positive management skill, so normally the main consideration is the need to reply as soon as possible. Net communication provides this ease also, e-mail on the net is easy and fast so there is tendency to respond immediately without taking unnecessary time to prepare well. In fact, numerous e-commerce manuals recommend replying within 48 hours. For some business transactions, replying within 48 hours may be too long while for others it could be too short.

Still payment and security are sensitive issues requiring serious assessment before responding, particularly when such requests are from unfamiliar markets or unknown parties.

Business on the net is no different from face-to-face deals in the sense that both require planning, preparation, patience, understanding people, needs of the other party, good motivational skills and decision making capabilities. It is very important to give due consideration to incoming and outgoing message and at the same time assessment of the impact of the message on the parties concerned. If the sender requires more time before replying, an interim message can be sent. It is good business practice to have open communication lines with dealing parties, while taking time to prepare and think well for upcoming business. Net communication can also be used as a supplement to face to face communication like making arrangements for face to face negotiations, such as travel bookings, fixing the agenda, selecting a location, agreeing on the number of people participating in the meeting and so on. The net is also expedient when negotiating a repeat order or a small transaction, which does not justify an investment in time, personnel and financial resources. Until e-commerce is fully integrated in the global economy and management is committed to this new form of doing business by restructuring their processes, executives should combine face-to-face interaction with Net-communication.

Finally, it will not be an exaggeration to say that nothing could have changed communication in modern business more dramatically than advances in technology. Changes in communication have, from time to time, enabled the business organisation to cope with the dynamic demands of the modern business environment. And surely we can say that changes in the communication world are not over, rather they will continue in the present and in the future also because of advancements in the technology. So, therefore, the subject matter of organisational communication cannot be discussed without taking into consideration the impact technological innovations have on the approach we are accustomed to. On these lines each chapter of this book is incorporated.

DOWNSIDE OF INFORMATION TECHNOLOGY

IT cannot be used to simply automate the procedures currently used in organisations. Of course, the expectation is that the changes will have considerable benefits, but these will often be felt only in the long or medium term. Commonly, the short term impact on the organisation and its profit is negative, as investment is undertaken, new procedures are drawn, and disruption occurs to the existing routine.

The impacts on employees are almost inevitably significant. Many people currently in the workforce have not been well conditioned for change by their education and training, and are not mentally well prepared for it. Employee's work-patterns, and the skills required of them, may be quite different from those that have been conventional. Capabilities in relation to computers and communications are vital. The conventional approach of deferring particular kind of transactions, and processing them occasionally in batches, may be replaced by on-demand handling of customers' needs. There may also be impact on working-hours such as timings beyond the traditional 9am-5pm time frame to give extended customer service. The location at which the work is performed may also change, with more performed on customer's site, or at home. All this is more relevant in the case of Indian work culture.

Not only this, these changes can result in major impacts on organisational structure as well. Increasingly, the primary focus is on business processes, and the hierarchy of managers and supervisors is being regarded as less important. In other words machines are more important than humans. Also, in any business organisation, the real possibility exists that information technologies can and will be misused and abused. New communication channels and computer capabilities provide opportunities for some people to use technology in ways not intended or even anticipated by the system's designers. So, technology has its dangers too. Laudon and Laudon[3] explains the risks of new information technology as " ...it will also be possible for you – but not necessary - to decentralize power in an organisation, invade the privacy of your employees, while you improve service to customers, reach markets served by your global competitors and cause widespread unemployment, engage in new kinds of criminal activity as your company seeks to protect itself from information disclosures, and create new kinds of products which eliminate older products and the employment of people who make those products." Obviously, it was not the purpose of technology developers to manipulate and corrupt organisational behaviour. Any new technology is designed to expedite the way we organise, handle, and communicate information but even then we are not free from the consequences of IT.

---

3. Laudon, K.C., and Laudon, J.P. (1994), *Management Information Systems: Organisation and Technology*, 3rd ed., Macmillan, New York, p. 700.

Job Layoffs

IT tools of several kinds are enabling organisations to perform functions with fewer resources, and in many industries this means that fewer humans are being employed. The rate of new job creation by emergent industries appears not to be high enough to take up the slack. The result is that, even when the economy is improving, unemployment levels are staying high, participation rates are falling, and more people are in part-time employment than was the case in the past.

With the introduction of computers in almost every activity of business, the job of many persons can be handled by only a single machine and with more accuracy and reliability. But this characteristic of computer has become a drastic threat to the job security of workers. Even the manual work is being handled by computers inside a factory resulting in layoff of workers. The retrenchment of workers and reduction in vacancies in organisations because of the replacement of manual work with computers, the problem of desk killing has taken birth. Workers' organisations fear that thousands of jobs will become redundant when computerization takes place on a very large scale. While there is some justification in this, however, there is another side to it; many new jobs will be created and the existing staff can be retained.

Lacks Personal Touch

Any latest means of communication cannot replace the old-fashioned face-to-face contact. Why? The answer is quite simple: all advance technological equipments lacks human touch. The click of a mouse cannot be compared with the shake of a hand. Every successful long-term business is based on personal relationships. And the personal touch cannot be replaced electronically. In the organisations, people have to feel comfortable with the quality of individuals they are working with. In the same way, not everything can be sold via e-commerce, delivered over wires or through a satellite up-link. There are services or goods such as childcare or dentistry where technology cannot help.

One of the tendencies of IT applications is that they deliver a great deal of what each individual needs at a workstation or playstation. So there is less reason for each individual to get up and walk around. Apart from being physically unhealthy, this also reduces people's direct interactions with one another.

Another negative impact is the reduced need for humans to work manually, arising from the productivity and efficiency from IT. For many people, this results in lowered self-respect, and reduces their commitment to themselves, their community and their society.

Continuous Monitoring And Upgradation

The tools of IT require continuous monitoring and upgradation as everyday new and developed systems are coming in the market. Take the case of computers, everyday new computers with more processing speed, more memory and better audio and video qualities at a reduced price, comes in the market. Even the latest machine bought today will become obsolete very soon because of this 'here today, gone tomorrow' nature of technology. To keep pace with this race, software vendors keep announcing the release of yet another version of their software even before the previous version has reached the users. A common man cannot afford to upgrade the machines and the software that fast.

Security Threats And Stress

A computer and the data stored inside a computer are never secure from unauthorised users unless some security mechanism is provided for safety of the system and security of the data. One such security mechanism is a password system where a computer allows a user to 'lock' the data and program files of that user with a user-fed secret password. The computer will allow access to these 'locked' files only when 'the authenticated user' is recognized through the correct password. Some computers have multi-level password system. The user is therefore always bothered about the security and the secrecy of his work on a computer and has to remember all the time the passwords. Passwords are required to be frequently changed to avoid any possibility of crackdown, especially when the computer is a part of some network or Internet. Sometimes a busy user may forget his own password and may lose permanently access to his data and programs. Experts say the explosion of passwords, access codes, PIN numbers, and the like has put an unmanageable strain on the brain and its capacity to remember. And it's getting worse. For example, assume that your local telephone exchange has added two new area codes in your city - meaning you have to remember ten digits, not seven, for most phone numbers. And as we start getting more and more codes to remember, as well as passwords and PIN numbers, it can cause tremendous stress. Unfortunately, computer security experts insist that passwords and PIN numbers are a necessary evil. Electronic thievery has reached to new heights, and stolen passwords are a leading culprit. Among the sophisticated tools in the arsenal of top electronic thieves are computer programs that plug every word in the dictionary, one by one, into a computer system until they match a password. This requires computer users to put a lot of thought into the passwords they create. This is not an ideal solution, because creating a hard-to-crack password usually means creating an equally hard-to-remember password.

Technostress

All the technological equipments whether they are faster computers, pagers or sophisticated cell phones — these things have opened a world of opportunity for many people, but the more accessible technology gets, the more it also has the potential to take control of our lives and invade when it is not required. Through these technological equipments any body has the access for intrusion in our private life and to destroy our peace of mind.

In a 1997 study, MCI Communications Corporation (a famous research organisation of USA) found that 59 percent of Americans experienced some form of hesitation, resistance or frustration with technology. In some cases, experts say, tech overload can even lead to job loss, divorce or suicide. So why do not we just say no? Actually, it is not that simple. In fact, we have no choice but to learn to deal with the technology or deal with the stress. Since most of us cannot afford to cut back on technology—because it saves us time, money and energy—we choose to deal with the stress. There are several other 'Technostress' indicators, including sleep deprivation, losing appropriate perception of time (usually while on the Internet), family and relationship strain, and tendency toward multitasking—doing several things in bits and pieces as opposed to sticking with one task until it is complete. Multitasking refers to the ability of a computer to handle several duties simultaneously. In the same way, due to these technologies, we have to carry many more tasks in our brain and switch much faster.

It is also true that for many people latest technological equipments are a symbol of status. People possess latest IT equipments not for the sake of their use but for status and appearance. All this contributes to the problem. The best solution to reduce this technostress is to assess what technology we really need to have, and to drop that we do not need.

❑❑❑

PART B

COMMUNICATION

2

COMMUNICATION: WHAT AND WHY?

The importance of communication can be gauged from the fact that we all are communicating in some form or the other almost every moment of our lives. All our behaviour throughout the day is communicating something. Whatever we are doing — talking, playing, walking, sitting, or even sleeping, communication is taking place. All the time a message is being formulated and transmitted. There is no way for 'no communication'. As one of the fundamental truths of communication holds that, "a person cannot *not* communicate." [1] It means we cannot stop communication. If a person is not speaking that does not mean that he/she is not communicating. Then, person's body movements, postures, facial expressions, clothing etc. conveys something meaningful to others.

We all live in a community or in a society. It is inevitable to understand the intricacies of human communication, only then we can apply it in a suitable manner which will lead to better understanding and good relations with others. The importance of communication has been recognized from the time immemorial. The oldest essay ever discovered, written about 3000 B.C., consists of advice on how to speak effectively. Similarly, the oldest book is a treatise on effective communication known as *'Precepts'*. This book was composed in Egypt about 2675 B.C. So, for thousands of years the need to share or to communicate had been felt. Different vehicles/channels were identified and subsequently improvised for the purpose of transmission of ideas and concepts. Man has the ability to communicate (its not that the animals do not communicate but human communication is more subtle and refined), which is much more than a composition of certain physical attributes, vocal chords, articulators, and so on. He has the ability to symbolise or to understand concepts in terms of images or symbols. It is this ability that helps him to communicate.

The word Communication is derived from the Latin word *communis* which means 'to share' that is, sharing of thoughts, concepts, feelings etc. Mainly it is sharing of understanding between two or more persons. A person can communicate with himself also, this type of communication

---

1. Paul Watzlawick, Janet Helmick Beavin, and Don D. Jackson, *Pragmatics of Human Communication* (New York, Norton, 1967, p. 48.

is known as **Intra-personal communication.** Intra-personal Communication is basically conversation with the self. It is individual's own reflection and contemplation. Ultimately, the level and depth of intra-personal communication decides the quality of inter-personal communication. An individual with no or low intra-personal contemplation is sure to have weak inter-personal communication capabilities.

When a person communicates with others it is a case of **Inter-personal communication**. Technically, inter-personal communication is communication between two persons. Usually, when we say communication we always refer to this kind of communication. It is more persuasive and influential. Why? The end goal of any inter-personal communication is to influence the behaviour of others. In fact, communication is all about influencing others. Then, there are other types of communication such as group communication or mass communication. In a group or mass communication an individual communicates with more than one person. It is one-to-many communication as against one-to-one in the case of inter-personal communication.

So, Communication is the process of sharing understanding or commonness — sometimes through spoken or written words and sometimes through such non-verbal means as facial expressions, gestures, and voice qualities. This way communication is much more than an understanding of the spoken or written language. We can say that all the human behaviour is communication. Even the silence is a means of communication. Therefore, it is a composition of symbols, signs, gestures, postures, words etc. as Ashley Montagu and Floyd Matson says "Communication is the name we give to the countless ways that humans have of keeping in touch — not just words and music, pictures and print, nods and becks, postures and plumages; to every move that catches someone's eye and every sound that resonates upon another's ear."[2]

Communication In Business

In the business world the ability to communicate effectively becomes more important because any type of organised activity demands communication. There is no other way to direct the work of the individual members and work groups of the business organisation. In laying out work assignments, changing the direction of work or projects that are under way, instructing subordinates, and coordinating the different activities of the organisation, the manager must communicate in some way. Therefore, the manager's world is a world of words. In fact a manager's job is communicating. Studies show that a manager spend as much as 90 per cent of his time in communicating. The average supervisor spends about 80 per cent of his time in communicating; some 10 per cent of the 80 per cent is spent in writing, 15 per cent in reading, 30 per cent in speaking, and 45 per cent in listening. A survey concluded that Chief Executive Officers (CEOs) spend 78 per cent of their time in oral communication, while third-level managers devote 87 per cent of their time to all types of communication. Second-level managers devote 81 per cent of their time similarly, and supervisors spend an almost unbelievable 74 per cent of their time in the same activity.[3] The more complex a business grows, the more important communication becomes because it is the main way to cut through the complexity to make the business understandable and workable.

---

2. Ashley Montagu and Floyd Matson, *The Human Connection*, New York, McGraw-Hill, 1979.
3. H. Mintzberg, *The Nature of Managerial Work*, Englewood Cliffs, NJ, Prentice-Hall, 1980, pp. 38-39.

COMMUNICATION: NEED AND GOALS

With the technological advancements the nature and methods of doing business are becoming increasingly complicated and the size of organisations has increased. As organisations have crossed national boundaries and are more dependent on efficient management, effective communication have become – and will continue to be – increasingly important. In every big or medium organisation, one needs to be a specialist in one or the other area. Some of us specialise in manufacturing, others in marketing, some in financing, and so on. When a specialist communicates with other specialist they talk a technical language all their own. Of course specialist's language saves time, yet the more technical nature of our work, the more we find ourselves unable to communicate with those who do not possess the same specialised knowledge. In the business situation the role of a manager, as he goes higher up in the hierarchy is to coordinate others, issue instructions, collate information, and then present the relevant information to the upper management. For successful accomplishment all these tasks require effective communication.

A well understood organisational structure helps employees in communicating properly. The authority lines and hierarchy levels must be clear to all those working in the organisation. The policies of the organisation should offer guidance to all; wise policy-making is dependent upon a good two-way communication system.

Effective communication is not a born trait. It is developed through exercise and training.

Communications to an extent possible should be included in training programmes. Training ensures proper orientation of the employees towards the organisation. The training programme should include an outline of the history of the company and also its aims. How good communication helps an organisation directly? By helping in achieving the organisation's objectives. Everyone should be aware of what the organisation wants to achieve. Every organisation has its own set of objectives, aims, or goals. Scott and Mitchell identified four major objectives that communication processes serve within organisations.[4] They are as follows:

1. Increasing acceptance of organisational rules by subordinates in allowing them to discuss attitudes, resolving conflicts and ambiguities among groups and individuals.

2. Motivating for greater commitment to organisational objectives and evaluating the performance of organisational personnel. Communication is the leader's major managerial tool to persuade followers and obtain cooperation.

3. Clarifying task responsibilities, identifying authority positions and providing accountability for performance. Organisational charts, information programmes, and standard operating procedures attempt to routinize decisions and provide a formal communication channel for management control in organisations.

4. Providing adequate data for decision-making. Communication is a vital information function for solving simple or complex problems and making accurate decisions to positively influence organisational performance. The emphasis for this goal is on technological accuracy and information processing activities that enhance operational output, rather than an emotional and feeling orientation.

---

4. William G. Scott and Terrence R. Mitchell, *Organizational Theory: A Structural and Behavioral Analysis,* Richard Dc Irwin, 1976.

Communication Defined

According to *The American Management Association* communication is "any behaviour that results in an exchange of meaning."

A special committee on communication in business (National Society For The Study Of Communication) defines it as "Communication is a mutual exchange of facts, thoughts, opinions or emotions. This requires presentation and reception, resulting in common understanding among all parties. This does not necessarily imply agreement."

Chester Barnard is of the opinion, "In exhaustive theory of organisation, communication would occupy a central place because the structure extensiveness, and scope of organisations are almost entirely determined by communication techniques."[5]

Goldhaber defines communication as, "Organisational communication is the process of creating and exchanging messages within a network of interdependent relationships to cope with environmental uncertainty."[6]

Wilson and others define it as, "Organisational communication is an evolutionary, culturally dependent process of sharing information and creating relationships in environments designed for manageable, goal-oriented behaviour."[7]

Although all these definitions are apt, they refer to communication in organisational perspective. According to one study, communication has more than one hundered definitions. The concept of communication, as it should be practiced, can be simply defined as any initiated behaviour on the part of the sender which conveys the desired meaning to the receiver and causes desired response behaviour from the receiver.

Communication: A Holistic View

A holistic view is when we try to see the 'whole' not the incomplete parts or components. If we try to get the holistic view of 'what communication is?' we are bound to have the following basic ingredients of communication that makes the whole picture. Following may also be considered as the essential features of communication.

More Than One Person

For the process of inter-personal communication to take place there should be more than one person or we can say involvement of at least two persons, a sender and a receiver, is required. Communication within one person will become a case of intra-personal communication. The speaker is called communicator and the target of the communication is known as communicatee. A person who speaks, writes or issues some instructions is the sender and the person for whom the communication is meant or who receives the message is the receiver or communicatee.

Message Is The Recipe

Without a message communication is incomplete. A message is the subject matter of communication. It can be the contents of a letter, memo, circular, order, instructions or the

5. Barnard, C; (1938). *The Functions of the Executive,* (Cambridge, Mass., Harvard University Press.
6. Goldhaber, G.M; (1993). *Organisational Communication*, 6th ed. Dubuque, IA, Brown and Benchmark.
7. Gerald L. Wilson, H. Lloyd Goodall and Christopher L. Waagen, *Organisational Communication,* New York, Harper & Row, 1986.

suggestions. However, it does not mean that 'no message, no communication', because in that case the act of communicating (without message) or the choice of media would become the message. As noted earlier "a person cannot *not* communicate."

Different Forms

Communication is neither confined to oral or spoken words nor it is limited to written message. Rather, it uses different forms or media to give meaning to the message. Communication includes any act or gesture made to convey any sense to the target of communication. In a nutshell, we can say that 'all the human behaviour is communication.'

Commonness

The essence of communication is 'understanding' between the parties however it does not mean that there will always be agreements or there will not be any conflict or dispute among the parties. The thrust here is on understanding or commonness, the message being conveyed by the sender should reach to the receiver in the same sense. Receiver may disapprove the idea or message transferred by the sender without affecting the process of communication; in that case he has received the message and understood it.

Feedback

Communication is a two-way traffic. The procedures or protocols of communication followed by the sender are same for the target or receiver of the message. The primary objective of a communicator is to generate a response or feedback from the receiver in order to have a clear understanding that the intended message has been received in the desired sense.

Multiple Directions

The flow or direction of communication in an organisation can be upward and downward and also from side to side and also in the shape of a diagonal. In the downward communication it flows from a superior to subordinates and in case of upward communication from subordinates to a superior. It also flows between two or more persons operating at the same level of organisational hierarchy or it may flow diagonally or cross-wise when communication is between the persons at different levels of authority and in different departments. The manager in a hierarchical system becomes a link in the communication chain. It is the organisational structure that gives direction to and imposes restrictions upon the flow of communications. Management decisions and directions flow from higher to lower levels in the organisation. Responses and reports from the lower level managers flow upward in the organisation. Managers also spend time communicating with their peers. Therefore, we see from the outset that communications must function effectively in a lateral direction, as well as downward and upward.

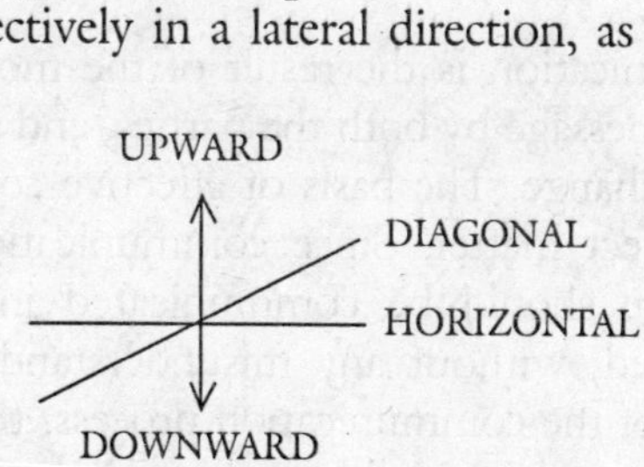

Fig. 2.1 Directions of Communication in an Organisation

Organisational Communication

Organisational communication may be formal or informal. Formal communication follows the authority flows according to the organisational chart or in other words, formal communication takes place formally according to the designations as described by organisational hierarchy. This formal system provides information regarding the organisation to the employees through different media. The formal network, made up of memos, reports, staff-meetings, department meetings, conferences, company newsletters, official notices, is highly documented and as such has very little chance for change.

The informal communication or the *grapevine* is the transmission of information through non-official channels within the organisation. The dictionary meaning for the grapevine is "the informal transmission of information, gossip or rumor from person to person." The grapevine is the informal and unsanctioned information network within every organisation. Grapevine or informal communication does not flow strictly according to rigid organisational levels rather it follows mix patterns of social contacts based on proximity and friendship. It flows from informal channels of communication, which are not provided in the organisation structure. These channels develop among members because of personal contact through working with each other.

All of the information within the grapevine is undocumented and is thereby open to change and interpretation as it moves through the network. The informal network of communication is less permanent and less stable than the formal organisation. This occurs because of the dependency of the network on informal leaders, whereas the formal network is set up through structured policies independent on individuals.

Informal communication can be more direct and faster than the formal channels of information since the information is not being screened or controlled. Grapevine often travels faster than formal communication. It is interesting to note that the grapevine is equally active both in management and among the workers. The grapevine serves many functions in an organisation. Grapevine network can carry useful information through the organisation with amazing speed. The grapevine is also capable of penetrating even the tightest security because it cuts across organisational lines and deals directly with people in the sphere. Employees get an idea of what the management is thinking and doing. It is useful in supplementing formal channels. It provides employees an outlet for their thoughts, fears, expectations etc. It also satisfies a natural desire to know what is really going on and gives employees a sense of belonging. It acts as an early warning system; grapevine allows people to think through in advance what they will do if the rumours become the reality.

Effective Communication

Effective communication is the result of the most accurate exchange of information, full understanding of the message by both the parties, and appropriate action taken upon completion of the information exchange. The basis of effective communication, whether oral or written, is clarity about the subject matter. Since communication is the act of creating understanding, therefore, the message should be communicated in such a way that it is received as the communicator intended, without any misunderstanding. Effective communication requires a thorough knowledge of the communication process, the environment in which it is taking place and an awareness about the possible barriers that may hinder the flow of communication. Understanding between the communicator and the receiver of the message is also very important. So effective communication is a function of so many variables, i.e.

EC (f) = (M, U, P, E, B)

Where M stands for Media,

U for Understanding between the parties,

P for Process,

E for Environment and related factors,

B for Barriers.

Effective communication and Good communication are used as synonyms denoting the same meaning but it is not so. Good communication means that the receiver of the message has understood what the communicator wished to convey, whereas the term effective communication goes two steps ahead; it includes the element of feed back and call for action on the part of receiver. So effective communication ensures that the desired result has been obtained. Good communication is a pre-requisite but does not ensure effective communication. Effective communication is a broad term and includes behavioural aspects like inter-personal behaviour, learning, persuasion, motivation etc.

Communication Styles

Today, all the means of technological communication whether it is a telephone, fax, e-mail, teleconference, cellular phone or any other advance media ensures us that we can communicate with anyone, anywhere and anytime. However, how we communicate that still remains a challenge. Whether it is a face-to-face meeting or an overseas transmission, communication is a complex process that requires constant attention so that the intended messages are sent and received. It is up to us to ensure that the messages we send are clearly understood by the recipient. Inadequate communication is the source of conflict and misunderstanding. It interferes with productivity and profitability. Everyone might have experienced times when they were frustrated because they just could not 'convey the desired thing' to someone. They felt as if they were speaking an unknown language or were on a different 'wave length.' Communicating effectively is much more than just saying or writing the correct words. How we communicate is affected by the frame of reference, emotional states, the situation, and preferred styles of communication. The basic process of human communication involves:

Perception: that is, the reception of incoming signals from the environment.

Evaluation: all the signals are evaluated on the basis of memory, past experiences, level of thinking etc.

Expression: evaluation results are expressed and transmitted in the environment.

For our present purpose we shall be concerned with the process of perception. Our perceptions are directly related to the senses — visual, auditory, or kinesthetic[8]. Although everyone uses all three styles or modes to interact with the world, most people have a primary one. Research indicates that most people are visually oriented, whereas the fewest number of

8. The word kinesthetic is derived from the term 'kinesiology' which means the science of body movements.

people are auditorially oriented. One thing is important to note here that, a person interacting in a particular style whether it is – kinesthetic, visual or auditory, does it subconsciously.

Let us consider each mode.

The Visual Style

In the visual style, visions dominate a person. There are people who view the world through their own mental visions. They interact with the world by creating mental pictures. They can be termed as 'Visually oriented people.' They will communicate in the manner as if they are visualizing something. For example, a visually oriented person will often make statements such as 'I do not see it that way' or 'You try to view the things from my angle.' When communicating, their eyes and facial expressions will go up to create a picture. They will use some words very frequently such as look, see, vision, picture, imagine etc. While communicating to these people, remember the importance of 'vision' for these people. If your boss is also visually oriented then present information using colourful pictures, charts, or displays.

The Auditory Style

Like visual oriented people, there are people with more auditory senses. Their perception always weigh audio signals more than anything else. They will make statements like 'I hear what you're saying' or 'It does not sound good to me.' So while interacting with the outer world their primary way is auditory. They like to discuss and listen to recorded information and music. During conversations or when responding to questions or making comments, you can always see their eyes will go over to the side, often repeating out loud or in their mind's ear the question or statement made. They will mostly use words such as hear, voice, listen, debate, talk etc. When presenting new information to them, take the time to discuss it and answer all of their questions.

The Kinesthetic Style

Then, there are others who try to express everything through body movements and gestures. They will not speak through their mouths only, rather their body movements will be more apparent than the spoken words. These people are doers and are quite demonstrative, preferring movement in their interactions. These people are very easy to recognize as their facial expressions, hand movements and motion of the body will be more active during a conversation. While communicating with these, make movements and gestures as if actually going through the motions of the conversation.

To ensure effective communication, it is important to learn how to communicate in another's particular style. To discover someone's primary mode:

- Listen to the words they frequently use;
- Watch their eye movements during a discussion;
- Observe their behaviour;
- Ask how they prefer to receive new information; and
- Be aware of your own preferences.

In this time of doing more with less and increased use of technology, it is imperative to do whatever we can to foster effective communication. By looking at the world from another's point of view we can make our communication effective. Listening and responding in a way that makes sense to others, will improve our relationships, enhance performance, increase productivity, and positively reinforce our personalities.

Why is communication difficult?

Data show that communication is difficult. Many people feel anxious about giving a formal presentation or talk in public. Some people rank the fear of public speaking ahead of such things as bankruptcy and even death. Communication is so difficult? Suppose you are in your office busy with your routine file work and suddenly you are informed that you have to give a presentation about the performance in the last quarter. How would you react? Formal communication and that without preparation makes many people apprehensive. Why communication is so difficult? Many of us shy away from speaking up for fear of negative feedback. In our quest to be liked we bite our tongue and look the other way instead of righting wrongs and correcting improprieties. Yet there are times when speaking up and speaking out is the right thing to do. Learn to speak your mind when it is time, professionally and with precision, to get the results you desire. There is no right way to speak. Each of us speaks in our own communication style. Some of us use long sentences and many words, others are short winded and direct. Learn to recognize how best you communicate and how best to communicate with others. This difficulty in communication is not only with verbal communication; the same problem exists in written communication also. Why? In our education system the emphasis is on quantitative methods and most of the students have had little practice writing or speaking formally. That is why, many feel more at ease with numbers, numericals etc. than with words. But it is a hard fact that the ability to communicate effectively is very much important in getting and marinating effectively any job or business.

What's your CQ ?

CQ is the Communication Quotient. Gone are the days when IQ (Intelligence Quotient) used to be judged in interviews and exams, these days it is your CQ that matters. For any job degrees, awards, knowledge of the subject etc. are essential, but how good a communicator are you? The answer will decide your future in great proportions. Every job description emphasizes it: must have excellent communication skills. In interviews, performance reviews many get marked down for it. Similarly, a manager/executive communicates with customers, clients, co-workers (both superiors and subordinates), vendors etc. On occasion he is also speaking with the media, members of association or even competitors. How well he is communicating with each? It means communication takes many forms. Each form of communication draws on different skills, each requires different approaches and sometimes even a different lexicon. So how is your communication quotient?

Find Your Quotient

Each question given below carries 2 marks. You have three options Strong, Average, and Weak. In terms of marks, one strong means you get 2 marks, average 1 mark, and weak 0 marks. So out of 40 marks if you get more than 30 marks you are a good communicator (but needs improvement), if you score less than 20 marks you are below average.

1. Can you make a small conversation with a stranger?
2. Can you join a group of strangers and converse with them for some time?
3. Can you ask things about themselves?.
4. Can you tell them about yourself?
5. Can you introduce two strangers to each other?
6. Can you discuss current events/news with strangers?
7. Can you give a prepared speech in your class/department?
8. Can you speak extemporaneously on any subject?
9. Can you make a sales presentation?
10. Can you interview someone else?
11. Can you be interviewed?
12. Can you train others?
13. Can you conduct a meeting as its leader?
14. Can you constructively critique another's performance?
15. Can you handle constructive criticism?
16. Can you assert yourself when necessary and speak up?
17. Can you negotiate/bargain effectively?
18. Can you co-exist with diverse personality styles?
19. Can you persuade others and engender their support?
20. Can you face verbal criticism and maintain control?

We are all developing our Communication Quotient on the job. Learn to recognize how different forms of communication require different skills. Make a point of analysing your style and the results it engenders. Where can you improve? Can classes, practice, or coaching help? Try to be a student of improved communication.

❑❑❑

3

Essentials Of Communication

INTRODUCTION

The thought of effective communication automatically makes effective communicator inevitable. Effective communication requires examination of one's inner personality, his/her attitudes and behaviour. All this will lead to certain adjustments that must be made in his/her own personality. People live their entire lives without ever thinking how to develop, learn, use, and control their own attitudes. The average person never tries to develop the attitude nor he ever tries to understand the importance of learning in personality development. He is so preoccupied in his own beliefs and ego system that he overlooks the environment in which he interacts with other people. An ideal communicator must understand the intricacies of human attitude. He must learn to manage his own attitudinal actions. Also, he should be able to manage and control reactions in the people to whom he wishes to convey his message. Someone has rightly said that the greater revolution of our generation is the discovery that human beings by changing their inner attitudes of their mind can change the outer aspects of their lives.

The tools for effective communication have been available for a long time. They merely have been obscured in the development of a one-sided technological society. The role of attitude is not limited to one single area of life rather it includes all the spheres whether it is personal or professional. A manager cannot be a good manager without a good attitude, a student cannot be a good student without a good attitude, a parent, teacher, salesman, anybody cannot be good in their respective roles in the absence of a good attitude. It is important to understand what is a good attitude and what is a bad attitude. A person with a good attitude will have certain personality traits like high expectations from others and also from his/her own self. He will be a positive thinker. On the other hand, a person with a bad attitude will have bad relations with others, he will have no harmony at work place and he leads a purposeless life. His behaviour will be bitter with everyone and he will be a pessimist.

Now the question arises from where we get this 'attitude.' The answer is simple, we develop our own attitude as we mature in age and experience. There are so many other factors that determine our attitude but primarily we can discuss three major determinants: Environment, experience and education.

Environment: All the positive or negative influences related with home, school, and workplace shape our attitude. Other factors related with the environment are cultural background, traditions, beliefs, religious rituals, social and political environment and media like television, newspaper, movies etc.

Experience: Our behaviour is the outcome of our experiences. Bad experiences make a person bad and good experiences results in positive and good behaviour.

Education: Education and qualification also play a major role in the development of attitude. Education does not necessarily mean formal school education rather it can be knowledge and training in any field.

Once the attitude is formed and developed (good or bad) it does not lead to the premise that the person will die with that attitude. Rather, attitude can be changed or modified in either direction — positive or negative. Of course, one should always strive for positive attitude.

It is important to understand that attitude change or development requires behavioural modification. Changing behaviour often requires giving up old habits and ways of believing and doing the things. All this is possible only through learning. Since acquiring new attitude or changing the behaviour is not easy, therefore, learning is very difficult. So we need to understand the process and nature of learning. Learning is an internal feeling and it cannot be imposed externally. Basically, learning is the discovery of personal meaning and relevancy. A person who is trying to learn, his/ her own background of experience provides a wealthy resource for learning and developing new patterns of behaviour. It implies, it is the individual's inner-self that has its richest resource for learning.

How Learning Helps In Personality Development

Learning is a continuous and integrated process occurring within the learner enabling him/ her to obtain personal goals. Conceptually, the process involves five distinct phases.

Unfreezing: If an individual wants to learn something, the first step is to 'unfreeze' or to undo his past knowledge, thinking, experiences etc. We cannot add water in an ice cube unless and until it is unfreezed. The same rule applies to human mind also.

Problem identification: It is the need, opportunity or some external stimulus from the environment which causes and demands a change in the personality.

Goal setting: At this stage, specific goals and objectives are set. The desired changes in the behaviour, attitude, knowledge etc. are stated clearly.

New behaviour: After the goals are achieved, an individual is able to learn and form new behaviour, knowledge, attitude etc.

Refreezing: Finally, it is a stage of 'refreezing' those newer learnings which have been found beneficial. Most importantly, the change in the behaviour must be permanent; otherwise there is no learning.

Personality and communication: Communication is an integral part of the human personality; it also draws a line of distinction between a human and an animal. Over the centuries, we have come to know that each of us is a blend of distinct personality types. As per Greek nomenclature, an individual's personality can have any or a combination of two or more of the four types of temperament - Choleric, Phlegmatic, Sanguine, and Melancholy.

The choleric type is sometimes called the Driver. As regards communicating, the choleric gets straight to the point and is not much concerned with the feelings of others.

The sanguine temperament is an outgoing, warm, people's person. They are talkers and are concerned with the feelings of others. The sanguine is loath to hurt others' feelings and will avoid conflict at almost any price.

The melancholy is highly organised, detailed, and critical. They are introverted and often moody. They often feel they are right because they have taken the time to carefully analyse whatever they are communicating.

The phlegmatic is the most silent of the four types. While generally calm on the surface they are the most likely to be anxious internally when communicating.

It is important to note that no one is of purely one temperament type. There are sixteen combinations of personality traits. If one can adapt his or her natural style to be more like the other person's style, he or she will find it easier to get their attention and, ultimately, better understanding with them.

So, it is evident that a properly understood and carefully applied personal perspective is the beginning for an individual who wishes to be a good communicator. The main aim here is to cite the important qualities of character and the factors responsible for its shape that go into the development of a communicator.

Essentials Of An Effective Communicator

With the technological advancements taking place everyday, the media and the methods of communication have tremendously improved. Today, technology is redefining everything, not only the definition of communication but also the role of a communicator has changed altogether. Gone are the days when speakers used to address a small group of people in an informal environment. But now, in an information age communicators have become the sources and dispensers of information. Communicators are not mere speakers only; rather they have wider responsibilities to perform such as promoting cooperation, fostering understanding, resolving conflicts and attainment of pre-defined organisational objectives. A manager's growth in the hierarchy of a business organisation also depends upon the effectiveness of his communication. Managers with excellent communication skills are treated as a valuable resource for the organisation and are taken in top-strategic teams.

Following are some of the qualities to be an effective communicator.

Self Assessment

The process of good communication starts with the self-assessment. It is the foremost requirement to examine one's self honestly and to make changes accordingly. Self-assessment will serve no purpose if the results are not to be implemented. Open feedback from others acts as a catalyst in this regard.

Be Highly Motivated

What is motivation? Motivation is the drive or need to do something. A good communicator without motivation can never be effective because it is the motivation that brings initiative and assertiveness in the behaviour. At the same time a highly motivated communicator without the element of loyalty is undesirable. In terms of communication, loyalty denotes proper use of listener's time and resources, accepting own mistakes and giving credit to others for their contribution.

Empathetic Thinking

Empathetic thinking is the thinking from other's viewpoint. It is against the rule of 'defending own self' time and again. Empathetic thinking comes when we consider other's viewpoint, thinking, environment etc. It is true that no one truly understands another's hurt, pain, sorrow, fear, or any other emotion unless he himself has either directly or indirectly experienced it. But, it is possible if a person has a good heart and he/she can think in terms of mankind. All this makes a communicator's role very tough.

Don't Change, Use It

The notion of Empathetic thinking leads to the principle of 'Do not change, use it.' When we truly understand other's circumstances, views, limitations etc., there remains no need of changing others. In the same way, any organisation's policies, procedures and people are hard to change. So, the wisdom lies not in changing but understanding the structure and then using it for your advantage. Here, Lord Krishna's principle 'Detached Attachment' applies fully. Whether it is a workplace or a war place we should be concerned with our 'karma' and not with the end results. So, a communicator's objective is not to change the basic make-up of people, organisations, policies, etc. He should try to learn and operate within the existing structure.

Lateral Thinking

Lateral thinking is the creative thinking. A communicator must be able to engage in creative thinking. Edward de Bono, who coined the term 'Lateral thinking', describes our traditional vertical thinking as digging the same hole deeper. Lateral thinking, he suggests, is digging a new hole somewhere else. In the same way communication as a science requires people who are able to dig new holes in unusual places.

Risk Taking

Digging new holes somewhere else also requires risk taking. We are in a world made for pioneers, a world full of endless possibilities where few things are certain. An effective communicator need people who are willing to make what might appear to be outlandish suggestions and try new and not yet proven approaches.

Self-Discipline

This is the limitation of English language that we have to add the prefix 'self' to the word 'Discipline.' In fact, discipline always comes from within. The Hindi word '*Anushasan*' is the right word to use here, which means 'discipline through self.' Discipline cannot be imposed externally. Not only for communicating but also for any form of success, 'self discipline' is a foundation stone. A person not able to control his/her own attitude, perception and actions, cannot control those of others.

Become A Multi-dimensional Thinker

An effective communicator is not confined to a single area of knowledge; rather he should be a multi-dimensional thinker. He should be open for new thoughts, ideas and new ways of looking at things. He should consider every angle, possibility, or combination of an idea or method of communicating it. All this is possible by recognising one's own limitations and then overcoming them.

Be Assertive

A communicator is very assertive in his expressions. Being assertive is not being aggressive. Assertiveness means calmly and boldly communicating your views or what you feel. Assertive behaviour requires consistency in what you say and what you do.

Be An Expert

Almost in every knowledge area, each individual is required to keep abreast of the constant changes in her or her learnings. A communicator to be effective must gather pertinent information, interpret it and apply it. The field of communication requires all of its members to be environmental scanners. They must be experts and keep up in their area of expertise, and at the same time be well-informed generalists. To use their expertise, they must connect with many other areas and make decisions based on fast-changing world. Therefore, a broad knowledge base is important. Being able to gather all of the needed information of course requires the ability to use technology also.

Develop Over Encyclopaedic Knowledge

The facts and figures can be gathered and stored by anyone. Only a true communicator can understand their true significance and apply it for the solution of relevant problems. In fact, he applies conceptual knowledge practically. The communicator first seeks insights, patterns, connections between ideas, significances, needs which must be fulfilled, problems which must be solved. Basically, he knows the difference between education and training.

Timing Is Important

It will not be an overstatement to say that communication is all about proper timing. In most of the business situations, people speak or react too quickly and in some cases communication is badly affected by delayed response. A good communicator does not forget the importance of right timing. It is also true that the art of judging proper time comes with experience and experimentation.

Be Flexible

A good communicator possesses all the above-mentioned qualities, yet he is very flexible and adaptable. He is able to readjust, retreat or react at a moment's notice. He is both benign and coolly calculating. Before reacting he consciously considers as many alternatives, possibilities, and probabilities for a situation as he can.

Winning Or Losing Communications

Conversations and discussions are, these days, no less than winning or losing battles. Often, when we communicate, we always try to win the communication situation by proving our points, knowledge etc. supreme and right. We want other person (who is also communicating) to lose the conversation. This phenomenon also applies to other communicating person. Everyone around us, if we closely observe, is trying to prove that he/she is right and the other person is wrong. This way, our discussions and interactions, generally, are ego and personality clashes. Most of us are "carried away communicators". We are blind in passion for proving our points right before the other person, lose the control over conversation which not only blocks the communication but spoils the personal image and relations also. And, we forget one thing, if we are winning the other one is losing also and one thing that is very clear, nobody wants to lose. In communication, even if we have proved ourselves logically right we may have lost the conversation completely. It should be remembered that in a perfect piece of communication nobody loses, everyone wins. It does not mean that there cannot be any disagreements; they are inevitable. The important thing is how we handle our communications so that others may not feel hurt. We should have a genuine concern for other's self-respect and ego.

Usually, when we converse we have different alternatives or styles of conversation making this battle of conversation to bring different results. We all want to converse in such a manner that the end result is: 'I am the winner'. Many people start off with the 'I am smarter than you'. They follow 'I' approach instead of 'You' approach, i.e. whatever they are saying is correct and whatever other intends to say is of no use. They can be termed as competitive communicators. This is a 'Win-Lose' style i.e. I win and you lose. However, all conversations do not need to be that way. There is an opportunity in most conversations for people to establish situations where both sides can get something out of it. This is an ideal 'Win-Win' style of communication. So, the effective communication situation is that where everybody has gained something and nobody has lost his/her pride and self-respect.

Following are the four major alternatives/styles that we have in any communication:

Alternative I: ***Win-Lose***

This style simply states that 'I am winner and you are loser'. I will converse in this manner that you will feel that you have lost the conversation. I will gain confidence in this conversation as I have proved my points right and on the other side as you have the feeling that you are a loser, therefore, you are likely to go away depressed and irritated. You may have a desire to gain revenge in the future communications.

Alternative II: ***Lose-Win***

This is the same situation as described above the only difference is that we have changed our shoes. Here I am a loser and you are a winner. You have proved your points in such a way that both of us have the feeling that you are a winner and I am a loser. So at this point I will probably be depressed, annoyed and frustrated and I may have an inner feeling to take revenge at the next conversation.

Alternative III: ***Lose-Lose***

In this alternative, no one is winner and both of us are losing. We are making the conversation impossible for the other to win. Both of us are putting hard to ensure that the other loses. In such situations, we both feel annoyed, frustrated and disappointed. But at the same time each of us may have a soothing feeling that at least the other is not a winner. It is a perfectly inelastic state where nobody is ready to compromise. In group communications this situation can bring the most detrimental result to inter-personal relations. This type of style gives birth to personal animosity and hostility, hence, should be avoided by all means.

Alternative IV: ***Win-Win***

This is the most desirable situation in all types of communications. In this case, at the end of conversation we both are winners. Both of us have gained something from conversation. The gains can be unequal. I may have gained more that you or *vice-versa*. But both of us have taken care that nobody loses. Each of us must have gained something, big or small, that is immaterial. Even when you do win, ensure the other side goes away with something to maintain self-respect. Therefore, the effective communicator will look for opportunities to facilitate the win/win situation. This is very important for teamwork and group communication. In conversations and discussions the central thought must be on problem solving instead of winning or losing conversation.

Practically, every conversation, discussion and negotiation cannot end in a win/win situation. But atleast, we should direct our efforts to achieve a common goal which enables subsequent interactions in win-win direction. In this regard relationship networking is also helpful and should be given due consideration.

GUIDELINES FOR EFFECTIVE COMMUNICATION

Answer basic questions

In business communication, the communicator should try to follow a logical approach as addressing a problem for which there may be no one right answer. Business communication tasks are evaluated based on the degree of effectiveness. As a communicator, you will often have to choose from a variety of options. To decide wisely, consider the context of communication. Logical approach is answering the most basic questions such as what is the purpose of communicating? Who is the receiver and what is his or her environment? What do I want the receiver to do? What should be the ideal message?

Business communication usually has the following purposes:

- to get information
- to give information
- to persuade or motivate receiver for something
- to give or take orders
- to enhance the goodwill of the company/product/speaker.

Therefore, one should be very specific about the reason for communicating. Failure to do so has resulted in many failed exchanges — the sales agent who describes the features of the product but forgets to ask for the order; the customer service clerk who sends a requested refund but annoys a customer in the process; the job applicant who, in listing qualifications, inadvertently supplies ready-made reasons for being turned down.

Know The Receiver

Mostly failures in communications are due to the wrong assessment about the receiver. People while communicating assume that the receiver will think the same way they do. As a result they produce letters or reports that are writer-based rather than reader-based, and speeches that miss their mark with the audience. Do not fall into this communications trap. Spend time assessing your receiver. And since people do not exist in isolation, also consider the receiver's environment, the context that may influence the receiver's response. Understanding the receiver's broader environment can in many instances make a dramatic difference in the effectiveness of communication. Moreover, anticipating receiver's response will help you to word your message so that it creates the impression you want and does not foster misunderstanding. All these analysis will help you create receiver-based communication that gets results.

Judge Your Timing

Judging timing for effecting communication may bring desired results. Whatever the communication, timing can affect its chance of success. Sometimes it is a good idea to delay the communication. You may be in a hurry to get results, but the receiver may be immersed in other matters. For example, your sales manager worried about giving an important report to the top-management may not be instantly responsive to your latest marketing idea.

Appropriate Media

Appropriate choice of channel and media for communication adds effectiveness in communication but there are no hard and fast rules about which channel of communication to choose. Communication in writing or orally depends on the context. Decisions about communicating, either individually or to a group, may depend on the personalities of the people involved. This is only through common sense that one can select particular media depending upon the past experience and according to the environment, for example, written communication is preferred when the parties want a record of the communication and the information is complicated or technical. But where quick result is required or where you want to persuade someone and the matter is sensitive oral communication will serve the purpose.

Immaterial of the fact whether you write or speak, the particular choice of medium can affect the reception of your message. According to Marshall McLuhan, "The medium is the message," simply means that the choice of medium influences interpretation of the message. So one should try to select the most appropriate media among the different alternatives.

Be Polite And Courteous

It is very important to communicate in a polite and courteous manner. Not only in oral communication but in written communication, this is to be taken care of. Letters, memos, and reports etc. can also convey different tones like enthusiasm, pride, modesty but courtesy and politeness are must. Even if you are angry for good reasons, you will be more effective if you do not make discourteous remarks.

Use The Proper Tone

Tone in the communication can entirely change the meaning of the message. An inappropriate tone can distort the meaning and can cause big problems. Through the tone we convey our inner feelings or emotions. We use a variety of tones in conversations with people we know well and sometimes not knowingly we use a wrong tone but that we know is not harmful as we know the other person and the same is also very close to us but in business we need to be more careful where the relations are professional only.

❑❑❑

4

FORMS OF COMMUNICATION

What is the form of communication? Simply, it is the media in which one transmits meaning and understanding. Fortunately, human beings have recognized the importance of communication. We can now only imagine that our ancient ancestors used some form of communication to convey a message from one person to another; such as a hand gesture, a signal, a grunt, or a scream. Symbols and written language developed over time. Today, many forms of communication have evolved with technology and the desire to convey accurate messages and information. The basic and foremost important forms of human communication are:

(1) Verbal communication

(2) Non-verbal communication

(3) Written communication

(4) Technological communication

(1) VERBAL COMMUNICATION

Human interactions and relations are a result of verbal communication. Verbal or oral communication is the basis of understanding between people. Some of the key components of verbal communication are sound, words, speech, and language. In fact, oral verbal language is the basic teaching and training vehicle and we well know that this remains the most important means of communication in education.

Verbal or oral communication may be one-to-one or it may be one-to-many.

(a) One-to-one communication : One-to-one communication or face-to-face communication is the most basic and direct form of communication. Face-to-face conversation is human communication at its most personal and intimate level. Or in other words it is the most effective, persuasive, and informative means of communication. It is known as one-to-one or face-to-face, simply, because it is the direct and personal communication of one person with another. When we speak, sign, or scream at someone that is directly in front of us, most of us are satisfied that our intended message has been transmitted as accurately as possible since we can accompany our message with facial expressions, body language, and various vocal or signal inflections. Face-to-face communication is the richest medium of human communication. Communicating this way keeps communication cycles extremely short. This is the most persuasive form of communication as the immediate and spontaneous feedback allows the communicator to respond according to the listener.

(b) One-to-many communication: As the name implies, in one-to-many communication one individual communicates with more than one individual. This form is useful when the same message is to be communicated to many persons at the same time. One-to-many is basically a form of mass communication where public at large is the receiver of the message. Electronic forms of one-to-many communication include radio and television. Instead of a salesperson knocking on every door to advertise his/her product, one advertisement on the television broadcast to millions of people, will do the job more effectively. The other main media of one-to-many communication is a computer connected to the Internet.

Verbal Communication In An Organisation

In the communication jargon, after all the technological advancements that have been done, communicators still rely on direct face-to-face communication to get the word out. We can think that if only words matter, why we bother to hold meetings or conferences? Why we do not do all the work with memos or through letters? The answer, of course, is that business continues to use direct face-to-face communication because nothing else can take its place. The speaker's tone, gestures, postures, and facial expressions may reinforce, amplify, or even contradict his verbal statement. All this is required for better understanding. Decades of behavioural science research support the importance of face-to-face communication and the significance of word-of-mouth in influencing people to change their minds and their behaviours. The evidence has been around for years and still, organisations place little emphasis on face-to-face communication. Managers, executives, public relations officers, marketing managers, and organisation leaders keep putting words on paper, often at great cost, and believing they have communicated.

Another biggest reason which emphasizes the importance of direct face-to-face communication, is the problem of Information Overload. In communication, more information does not necessarily mean better communication. We now have so much information that dealing with it presents a challenge for individuals as well as for organisations. The free flow of information within an organisation is an ideal to be achieved. When the information received far exceeds that required, the recipients cannot give proper attention to what is really needed. Much valuable time is devoted to the sorting and selection process. There is, always, a limit on the number of messages an organisation can handle effectively. Ever faster and more voluminous flows of information can impair rather than facilitate decision making, especially when rapid changes in technology and frequent changes in the strategies and missions of organisations themselves accompany this flood of facts, statistics, and reports. There is so much new information available in so many new channels that traditional mass communication is becoming less and less effective in reaching mass audiences. Now, only direct verbal communication is available that is still popular and effective.

Not only in a business organisation but social trends also point to the need for face-to-face communication in order to change people's attitudes and behaviours. Due to globalization and liberalization, minority groups are growing in size and number. Even majority groups are being splintered by special interests and differing lifestyles. Communication needs to be personalized much more often to match the varying needs of people who make up our audiences. Messages should relate to their specific interests. All this is possible through face-to-face communication.

Improving Verbal Communication

Improving verbal communications requires first that we understand that communication is rarely perfect or clear in and of itself. We must learn to listen better and speak more clearly. We must also check whether our message is delivered correctly and whether we have heard a message clearly. Carl Rogers notes that, "The whole task of psychotherapy is the task of dealing with a failure in communication. . . . the major barrier to mutual interpersonal communication is our very tendency to judge, to evaluate, to approve or disapprove, the statement of the other person, or the other group. . . . Real communication occurs when we listen with understanding to see the idea and attitude from the other person's point of view, to sense how it feels to them, to achieve their frame of reference in regard to the thing they are talking about."[1] Improving speaking and listening skills can have major impacts on leadership, teamwork and internal communication, as well as public relations, marketing, and grass roots success. It is believed that more than 50 percent of an internal communication or public relations programme should involve verbal communication tactics.

In verbal communication, etiquette is very important. To be an effective communicator, one must speak in a manner that is not offending to the receiver. To be successful in the business world, a person must use proper verbal etiquette. One important aspect of verbal etiquette is a proper introduction. Every day we encounter people in a variety of business and social situations. The way we meet and greet them creates lasting impressions and paves the way for a productive encounter. Introductions project information. Besides the obvious elements of name, title, and affiliation, an introduction conveys a level of respect and reflects how the person making the introduction views the other person's status.

The most important point about introductions is to always make them, even if you cannot remember names. Failing to do so causes embarrassment and discomfort. If given a choice, most people would prefer you to make the introduction incorrectly, even if you forgot their name, rather than stand there unacknowledged and disregarded.

Another important aspect of verbal etiquette is the way in which people address others in a business setting. Once introduced, improperly addressing superiors, colleagues, customers and clients, or subordinates at future meetings may create tension and will create a negative impression. Generally, it is appropriate to address subordinates and others with whom an informal relationship has been established by their first name. In formal relationships, or when the relationship status is unknown, it is necessary to refer to the individual using the appropriate gender-specific title. When gender-specific titles are necessary, use Mister (Mr.) to address men, Miss or (Mrs.) to address married women, and Miss (Ms.) to address women who are single or whose marital status is unknown.

1. Carl Rogers, *On Becoming a Person*, Boston, Houghton Mifflin, 1961, p. 226.

Following are more specific rules for addressing others in business settings:

Superiors: Always address superiors with the appropriate gender-specific title, for example Sir, Madam etc., unless he/she gives express permission to do otherwise.

Colleagues: It is generally accepted procedure to address colleagues by first name. Exceptions arise when the relationship is formal or unfamiliar.

Subordinates: If the superior has developed an informal relationship with the subordinate, use of first names is permissible. But where the relationship is formal or unfamiliar, the appropriate gender-specific title should be used.

Customers and clients: Most relationships with clients or customers are formal, dictating appropriate gender-specific titles. But over the time period, if an amiable relationship has been established, the use of first names is permissible.

The other important aspect of business etiquette is proper telephone procedure. Since much of today's business is done over the phone, using correct telephone etiquette is more important than ever. Lasting impressions may be formed during and after telephone conversations, and business people, in order to be successful, must maintain a positive impression. This dictates that people use proper telephone etiquette.

THE ESSENCE OF ONE-TO-ONE COMMUNICATION: INTERPERSONAL SPEAKING

The actual origin of language is subject to considerable speculation. Some theorists believe it is an outgrowth of group activities such as working together or dancing. Others believe that language developed from basic sounds and gestures. Over 3,000 languages and major dialects are spoken in the world today. The development of languages reflects class, gender, profession, age group, and other social factors. The huge variety of languages usually creates difficulties between different languages, but even within a single language there can be many problems in understanding. Through speaking, we try to eliminate this misunderstanding, but sometimes this is a very hard thing to do. Just as we assume that our messages are clearly received, so we assume that because something is important to us, it is important to others. But, it is not at all true. Many problems can arise is speaking and the only way to solve these problems is through experience.

Speaking can be looked at in two major areas: **interpersonal and public speaking**. Since the majority of speaking is an interpersonal process, to communicate effectively we must not simply clean up our language, but learn to relate to people.

Interpersonal communication is an essential part of business and when it is executed correctly, good things happen. Because speaking is such an indelible activity, we tend to do it without much thought. But, that casual approach can be a problem in business. A casual comment can create an image in someone's mind that cannot be replaced even when we meant something totally different. When it comes to oral communication, our goal should be to take advantage of its positive characteristics while minimizing the dangers.

Speaking can be used as a tool to accomplish our objectives. But, first we must break the habit of talking spontaneously without planning what we are going to say or how we are going to say it. We must learn to manage the impression we create by consciously tailoring our remarks and delivery style to suit the situation.

Following are some points, which will make your verbal communication effective:

- Remember to become aware of what you are saying.
- Apply the same process you use in written communication when you are communicating orally.
- Before you speak, think about your purpose, your main idea, and your audience.
- Organise your thoughts in a logical way.
- Decide on a style that suits the occasion and then edit your remarks mentally.
- As you speak, watch the other person to see whether your message is making the desired impression. If not, revise it and try again.

Remember that various situations call for different speaking styles, just as various writing assignments call for different writing styles.

THE ESSENCE OF ONE-TO-MANY COMMUNICATION: PUBLIC SPEAKING

The other major area of verbal communication is public speaking. From the origin of time, it has been obvious that some people are just better public speakers than others. Because of this, today a good speaker can earn a living by speaking to people in a public setting. Some of the major areas of public speaking are speaking to persuade, speaking to inform, and speaking to inspire or motivate. But speaking before public is not that easy. Many people are afraid of speaking. They expect that they will make mistakes that cause catastrophic ruin. The truth is: You will make mistakes and the mistakes are not fatal. We all learn and grow from our mistakes.

Key Points For A Better Speech

Some basic communication tenets to keep in mind in public speaking situations are as below:

(1) Understand The Subject Matter

Collect all the information, ideas and material on the subject or topic on which you have to make a speech. Without proper understanding of the subject matter speech cannot have good impression on the audience. Always remember: Good preparation is 90 per cent of effective speaking.

(2) Don't Memorize

A good speaker never tries to cram or memorize the talk word for word as this may limit the scope and thinking area for the speaker.

(3) Make An Outline

The subject matter of the speech may be very comprehensive, so, it is advisable to make an outline for important points in the speech.

(4) Judge Your Audience

Before making speech try to judge the knowledge and understanding level of your audience.

(5) Enunciate Effectively

For many, English is a second language. Focus on the consonants of each word. Enunciate means to pronounce clearly and distinctly. A particular word may sound similar to some other words. So what is needed is that the audience gets the right word. Give thought to the way you enunciate.

(6) Don't Rush

Speak clearly and audibly at all times. Do not rush your presentation. Pare its content down if you have too much to cover in the time given.

(7) Opening And Closing

Opening and Closing of speech is much important than anything else. So how you open up with your speech and how you close your communication with the audience will largely determine the effectiveness of speech.

(8) Sum It Up

Close the talk with a brief summary and speak main points once again. Follow the rule: Tell them what you are going to tell them, Tell it to them, and then Tell them what you told them.

(2) NON-VERBAL COMMUNICATION

Discussed in detail in Chapter 7: Communicating Non-verbally.

(3) WRITTEN COMMUNICATION

The difficulty in communication is not only with verbal communication, the same problem exist in written communication also. Generally, it is understood that written communication is more difficult than verbal communication because one has to get the message correct first time; one cannot have the advantage of immediate feedback and non-verbal cues such as facial expressions, gestures etc. are also missing. There are other reasons that make written communication difficult. In our education system the emphasis is on quantitative methods and most of the students have had little practice writing or speaking formally. That is why, many feel more at ease with numbers, numericals etc. than with words. But it is also true that the ability to communicate effectively is very much important in getting any job or doing any business.

Many managers and executives lack the ability to express their ideas even in simple language and many others feel that the pompous and artificial language, they use, is the main cause of all their communication problems. Today, for many business people, their communication is not only incomprehensible to the people they are trying to reach but also wasteful in terms of money, energy and time, besides creating plenty of misunderstanding. Professionals and managers require strong writing skills as they are, mostly, asked to prepare reports, advertisements and technical manuals for company and customer use.

In verbal communication, one can afford to be spontaneous, since the instant feedback of the listener allows you to correct any mistakes immediately. An angry or skeptical look, or even a raised eyebrow, will point the way to changes. But in written communication, we do not have that kind of instant feedback. Since changes and corrections are almost impossible once a message has been delivered and read by the receiver, therefore, it is important to try to avoid errors beforehand. Careful planning and proper attention to the message can avoid errors and misunderstandings in communication. In the business world, where the results of casual mistakes may be more dangerous than in the everyday social life, it makes sense to give forethought to what we are communicating. Planning is especially important in written communication. In a good piece of written communication, the facts are arranged in an orderly, logical, and concise manner. Most business writings become bad because of disorderly arrangement of facts or lack of conciseness. Many writings may have grammatical and spelling errors. The following will briefly explain how to target your writing, structure an outline and write your piece effectively.

Think About The Reader

It is essential to have a clear idea of who your reader is. You should know why he or she is going to be reading your piěce, where and when they will be reading it, and what they will want to get out of it. Knowing this, and knowing what information you want to convey allows you to decide an aim for the written communication. You should focus all decisions on content, structure, style and presentation on meeting this aim.

First, Make The Outline

Once you have decided the aim of writing, you are ready to prepare an outline. This allows you to start to organise the information for a coherent structure. If you start writing without an outline you are in danger of producing a disorganised, chaotic mess that confuses your reader and fails to make the desired connections in his or her mind. Once you have selected information and organised a structure, prepare an outline of the written document. The shape of this should be obvious from the structure you have given your information. The introduction should help the reader to prepare an overall picture of the intended message.

Now, Start Writing

When you have prepared your outline, it is time to start writing. The easiest way of doing this is just to let the words and ideas flow. Move quickly through the piece without editing or reviewing it. This will help to keep your creativity flowing without it being crippled by self-criticism. Only when you have finished a section should you review it. At this stage, you may decide to reorganise it, edit it, change it, and add or delete information. As you review it you should check that what you have written meets the objectives you set and gives the reader the information they want.

Finalise It

The style of the communication should be completely focused on the reader's needs. Language used should be pitched at the appropriate level for the reader. People generally prefer information presented in short sentences with little or no jargon. You may be tempted to write in a way that you think will impress your readers, using long words and complex sentences. All this shows is that you are not able to communicate ideas clearly and simply. It is likely that material written like this will not be read at all. If you need to use technical language that may not be understood, include a glossary.

Remember that you have responsibility for the clarity, effectiveness, and focus of your communication. Beyond this, style will emerge on its own without you needing to worry about it.

Writing In An Organisation

The written communication in any organisation depends, entirely on its policies and philosophy about writing and speaking. Big industrial houses place a priority on written communication. Even the routine communication from one level to another takes place through written inter office memos. On the other hand small firms having less number of employees place less emphasis on writing, the usual communication is done through phone or direct face-to-face conversation. There are industries in particular — for example, insurance, banking, and accounting — tend to follow writing cultures. The nature of their work and certain legal requirements, force these industries to use formal written communications, such as insurance policies, auditing reports and financial statements etc. Companies with many layers of management also follow writing cultures because the different authority levels make working and communicating face-to-face or over the phone very difficult.

Then on the opposite, there are organisations that follow purely oral cultures. These companies are usually small entrepreneurial and family-run business houses having less number of employees and simple structure of management. In the same way, new firms and those run by an individual also rely on verbal communication.

WRITTEN COMMUNICATION: IS IT OUT DATED?

Technology is becoming increasingly a part of most business environments and can assist businesses with everything from inventory control to draft letters. Writing in the work place is done more and more with the aid of computers. Almost all the biggest and medium sized organisations are planning to automate their offices. Even in a small company's office we see computers assisting in business writing. Computers helps in several ways, for example, word processing, electronic mail, graphics for displaying information visually and for composing and sending messages from one terminal to others. This is not all! We live in a world of instantaneous communication. Fax machines in the offices of one country receives the messages from another country and that too, in a few minutes. Electronic mails are received and sent from one country to another in no time. Telephone and cellular technology knows no physical distance on the earth. In short, we are living in an IT age where traditional means of business communication seems out of place. In such a time, is written communication out dated? The answer is — 'No, it is not'. Of course, we should make full use of all the latest technology and equipments in our communications. But it does not mean that traditional written communication is out dated and of no use. In situations, where there is an emergency, or where time is important, and instantaneous communication is required; we should use the facilities available. But where there is plenty of time, or the subject matter requires comprehensive details and where the telephonic communication does not serve the purpose, the written communication is cost-effective, more certain and more reliable than the electronic method. One thing is sure that written communication cannot be entirely replaced by any other means of modern communication. Following are the other reasons that emphasize the importance of written communication in business:

1. Written communication serves as a permanent and tangible record of a business transaction.
2. Unlike verbal communication, written communication leaves no scope for confusion and misinterpretation.

3. Written communication can be produced as evidence in the courts of law. Moreover, in business contracts the terms and conditions can be mentioned and analysed in detail. That leaves no room for future ambiguity.
4. It is suitable for lengthy as well as long-distance communications.
5. Till date, it is formally recognised official method of communication in business and other organisations.

A written message is useful only when it is properly and timely read. Good communication skills also include efficient reading skill. In today's time, proper and careful reading is rather more important. The technological revolution in the area of communication has resulted in abundance of information and paperwork. Thus, information overload is the obvious evil of this advancement. These and other implications of technology on business communication are discussed throughout this text.

TOOLS OF WRITTEN COMMUNICATION (BUSINESS WRITING)

Examples of typical written communication, in a business firm include the following:

(a) Business Letters

(b) Memorandums

(c) Reports

(d) Electronic Mail

Let us discuss all these major organisational tools of written communication, one by one.

(A) Business Letters

A business letter is a written message sent to someone outside the organisation. Being an effective communicator requires knowing how to write good business letters. The main reason for writing good letters is that your writings reflect you. A badly prepared letter distorts the image of the person or organisation in the mind of the reader. On the contrary, clearly stated views and good written communication skills represent a strong organisation.

To be an effective communicator, you must know when to send a letter as opposed to a memo. Letters generally go to people outside an organisation, while memos go to people inside an organisation. However, sometimes in large organisations, people will send letters to different departments instead of memos. The only other major distinctions are the audience and format.

Good grammar and use of punctuation is essential in an effective letter. There is no excuse for poor grammar, spelling, and punctuation in business letters. Do not rely on spelling and grammar checkers to find all of your errors. A letter submitted with an error that is overlooked states that the letter was not important enough to double check, and can show a lack of effort.

(B) Memorandums

A memorandum or memo is a major tool of written communication in an organisation. A memorandum is a written message sent to someone working in the same concern. A memorandum serves as a permanent record for future in case a dispute arises. The purpose of a good memo is to inform employees of an event or a change of some kind. The memo is a brief message that is usually two to five paragraphs in length. A memorandum or a memo is a media of written communication between persons, between the departmental head and his subordinates, or between one departmental head and another (in which case it becomes an IOM- i.e. inter-office memorandum).

Sometimes, a memo is misunderstood in business and government circles as a curt, almost threatening or bad-news-message, an official note from a person in authority to a subordinate, asking for an explanation for some action, or to show cause message. It is true that there are bad and threatening memos but most memos are mere instructions or conduits of routine information. Memos can become complex and impersonal in large organisations where the personal touch is difficult to maintain. Mostly the memos are used for the announcements of meetings, changes in timings, changes in procedures, upcoming events, time-tables, schedules of production, changes in position and amendments to practices which are not likely to attract any serious resistance from any section of the organisation.

The starting paragraph should describe the most important accomplishment or concerns, and this should be summarized in one or two sentences. Other paragraphs should give background to the readers so they can better understand your statements. You may also need to describe your experiments, calculations, assumptions, or remaining tasks. You may also want to have a paragraph where possible actions that need to be taken are presented and a summary of the topics is reviewed.

(C) Reports

A report is a written document in which a problem is examined for the purpose of conveying information and facts, reporting observations, putting forward new ideas, and also, making recommendations. A report is an orderly presentation of facts and figures that assists in decision-making and problem solving. Business reports can be of different types, for example, organisational policies, status reports, minutes of meetings, annual reports, financial reports, performance appraisals, press releases etc.

Reports are vital to the management process, whether their content relates to commercial or public activities. If management is concerned with long-term planning and overall policy, then it must be informed fully about the effects of the decisions it has made. It must also respond to suggestions for future actions. The instrument which makes all this possible is the report. Clearly, then, the ability to produce a good written report is an essential part of the repertoire of the effective manager, and it is worth spending time considering the main aspects of this key area.

A report may serve one or all of the following functions:

To convey ideas or information, to influence decision making, to initiate action, to serve as a persuader. Most reports, however, are selective, subjective and, to a greater or lesser degree, persuasive. In these cases, the role of the report is to be not the end of a process, but the beginning of a new one.

It should be remembered when writing a report that, as with any form of written communication, a permanent record is being created. Reports will usually be filed as they represent research which may prove valuable to the organisation.

A good report requires a subject, a writer, a reader, a structure, and a purpose. The over-riding consideration is that the report must communicate. It must be persuasive, decisive and action-centred. Indeed the writer's purpose is accomplished when the reader reacts as the writer desires.

(D) Electronic Mail (E-mail)

E-mail is a message transmitted electronically over a computer network most often connected by cable, telephone lines, or satellites. The traditional mails through post can take several days to reach its destination within the country and several weeks to go around the world. Perhaps that is why it is referred to as 'snail mail', now-a-days. E-mail or electronic mail is a very fast media of written communication. It is less expensive and saves time and money. Moreover, it is very easy to use. You can send e-mail to anyone with an e-mail address, anywhere in the world. The recipient's computer receives and stores the message almost instantaneously after it is sent. The recipient may read, respond to, file, or discard the message — all without the use of paper.

E-mail is not a replacement for the traditional postal service, phone or fax but a complementary communication media. It saves paper, postal fees and provides the ability to quickly respond to present and prospective customers of a business organisation.

Communicating by e-mail is no different from writing on your company letterhead. A business communication is business, period. A certain degree of formality is required. Just because e-mail tends to be more immediate and personable, it does not need to get personal. If your correspondent uses your first name, then by all means use his. Many people do not want such immediate informality in a business situation, especially in the international arena.

E-mail is the perfect tool to use for honing your non-verbal communication skills. Remember to use the same language unless there is profanity included. Be aware about the tone you are using. In response to the tone of customers, mirror their tone briefly in a positive way and finally slow down the tone. People like people who are like themselves. When replying to a customer relate to their interest or background such as life, work, family etc.

E-mail is one of the fastest ways to attract or lose customers because it delivers information fast to a single person or a mass of people. Company news and gossip, customer praise, complaints, and misrepresentations can all be communicated over the Internet in minutes, where in the past such communication would take days or months, if ever. The sheer volume of exchanged information has exploded since e-mail use has shot up over the past few years. The capacity to respond to quickly and easily has inspired many business owners and many customers to offer and ask for information and feedback that they might not even have attempted to provide before.

TYPES OF A REPORT

A report can be oral or written. Oral reports are also termed as 'informal reports' and written reports as 'formal reports'. An oral/informal report takes very less time for preparation and, in the same way it does not take much time of superior. These advantages, however, are more apparent than real. An effective oral report should be carefully prepared. If it is not carefully prepared, it may take a considerable period for discussion in order to bring out all the facts. The real advantage of an oral report is the chance to discuss the problem and to have two-way communication between you and your superior. The principal disadvantages of oral reports are that there is no record of the report and it is difficult to transmit the report to others.

A good written/formal report takes time and proper care to prepare. A report is not prepared for temporary use; rather it has the advantage of providing a permanent record in the files. In addition, it permits referral of the problem to higher authority. It is also possible that your superior may not have the authority to approve some or all of the recommendations that you make. In that case, the report is sent to the next higher level for implementation.

Report Writing

One should be clear about the subject, scope, and purpose of the report. The report writer must start from a clear perception of the needs, interests and requirements of the reader, who is the other end of the communication chain. As with any written communication, you must establish what your reader wants to know what he/she knows already, and what kind of terminology he/she will understand. Report writing entails the collection, organisation, and interpretation of information. Proper time and efforts should be made in the preparation, justifying the purpose of the report. When gathering information, always bear in mind the report's purpose by asking yourself:

What do I need to know?

Where do I find the information?

What graphical/numerical information should I present?

In what order should I present my material?

Before you start writing, arrange the order of presentation of each section, as well as the order within each section of the items to be discussed. Remember, you are aiming for a document which is clear, concise, and relevant. A combination of a sound framework, a clear style and an attractive appearance will encourage the reader to study the report and will make it easier to understand.

Elements Of A Report

Patterns used for reports may vary, but as a general guide the arrangement will be likely to adopt the following order:

Title Page

Contents Page

Summary

Introduction

Findings

Conclusions

Recommendations

References

Appendix

This suggested format must, of course, be used flexibly; some headings may not be appropriate for some types of reports.

Title Page

This should contain the name and status of the author, the department, and the date of issue. This page also includes the name and designation of the person(s) to whom it is submitted. The title of the report should be short, clear, and unambiguous.

Contents Page

Contents page shows the contents of the reports along with their respective page numbers.

Summary

The summary, or précis, should present the context of the report and the most important findings and recommendations. It functions both as a guide to the reader as to whether the report is of any interest to him/her, and as a time-saver for busy managers (often initial decisions are based on a reading of the summary, together with an examination of the recommendations). Writing an effective précis is an excellent test of the skills of concise, clear writing. Your aim is an overview, not to convey the minute details.

Introduction

The introduction should contain the authorising person or body requesting the report, the author or group responsible for the investigation, the purpose or reason for the report, the methods of enquiry — that is, sources and the form of enquiry used, an explanation of the arrangement and grouping of the data presented in the rest of the report, the general background to the report's subject — just enough to enable the reader to understand and follow the report.

Findings

This section of the report presents the results of your investigation and the facts you have discovered. If your findings are lengthy and/or complex, you might find it useful, both for yourself and for the reader, to end each sub-section with its own conclusion. These can be gathered, restated, and analysed in the report.

Conclusions

The conclusions are a summing up which states the results of your investigations. In other words, they are the answer to the questions raised at the beginning of the report.

Normally this section shows the writer for the first time drawing together all the threads of his/her report. No new information should appear here since you are considering the evidence presented in your findings section, and coming to a conclusion based on it.

Recommendations

This section is considered as the 'centre point of attraction' of any report. Recommendations serve as the basis for action. Recommendations should state how the conclusions should be acted upon, and what (if any) other studies should be undertaken or continued. If your report is properly written, the reader should be able to anticipate the recommendations from your conclusions. And very importantly, recommendations should always take into account the practical difficulties involved in their implementation, together with the financial implications.

Appendix

An appendix, while not always essential, is considered to be an integral part of a report. It follows the body of the report and should be treated as the equivalent of a new section (usually with separate pagination).

The appendix should contain only detailed information of the kind that would interrupt the flow of material in the body of the report and distract your reader's attention.

Reference materials of secondary importance may also be included in an appendix to avoid making the text of the report unduly bulky. Other items include documents, general reference tables, results of experiments, statistics, forms or questionnaires used, and worksheet tabulations.

When the appendix material can be sorted into several distinct topics, each topic should be presented as a separate appendix.

GUIDELINES FOR USING E-MAIL

E-mail has become, now-a-days, a formal method of business communication. Following are the guidelines for effective use of this media:

While drafting an e-mail, do not type in all capital letters. This is perceived as shouting.

Limit line length to 65-70 characters across. Otherwise some e-mail programs will wrap the text at wrong points or not wrap it at all.

Consider carefully what you write; it is a written permanent record and can be forwarded easily to others.

Do not attach large files (over 500KB) as attachments with e-mail.

When sending a web site address, always type it in the form of *http://...* because some e-mail programs will permit the user to click on a web address to go right there. Without the *http://* prefix these programs will not recognize it as such.

Write descriptive subject lines. Many busy people will only open messages with captivating subject lines. Think creatively.

Do not quote back an entire message when only responding to one or two points. Delete the excess and make a note at the top before starting the quotes. Some e-mail programs will automatically set up to quote the original message when replying and put you at the end of that message. This is very annoying to your recipients.

When forwarding messages, put your comments at the top of the message.

Do not over use acronyms like BTW (by the way) or IMHO (in my humble opinion). Not everyone is experienced with this jargon.

Read over your e-mail before you send it. Although e-mail is a more informal method of communication than writing a letter, be sure to make your points clear and concise.

(4) TECHNOLOGICAL COMMUNICATION

With the development of technology, increased use of technological or electronic communication has become increasingly popular. In this section, we are going to list all those forms of communication which are available only due to technological advancements. Today, we cannot even think of the survival of communication without the aid of technology. Let us discuss how it is different from the conventional face-to-face communication. Since e-mail has emerged to be widely used method (after telephone) of technological communication and for the purpose of simplification also we are taking e-mail as a major technological tool for comparison.

No Boundaries

Technological communication has no boundaries. The biggest advantage of electronic communication is that it knows no time and space limits. People in one part of the globe can communicate with others in another part within no time. Anybody can communicate from office, car, home, or anywhere else. All this is possible only with the help of technological advancements in the area of communication.

Better Communication

Studies[2] show that sending and receiving e-mail messages at work increases employees' commitment to their working organisation. Studies show that compared with face-to-face groups, it is easier to join and feel like a participating member of an electronic group on the Internet. Research also indicates that employees prefer electronically communicating with their bosses and supervisors when they have to negotiate or solve problems and that people are more likely to contribute to an electronic group than they are to speak out during a meeting. This allows the boss and/or group to make decisions with better information than if they were only restricted to face-to-face communication.

It Is Mostly Text Based

Another feature of technological communication is that it is mostly text based. In a face-to-face communication, people use not only words, but also gestures, facial expressions, and body language etc. to convey intended meaning. And all this is not insignificant in understanding the true meaning of the message. But, in e-mail only words can be used to convey all the emotions and feelings.

Formal Channel Of Communication

Today, e-mail has been accepted as a formal channel of written communication. Moreover, unlike face-to-face interaction, e-mail can be stored easily for future reference. In normal circumstances, it is the fastest method of sending and receiving written messages.

Now we discover other technological tools of communication.

(A) Telephony

Though the telephone lacks a visual channel, it is a relatively rich medium (after direct face-to-face interaction) for communication because feedback is fast and messages are personally focused (the only exception being group telephone meetings). The telephone is one of the early technological developments that revolutionized the nature of human communication. Telephone, even today, is a major channel of verbal communication that covers the constraint of distance. Today, a telephone device contains redialing, number storing, call-waiting, and other features for

2. Lee Sproull and Sara Keisler, *Electronic Communication*, 1992, Cambridge, MA, The MIT Press.

the IT office. Through telephone wires data is also sent and received from one computer to another. Telephone lines also provide the basis for dial-up connection to Internet. All these strengths of telephone technology have significant potential for business communication.

Cellular Phone

The cellular telephone, a significant development in the area of telephony, was developed by AT&T in 1946. The cellular telephone carries messages via regular telephone lines. Large city areas are divided into smaller geographical sub-areas called 'cells'. These cells are connected to one another through sub-area antennas, transmitters, and individually assigned frequencies. A computer transfers a call automatically to successively adjacent cells, without the caller's or receiver's knowledge.

This service is growing rapidly and is available in almost all the parts of India. The Planning Commission, in its Ninth Plan projections, has predicted a spectacular rise in the use of mobile phones and pagers. According to the Ninth Plan, the number of cellular phones will increase to 3 million, up 12 times from 2.5 lakh at present.

Cellular phones are extremely useful to business persons as this service provides complete mobility. They are also beneficial to anyone who finds him or herself helpless without access to a conventional phone. Obviously, the cellular telephone has changed the business communication environment. On the plus side, cellular telephones allow instantaneous communication with improved quality and quantity of information. In effect, technology has brought business communication to the driver's seat. On the negative side, equipment and operating costs are high compared to conventional calling. However, costs are decreasing as technology develops, competition and customer base increases.

Pager

A pager is much cheaper than a cellular phone and is, therefore, much more popular in a country like India. A pager enables a person to receive messages from anyone with access to a telephone. To send a message a call from a phone is required to access to local network operator. This network operator dials the pager's number and gives the message. The operator uses an elaborate network of computerized transmitters dotting the city and within seconds the pager receives the message.

Voice mail

Voice mail is a telephone answering system which records the verbal message of the caller. So, even if the receiver is not available on phone, his messages are received by the voice mail system. Voice mail has become an essential IT office tool, speeding up, and improving communication in today's dynamic business environment. Initially, voice mail was met with resistance at first. But slowly and gradually people realized the functions and importance of voice mail system and accepted it as an effective communication tool.

The advantages of voice mail system are – the message is stored and can be sent to different persons at the same time. The receiver does not require a computer, rather simple telephone equipment. It is particularly useful in sending short and routine messages.

How To Make The Best Use Of Telephone?

Today, the telephone is a vital business tool. Everyone uses the telephone, but only a few people know how to make sure the caller will want to continue doing business with your company. People are unable to see you or interpret the meaning of such non-verbal cues as gestures, body positioning, and facial expressions. In a business environment, the first contact you ever have with a customer is often over the phone. He or she will be forming an opinion of you from this first contact. It is very easy to give a poor impression by being disorganised and unprofessional in the way you use the phone. Conversely by using it effectively you can appear very sharp and competent.

Therefore, communicating clearly over the phone is very important. Your voice and attitude are the tools to enhance your telephone conversations. Your voice should reflect — courtesy, audibility, and friendliness. Also, the attitude towards the receiver should be positive.

We now discuss the skills that are required to be sharp and professional when talking on the phone

Know Your Objective

When making an outgoing call, you should be clear about the objectives of your communication. Always ensure that you have all the documentation you need to achieve your aim. This saves both your time and the time of the person you are talking to.

Read The Receiver

While talking try to read the receiver. Do not speak much and give the receiver also a chance to open up. Judgement about the receiver will prove beneficial in forming understanding and rapport.

Don't give wrong answers

Do not give wrong answers or hasty suggestions. If someone relies on you when you are guessing, and you guess wrong, then they will never trust you again. If you do not know something, say you will get back to them with a firm answer. And always try to give concise answers to questions. Long rambling answers are unprofessional, dull, and confusing.

Always Call Back

Timely made return calls shows etiquette and respect for others. There is nothing more frustrating than waiting for an important call that is not returned for many hours. By not returning a call you are showing a lack of concern for the other and moreover, it may also offend the feelings of that person.

Don't Over Socialize

Do not over socialize on phone. It wastes time and it may also convey idleness or lack of work on your part. In any organisation, a phone is always subject to be misused and misutilized. This is more true in case of India, people in the govt. and public sector seldom use phone for the intended purpose. Over socializing on the phone and that in the working hours should be curbed.

Remember The Time

While making a call, respect the time perception followed in the culture of the receiver. Do not make a call very early or very late. If you are calling in the morning, give the person you are talking to a chance to get a cup of tea etc. and settle in before you ring them. Do not take up people's time when they want to leave the office.

Don't Harass People

Frequent phone calls to the same person may be very disturbing. If someone is doing a job for you, do not ring them every few hours to find out how it is going. This is irritating and stressful, and slows achievement of the job.

Conclude Nicely

At the end of a call, summarise the points made. This ensures that both people agree on what has been said, and know what action will be taken. At the end of the conversation say pleasing words such as good-bye and replace the receiver gently. The person making the call should end the conversation.

Many of these points are simple courtesies. Always bear in mind that the time of the person you are talking to is limited, and that person is forming an opinion of you and your organisation's efficiency while you are on the phone.

(B) Tele-conferencing

A tele-conference is a 'telephonic' meeting in which the people can communicate using telephones and computers. The people talking cannot see each other but can speak or listen to all the people at the same time. Tele-conferencing is a money saving and time efficient way to conduct business. Tele-conferencing can help you collaborate, exchange, and present information faster and more effectively with your clients and colleagues. Meetings are, this way, easy and convenient. With the aid of Tele-conferencing a business can be more efficient, more productive, more responsive and ultimately, more profitable. Although the performance of Tele-conferencing is acceptable over high-speed links, its quality is heavily dependent upon Internet traffic. At high-traffic times, connections are usually of mediocre quality.

The next technical advancement in Tele-conferencing is Video-conferencing.

(C) Video-conferencing

Today, with the help of technology, two-way interactive communication is possible ignoring all the physical distances. Big industrial houses create 'virtual meetings' with people in distant geographical locations. Video conferencing enables a meeting or discussion between two or more groups of people who are in different places but can see and hear each other using telephone lines or through satellite. Therefore, Video-conferencing is face-to-face communication via computers using web cameras, microphones, speakers, and communication lines to transmit compressed audio and video data. Participants sit in front of a web camera and speak into a microphone. As this occurs, the data compresses and transmits to another participant who receives the data by viewing the video on a computer screen and hearing audio via the speakers. In this system, audio and video are combined and transmitted via satellites or phone lines. The telecommunication network carries pictures and sound and such conferences can take place around the world. Placing a video call is very similar to placing a telephone call. Once you are connected you see the other person in colour video and it may even be possible to transfer files to one another.

It is estimated that there are around 500 public video conferencing centres in Europe. In addition, thousands of companies around the world have now their own in-house video conferencing facilities. In India Videsh Sanchar Nigam Limited (VSNL) has four public video conferencing centres in Mumbai, New Delhi, Kolkata and Chennai.

Video-conferencing in an organisation serves many functions. It brings in professionalism and heightens the motivation level of employees. The excitement of using new technology and interacting with others increases motivation. Moreover, Video-conferencing is usually easier than visiting; therefore, communication can be more frequent as well as save time and resources. Hence, it increases connection with the outside world. It also improves communication and presentation quality. People perceive video guests as important and are, therefore, more conscious of their appearance and oral communication. Video-conferencing also increases depth of learning. Employees learn to ask better questions as well as show more depth of understanding when interacting regularly with professionals. This can be helpful to trainees in that they are learning from a primary source rather than from a textbook.

Video is advantageous when visual information is being discussed, but may not provide substantial benefit in most cases where conventional audio telephones are adequate. In addition to supporting conversations, video may also be used in less direct collaborative situations, such as by providing a view of activities at a remote location.

(D) Intranet

The latest trend in networking is the development of 'Intranet' or 'Corporate Networks' which have started changing the concept of work place itself from home to trans border offices. The intranet within a company provides data and information to employees and others with authorization to access. These networks are specific to the corporate which use them and are used for internal communication of that corporate by installing servers which talk to each other and update each other using public networks.

Intranets use the same communication protocols and hyperlinks as the Internet and thus provide a standard way of disseminating information internally and extending the application to remote business locations. The difference between the Internet and a private Intranet is who is allowed access. The Internet is available to everyone. An Intranet is a private network that uses Internet technology. Information stored within the Intranet is only accessible to individuals within the organisation. Those who are allowed access can include management, employees, and customers, and even these individuals can be limited in the amount of information they can access.

An intranet provides many benefits:

Intranet provides easy e-mail facility for participants, coordination efforts among projects and teams, free flow communication between company and customers, centralized and standardized database, effective group communication, online help for employees and customers, and reduced documentation.

(E) E-mail

E-mail, or electronic mail, is a message sent through a computer. E-mail is delivered to the recipient's account within seconds under normal circumstances. E-mail can be distributed to lists of people, called list servers, as well as to the individuals. E-mail is less formal than letters and can be sent to an overseas client, a co-worker or manager, or a distant relative in the matter of seconds. E-mail is now one of the fastest ways to gain or lose potential customers because of its ability to deliver information fast to an enormous amount of people.

E-mail facilitates two-way communication with your customers, any time, anywhere, with ease and cost-savings that is transforming the ways companies communicate everywhere. Customers can inquire, complain, send referrals, suggest improvements and even buy. How easy are you making it for your prospects and customers to work with you? However, the lack of body language, tones of voice, and shared environment, e-mail is not as rich a communication method as a telephone conversation or face-to-face. It may be difficult for your correspondent to tell if you are serious or kidding, frustrated or euphoric, happy or sad. Sarcasm has the most potential to offend and can be particularly dangerous to use in e-mail. Avoid sending e-mail that might be upsetting to the recipient. Although expressing human emotions, moods and personalities is difficult to convey when using e-mail but these days, *Emoticons* (these are the pictorial symbols showing different human emotions) have been developed as shorthand to help communicate feelings, emotions and show some personality where desired.

The advantages of e-mail are:

It is reliable and provides an immediate response. It reduces transit time and paperwork. It is faster than conventional postal service or any next day delivery service. It is cheaper than most long distances phone calls.

How to make best use of e-mail?

The wide uses of e-mail presents great dangers and opportunities to any kind and size of business. How can we ensure that we are using it to its fullest, and will not be abused in its use? There is no guarantee with e-mail, but following are the steps one can take to make best use of this tool:

- Unless you have your own Internet access through an Internet provider, be sure to check with your employer about ownership of electronic mail. Laws about the ownership of electronic mail vary from place to place. Also respect the copyright on material that you reproduce.
- Unless you are using an encryption device (hardware or software), you should assume that mail on the Internet is not secure.
- Do not send large amounts of unsolicited information to people. If your mail system allows you to forward mail, beware the forwarding loop. Be sure you have not set up forwarding on several hosts so that a message sent to you gets into an endless loop from one computer to the next to the next.
- Be sure not to send heated or negative messages even if you are provoked.
- Mails are subject to forgery and spoofing of various degrees of detectability. Apply common sense reality checks before assuming a message is secured.
- Make things easy for the recipient. In order to ensure that people know who you are, be sure to include a line or two at the end of your message with contact information. An address file can be created ahead of time and it can be added to the end of the outgoing messages. In Internet parlance, this is known as a ".sig" or "signature" file.
- Be careful when you are addressing a mail. There can be addresses which may go to a group but the address looks like it is just one person. Make sure to whom you are sending.

- Avoid lengthy e-mails. Get to the point. In problem situations do not attempt to confuse but rather make your message short and clear. You risk losing the attention of your reader if your message is too long.
- Never send chain letters via electronic mail. Chain letters are forbidden on the Internet.
- Remember that people with whom you communicate are located across the globe. If you send a message to which you want an immediate response, the person receiving it might be at home asleep when it arrives. Give them a chance to wake up, come to work, and login before assuming the mail did not arrive or that they do not care.
- Remember that the recipient is a human being whose culture, language, and habits have different points of reference from your own. Remember that date formats, measurements, and idioms may not travel well.
- Do not include control characters or non-ASCII[3] attachments in messages unless they are MIME[4] attachments or unless your mailer encodes these. If you send encoded messages make sure the recipient can decode them.
- Mail should have a subject heading which reflects the contents of the message.
- If you include a signature file keep it short. Rule of thumb is no longer than four lines.
- If you think the importance of a message justifies it, immediately reply briefly to an e-mail message to let the sender know you got it, even if you will send a longer reply later.
- Reasonable expectations for conduct via e-mail depend on your relationship to a person and the context of the communication. Norms learned in a particular e-mail environment may not apply in general to your e-mail communication with people across the Internet. Be careful with slang or local acronyms.
- The cost of delivering an e-mail message is, on the average, paid equally by the sender and the recipient (or their organisations). This is unlike other media such as physical mail, telephone, TV, or radio. Sending someone mail may also cost them in other specific ways like network bandwidth, disk space or CPU usage. This is a fundamental economic reason why unsolicited e-mail advertising is unwelcome and is forbidden in many contexts.

(F) Discussion groups

Another way to communicate with others in the global community is through online discussions. There are two types of discussions: real time and bulletin boards. In real time, discussions are interactive. You type messages that the other participants can immediately see and answer. Chat rooms are an example of real-time discussions. Chat is a form of instant communication that uses

---

3. ASCII is a universal computer code for English letters and characters. Computers store all information as binary numbers. For example, in ASCII, the letter 'A' is stored as 01000001. ASCII also refers to a method, or protocol, for copying files from one computer to another over a network, in which neither computer checks for any errors that might have been caused by static or other problems.

4. MIME or Multipurpose Internet Mail Extensions is a standard for defining the types of files attached to standard Internet mail messages. The MIME standard is used in many situations where one computer program needs to communicate with another program about what kind of file is being sent.

technology like that of e-mail. Technically, chat rooms are termed Internet Relay Chat (IRC). It is a set of protocols which allow two people to have an interactive dialogue via computer. Participants engage in text-based interaction that resembles the immediacy of in-person face-to-face encounters. Chat rooms are very numerous and diverse. Most chat services offer other functions as well, such as free e-mail, web pages, and discussion boards. Online chatting requires that participants respond immediately; they do not have much time to think about what to say or how to say it. However, chat rooms allow group members to engage in real-time discussion without needing to be in the same physical location. Most chat rooms are topic oriented and sometimes have a room leader. This person is there to monitor conversations and to facilitate the subject matter. In a country like India, this media of communication is not used, as it should be. Teenagers and young people waste their time, money, and energy on chatting with strangers.

Bulletin boards are ongoing postings that anyone can read and reply to at any time. Newsgroups are an example of bulletin-board discussions. For bulletin-board discussion groups, you will have to subscribe to a 'list' by sending a simple e-mail message. You will then receive messages posted to the bulletin board in your Inbox. Bulletin boards are an excellent way to keep up with current discussions about topics of interest to you. Discussion groups are available on almost every topic from literature to technology. If used properly, it is an excellent way to share the knowledge and information.

(G) Internet

The Internet is a network of networks in which different servers located around the world are connected to each other. It is a vast information system connecting millions of computers worldwide allowing people to communicate, conduct business, research, shop, etc. The Internet has rapidly changed from a network connecting scientists and engineers to a network connecting everyone. The designers of the original Internet could not possibly have foreseen the current success of their creation.

The Internet is widely used by corporate world over to publish information about themselves and their products. The network uses a special protocol called 'Hyper Text Transmission Protocol' or HTTP for connection and communication. The information published uses a Hyper Text Mark Up Language (HTML) which enables link between one part of the text stored on one server to other text stored on other server. Technically, the Internet is a collection of networks which is inter-connected using a particular set of standards popularly referred to as TCP/IP or Transmission Control Protocol/Internet Protocol, but more correctly called the Internet Protocol Suite (IPS). The total number of nodes or computers it connects is in the hundreds of thousands, and the number of people is in the millions. The Internet has brought revolution in information distribution and also social communication by making it instantaneous and yet at very much reduced cost. There is a good chance that every piece of information we would ever need is on the Internet, we just need to learn how to access it.

The functions and uses of Internet are: Bulletin board discussions, information search resources, e-mail, news, classifieds, personals, yellow pages, travel information, weather forecasting etc.

For more details on this topic please refer to the Chapter 14: Internet.

❑❑❑

5

COMMUNICATION MODELS

The behavioural science is not as exact and predictive like physical science. However, theories and models help us in understanding what is happening, what is the change and what should be done. As someone has rightly said, "There is nothing so practical as a good theory." Good theories and models simplify the working and process of any phenomenon for our understanding and examination. They are usually based on certain assumptions and conditions to reduce the complexities and, thus, to make the models and theories easier to understand. Models are the simple representations of how things work. A model is the approximation or abstraction of the reality. Models do not represent each and every aspect of reality but they take only relevant components for understanding. In other words, models deal with the relevant variables, and often only the relevant variables that have a major impact on the given phenomenon.

In communication, we often use models to try to present a simplified version of human communication, containing the essential components only. These models help us to find out the factors which are common to all forms of communication. With this, we can easily judge how successful a communication has been, or where it went wrong if it was not effective and what to do to improve it in the future. This way, a model helps us in understanding the intricacies of communication process. In communication literature, there are different models based on different set of assumptions and variables. Some of the popular models of communication are discussed as below:

1. Aristotle's persuasive model
2. Shannon and Weaver's transmission model
3. Berlo's model
4. Lasswell's model
5. The process model\Two way model

1. Aristotle's Persuasive Model

It is generally understood that the primary goal of communication is to exercise influence through persuasion. Probably the oldest communication models were of the persuasive type and the first basic model on persuasive communication was Aristotle's *Rhetoric*. It is believed that it was the first formal exposition on communication in the western communication theory. Aristotle observed mainly persuasive forms of communication. This may have led him to see communication as a one-way process flowing from a sender to a receiver.

Aristotle considers three elements in communication — the speaker, the speech, and the audience. The different forms of communication are:

- Arguments in the courtrooms
- Legislative assemblies, and
- Public meetings where speakers praised men and events

As per Aristotle, successful persuasion takes place when a speaker uses the right techniques to present the right message to the right audience. Once a speaker knows the interests or needs of his audience, communication is a matter of using the right techniques to get the desired response. In many ways, this is the basic model of communication and this model is still the foundation of most mass communication and the same concept of communication and its effectiveness we all carry in our minds. If you say the right thing and speak well, your audience will be convinced because you have put your ideas into their minds. But, if they are not, you can always try other techniques, arguments, facts, etc. until they get your idea as you mean it. It implies that the communicator is right in his or her approach and the fault, if any, is of the listener. The greatest shortcoming in Aristotle's theory was his assumption of persuasion as a one-way process flowing from the speaker through his messages to the listener. He did not give any attention to the listener's behaviour or response. Listener's persuasive skills are assumed to be absent.

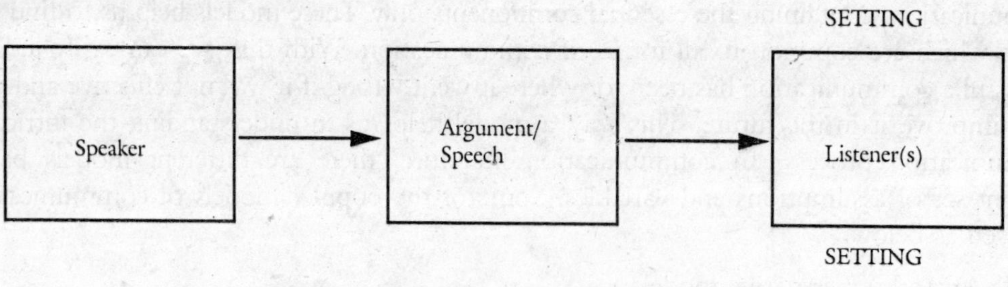

Fig. 5.1 Aristotle's Persuasive Model of Communication

Aristotle recognized the role of setting in communication. It is one of the major strengths of Aristotle's model. He observed that the situation in which one communicates has a profound influence on the communicator and the message which is being conveyed. To be effective in persuasion the speaker must try to analyze the audience and the setting accurately. According to Aristotle, the analysis of setting (purpose and location where the speaker is persuading) cannot be ignored in persuasion.

He strongly emphasized the speaker's need to consider the characteristics of the listener, such as the age and frame of mind. He also realized that other factors such as economic status, individual's primary goals have a profound effect on the reception and process of persuasion.

Preparation Of The Message And Its Delivery

Message preparation and the choice of information in the message are also very important. Speaker cannot persuade a listener in a courtroom using the same type of message prepared for a ceremony. So the choice of relevant information is essential for the preparation of a message. Preparation of the message involves:

Invention- Choice of information to be used in the message;

Arrangement- Organisation of the information in an effective manner.

Delivery- Persuasion will not be there if the presentation of the message is poor. So it requires practice for good delivery of the message.

Aristotle's model highlights another important area i.e. the message and the way the sender delivers it. When using this model as an analytic tool, we need to identify all the parts of the message, the order in which the sender presents them, and the sender's manner of expressing them. A complex, multipart message may not be received or accepted as fully as a simple one.

Types Of Proofs

Further, Aristotle believed that effective persuasion not only depends upon accurate and logical information but also on probability and doubt, therefore, one must use evidences or proofs of both the scientific and the unscientific type. Proofs for Aristotle were of three types:

Logical (scientific) i.e. using real facts, data, quotations etc.;

Emotional (unscientific) i.e. referring to illustrations, stories, examples etc.;

Ethical (unscientific) i.e. quoting speaker's own experiences and knowledge.

Strengths and weaknesses of model

Aristotle's model is also known as 'One-way model' of communication as he perceived communication as a one-way process flowing from a sender to a receiver.

Aristotle's model is oversimplified. The major weakness of this model is that it totally ignores listener's role in communication and persuasion. In every communication, there is some kind of response from the audience. Even if there is no active response from the listener that also conveys many things to the speaker, for example, it can be lack of interest, improper language etc. The one-way model also fails to explain anything about the sending and receiving process in the communication.

The Aristotelian model is considered as the most basic and fundamental model of communication theory. It gave birth to many modern models. It is still widely read in the disciplines of speech and communication. It is now believed that the application of this model is much more important to written communication than to oral. We can see the reflection of this basic model of persuasion in the modern models of communication.

(2) Shannon and Weaver's Transmission Model

The most popular model of communication is the 'Transmission Model' of communication developed by Claude Shannon and Warren Weaver. The model is based on Shannon' s work in the Bell Telephone laboratories and it was published in the year 1949.

Shannon and Weaver were principally concerned with communication technology, but now their model is applied and frequently discussed in the area of human communication. This model reduces communication to a process of 'transmitting information'. The emphasis here is very much on the transmission and reception of information. That is why, this model is also known as 'Information Model' of communication. This is worth noting that information theory, or statistical communication theory was initially developed to separate noise from information-carrying signals. That involved breaking down an information system into sub-systems so as to evaluate the efficiency of various communication channels and codes. This model has been the most influential model of communication which has yet been developed, and it reflects an understanding of what communication is.

The main features of this model are that the language in which information is carried down the channel is not the same as the representation of that information at either source or destination and distortion may occur at encoding or decoding and along the channel. Its main consequence is that the message received is not the same as the message sent.

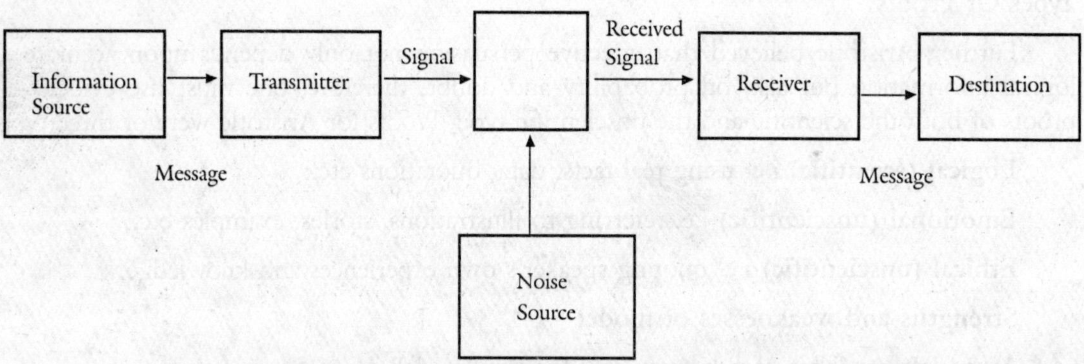

Fig. 5.2 Shannon and Weaver's Transmission Model

Claude Shannon and Warren Weaver were not social scientists but engineers working for Bell Telephone Labs in the United States. Their goal was to ensure the maximum efficiency of telephone cables and radio waves. They developed this model which was intended to assist in developing a mathematical theory of communication. Shannon and Weaver's work proved valuable for communication engineers in dealing with such issues as the capacity of various communication channels in 'bits per second'. It contributed to the computer science and it gave birth to the mathematical study of 'information theory'.

Elements Of The Model

The model assumes communication as a system composed of five essential elements and 'noise.' Shannon and Weaver's model has five elements:

1. An information source
2. A transmitter
3. A channel
4. A receiver
5. A destination

The model describes a one-way communication process going from source (sender) to destination (receiver). All human communication has some source, some person, or group of persons with a given purpose or a reason for engaging in communication. A person as the source has to express his purpose in the form of a message. That message has to be formulated in some kind of code or language for the purpose of communication. This requires an encoder. The communication encoder is responsible for taking the ideas of the source and putting them in understandable code, expressing the source's purpose in the form of a message. The message of the source is what communication is all about. Whatever is communicated is the message. The Shannon-Weaver Model, in common with many others separates the message from other components of the process of communication. The choice of the appropriate channel is also vitally important in communication. Through the channel message is passed to the receiver, a destination to whom the message was originally intended. Actually, Shannon used the term 'destination', reserving the term 'receiver' for what we call in other communication models 'decoder'.

The sixth element, noise is a dysfunctional factor. Noise is any interference with the message travelling along the channel which may lead to the signal received being different from that has been originally sent by the communicator. So, noise is anything in the message the receiver perceived that was not part of the message the sender originally intended. Shannon and Weaver are primarily concerned with physical or mechanical noise in the channel, i.e. unexplained variation in a communication channel or random error in the transmission of information. The concept of noise makes some allowance for the way in which messages may be distorted. This reflects Shannon and Weaver's concern with accuracy and efficiency.

Advantages And Weaknesses Of The Model

The Shannon and Weaver's model is simple and quantifiable. Such advantages made this model attractive to several academic disciplines. It also drew serious academic attention to human communication and information theory, leading to further theory and research.

Shannon and Weaver adds another aspect to Aristotle's model. Like Aristotle model, however, communication is represented as a linear sequence, that is, there is a sender (speaker), who encodes messages (selects the right words), and uses certain channels of communication to get that message across to a receiver (listener) who decodes the message. What makes their model more realistic and less predictive than the rhetorical model is their concept of noise. Noise is anything that interferes with getting the message, as sent, into the mind of the receiver. They realized that anything can interrupt or intrude while one is communicating, creating distortion and reducing the fidelity (faithful reproduction) of the message in the mind of the receiver.

Although the concept of noise was a step forward, the model is still limited by its basic linearity — communication happens in a straight line from sender to receiver and their focus on noise was that it existed primarily within the message. It looks at communication as a one-way process. It assumes a secondary role to the receiver who is seen as absorbing information. There was no provision in the original model for feedback i.e. reaction from the receiver. Later theorists added a 'feedback loop', but the original Shannon and Weaver's model remains linear. Shannon and Weaver's transmission model is an instrumental model, in that it treats communication as a means to a predetermined end.

The transmission model is not merely a gross over-simplification but also a misrepresentation of the nature of human communication. This is particularly important since it underlies the understanding of what communication is. The transmission model fixes and separates the roles of 'sender' and 'receiver.' But, communication between two people involves simultaneous 'sending' and 'receiving.' In Shannon and Weaver's model, the source is seen as the active decision-maker who determines the meaning of the message; the destination is the passive target.

Also, Shannon and Weaver's model has been criticized as being very mechanical in its style, (after all, they were electronic engineers) particularly in terms of its reliance on language like transmitter and receiver to describe human interaction.

(3) Berlo's Model

David Berlo's model is popularly known as the SMCR model i.e. Source — Message — Channel – Receiver model. Berlo's model proposes that there are five elements within both the source/encoder and the receiver/decoder which will affect fidelity.

Being based on dyadic communication (communication between two persons), this model is different from transmission models. It stresses the role of the relationship between the communicator and the receiver as an important variable in the communication process. A greater emphasis has been put on the factors to be taken into account at each end of the communication. Therefore, this model interprets that the message will be more effectively encoded and decoded, if the communication skills of the sender and the receiver are highly developed. As per Berlo, in any conversation, we can easily determine communication skill level, personal characteristics etc. of both the source and the receiver. The basic limitation of this model remains, its inability to judge the competence of both the parties in communication, and to make any firm predictions about the likely success of the communication.

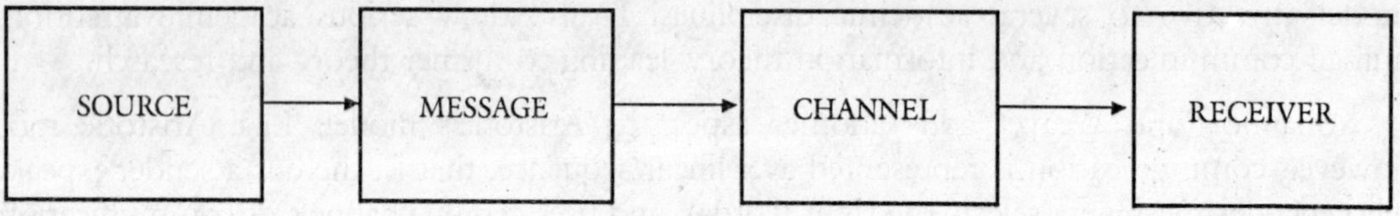

Fig. 5.3 Berlo's Model

The communicator's (encoder) communication behaviour is affected by his/her knowledge, perceptions, attitudes, the ways in which he or she can produce or control messages, the choice of communication channels and the subject matter. All these factors apply equally to the receiver (decoder) also. But, in Berlo's model, the receiver's (decoder) role is passive. It is the role of the communicator to control and regulate the flow of communication. The model also includes a feedback loop which reduces the element of linearity.

The basic merit of Berlo's model is its ability to put light on the factors that are responsible for the unpredictability of communication. Therefore, it is useful as a broad framework for the audience research.

(4) Lasswell's Model

Harold Lasswell, an American sociologist's model of communication is concerned with answering the question, 'Who says what in which channel to whom with what effect?' Lasswell's research in communication is closely related to behaviouristic approaches. Lasswell's model is primarily concerned with mass communication, therefore, his model is concerned with the messages present in the media.

Lasswell's model consists of five major components. Since Lasswell's model is primarily concerned with mass communication, so it emphasizes to find the answers to questions concerned with 'Who' (communicator), Says what (message), In what channel (channel), To whom (receiver), With what effect (the result or effect). The answer for 'Who' is the area for Control Research, 'Message' is for Content Research, the choice of 'Channel' is Medium Research, the 'Receiver' is Audience Research and the 'Effects' of communication are analysed under Effects Research.

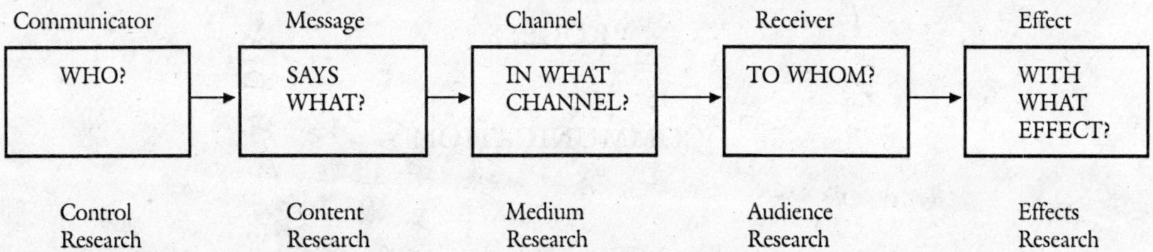

Fig. 5.4 Laswell's Model

In our routine communication, we are usually not conscious of thinking about our messages. But in the area of mass media, the message and its contents are very important. The message is transferred through the channel or media. In every communication, the choice of medium or channel is very important. In mass communication the choice of appropriate medium requires thorough investigation. Not only the medium but also the analysis of the receiver or target audience requires attention. Lasswell's model is also concerned with the effects of communication. This introduces the question of media effects. Communication always has certain objectives to achieve. The effects of the communication can be judged only with the help of feedback. In short, this model is quite simple and easy to understand. It is most widely quoted in the area of mass communication.

(5) The Process Model/Two-way Model

The process model explains communication as a process or flow. This model combines ideas from several communication theorists and it is the most common and basic approach to understand what communication is.

COMMUNICATION AS A PROCESS

The person who initiates the communication process is referred to as the communicator (sender/writer/speaker). The communicator first of all formulates an idea about the subject matter of communication. Even before the generation of an idea there must be a stimulus, an event that creates within an individual the need to communicate. This stimulus can be internal or external. An internal stimulus is simply an idea that forms within the mind. External stimuli come from outside world through sensory organs — eyes, ears, nose, mouth, and skin. This stimulus can be facts, views, suggestions, opinions, or any information which the sender wants to communicate.

The idea is then translated by him into words, symbols, and some other form of message, which he expects the receiver to understand. This process of conversion of subject matter into symbols is known as encoding of the message.

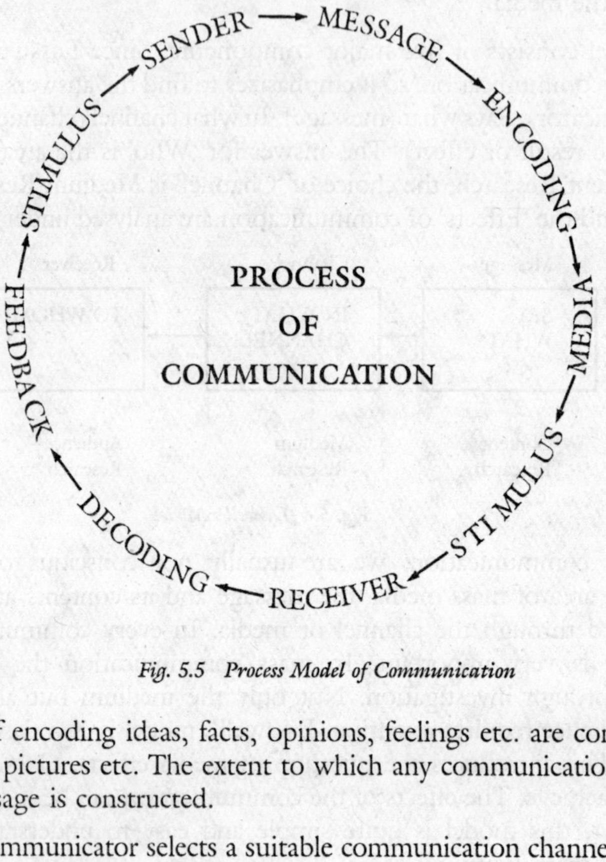

Fig. 5.5 Process Model of Communication

In the process of encoding ideas, facts, opinions, feelings etc. are converted into symbols, signs, words, actions, pictures etc. The extent to which any communication is effective depends on how well the message is constructed.

After this, the communicator selects a suitable communication channel for the transmission of the message to the receiver. Communication channel means the medium or media through which the message passes. Oral messages might be transmitted through face-to-face conversation, telephone conversation, voice mail etc. Written messages might be conveyed through an office memo, a report, a letter, notice, electronic mail etc. And non-verbal messages might be transmitted through facial expressions, gestures, or body movement. The receiver of the message also known as Communicatee (listener, reader, receiver) receives the transmitted message and at this point control passes from the sender to the receiver. Receiver decodes the message and interprets it. Decoding is the process of translation of an encoded message into that language which is understandable to the receiver. Depending upon the perception of the receiver, he or she interprets the message. Every person has a unique perception about things based on his or her individual experiences, emotions, knowledge, customs, status, and a number of other factors. If everyone around us had the same perception about things, communication would have been much easier. The manner in which the sender and receiver perceive the same word could give rise to difference in encoding and decoding. After decoding the message receiver formulates his message (reply), encodes it and transmits it to the original sender (now receiver). This is known as feedback and it is the most important element in two-way communication. The meaning of the term feedback in communication is the verbal or non-verbal response received from the individual to whom a message is directed. Feedback suggests that communication includes a return loop by which the sender obtains reactions from the receiver. In the absence of feedback, no communication can be termed as effective communication. The term feedback has an interesting history in communication. In 1961, Norbert Wiener in his book *Cybernetics* proposed a concept called cybernetics. This is a process model based on built-in monitoring of the environment and modifying components of the overall system. In other words, the system has in its processes the ability to sense stimuli from its environment and to implement adjustments to the system to make it more responsive. Electronic fuel systems on automobiles and thermostats in home air conditioning systems are good examples. In cybernetics, feedback refers to the ability of man and some machines to detect an error or deviation from what is desired in an operation and to feed back that error to a control mechanism, which then makes the necessary correction. The idea was incorporated into the human communication model and suggested that understanding could only be evaluated if the sender receives feedback as a measure of the receiver's understanding.

❑❑❑

6

Business Writing And Presentations

Business writing is the written communication in any business organisation. Writing is crucial to any business organisation as it is the major source of documentation. In a business organisation, through written communication, people can exchange information, make recommendations, motivate, consult, plan, give and take orders. Business writing is the permanent record of business communication. Letters, memos, and reports are the most common forms of business writing. Business letters are written when dealing with outside people and organisations. Memos are media of internal organisational communication. For major projects and proposals, reports are written to convey information and to gain approval. (All these tools of business writing are discussed in the Chapter 4: Forms of Communication)

Writing is the major means of communication within an organisation. It is estimated that a manager's 30% of work-time is engaged in written communication. Thus, it is absolutely vital for a manager to actively develop the skill of writing; not only because of the time involved in writing, but also because his whole career may depend upon it. But some people falsely believe that successful business people need only good ideas, because a subordinate or a secretary will translate those ideas into a clear and precise written document. With the changing role of technology in communication, the chances are that managers will do more and more of their own writing, from inputting their ideas at a computer system to making corrections on the final draft.

Is writing effectively so important in business world today? Let us answer this question.

Writing Is A Part Of Every Job

Almost every job requires some writing. So writing is a part of every job. It is through writing that rules and procedures can be explained, decisions can be confirmed, policies can be recommended, products can be promoted, orders can be issued, and many other necessary tasks can be performed to carry on business. Even for people like advertising executives, corporate planners, marketing research analysts, public relations managers etc. writing and the working are the same things.

It Gives Freedom And Flexibility

Writing allows freedom and flexibility to the readers. It allows readers to decide when and how much they want to read. They have a chance to 're-read' if necessary and to reflect upon a message or proposal. Business proposals or reports cannot be prepared and narrated orally but they require strong writing skills. Often reports and proposals are based on technical and complicated data which is very difficult to present orally to the management. The written media gives the reader full freedom and flexibility to read the document at his or her convenience.

WRITING HELPS IN CAREER DEVELOPMENT

Effective writing skills are also desirable for a good job and job promotion. A person with good written communication skills always has good chances of promotion and success in any organisation. Hundreds of students with good academic records graduate every year from colleges and business schools. But only a few of them can communicate effectively through writing. Many of the students do not even know how to write their resumes or job applications.

The Words Have Power

Writing is very powerful — and for this reason, it is said that the pen is mightier than the sword. The power comes from its potential as an efficient and effective means of communication. Good writing will assist you in achieving many goals. In writing, you are allowed to communicate conversationally, convincingly, and clearly. The oral communication relies entirely on human memory, which is an unreliable vehicle, whereas the written communication can be easily stored and saved for future use.

It Helps In Solving Problems

Writing also helps in solving problems and making decisions. In other words, writing can be used as a way of thinking. Studies have proved that writing helps in making thinking clear and in solving ambiguous problems. When we try to write down a problem, we need to define and think about the problem in a logical manner. This process brings all the hidden aspects of the problem on the surface and the writer easily finds the solution.

Essentials Of A Business Writer

Effective business writing requires more than fundamental writing skills, and there is no substitute for a well-written document. In oral communication, the listeners can interrupt to clarify something they have misunderstood. In written media, this luxury is not available. One must write clearly and in a way that is understood by all the readers.

We are often encouraged to write just like we speak. But written language and spoken language are not the same and the differences are important when we write for the business. Contrary to the popular belief, we should not write as we speak. When we prepare written material for advertisements, business letters, magazine articles etc. we have more time to organise our thoughts than we do when we talk. Consequently, our readers expect us to use that time to review what we have written, clean up the language, and clarify the sentences that may be confusing. Also, one should avoid regional dialects and expressions in the business writing. They may work fine for a local audience, but in business, the written words may be read by the potential customers all over the nation and probably all over the world. Writing well makes a business look good and helps build customer confidence. It is also true that most of the customers only know a business organisation through their written communication.

Problem Solving Aptitude

A business writer should have problem solving skills. Logical and problem solving aptitude helps in drafting a good piece of written communication whether it is a memo, a report or a business letter. A person with problem solving aptitude takes a problem and mentally goes through all the information that is relevant and decides what is the optimum solution under the current circumstances. A solution-oriented person identifies the problem, collects the required data, and finds the solution and he follows this aptitude in writing too.

Verbal Skills

Good verbal communication skills are also helpful in writing. The art of conversation and arguments can be applied in writing as well. The ability as a speaker to assert your viewpoint and motivate others to follow your logic helps you in becoming a persuasive writer.

Writing Skills

Writing skills and the command over communicating language are the fundamental requirements to be an effective writer. In schools and colleges, students write paragraphs, essays, and exams. Assignments and reports are prepared for the class. All this helps in acquiring good writing skills. The other important thing is the knowledge about the language. In India, English is no more a foreign language now. Rather it is the most popular formal business language in vogue. Whatever is the language, one must try to master its use both in oral and written communication. We all want to qualify as quickly as possible, but there are no short cuts in learning, and conscientious work over a long period is the best way to ensure success.

Love For Reading

Written communication is successful only when it is read. In today's technological age, the abundance of information has created the problem of information overload. The information overload is one of the necessary evils of our times. (These and other implications of technology on business communication are discussed throughout this text.) Everyday we receive so much of written information that it is almost impossible to go through each and every item. The respect for written words can come only when we have love for reading. Anyone fascinated by language can apply this love of words in developing business-writing skills.

Seven C's Of Communication

For effective communication, oral or written, there are generally accepted certain principles. These principles guide the communicator for the choice of appropriate words and for the better quality of presentation skills relevant for the purpose of communication. Among the principles, the concept of "Seven C's" is very important. These C's are completeness, conciseness, consideration, concreteness, clearness, courtesy and correctness. These principles are universal in nature and can be applied to all forms of communication.

(1) Completeness

A message (oral or written) must be complete in all respects. It must contain all the facts, figures, data, views which are required to be conveyed to the reader or the listener. It is very important to note that in inter-personal communication, the sender and the receiver, always differ in their nature, understanding of things, experiences, academic backgrounds, viewpoints, attitudes etc. So, while drafting the message, the communicator should take into consideration all these factors and must try to include all the relevant information to bridge the distance for better understanding. A complete business message serves many purposes – it avoids additional future communication for clarity and explanations and build good image of the organisation. A complete message leaves no room for misunderstanding resulting into better relations and avoiding the chances of litigation.

(2) Conciseness

Conciseness simply means conveying the full message without being wordy. A short and concise manner of expression is essential. This should aim at saying as much as possible in as brief a form as is consistent with clearness and courtesy. A message must be complete before it is sent to the receiver, at the same time it must avoid unnecessary and lengthy details without sacrificing the desired quality of the message. A message with unnecessary and purposeless details causes wastage of time both on the part of the sender and the receiver and makes the meaning poor and ambiguous. A concise message requires proper understanding of the subject matter to be conveyed, relevant choice of words and balanced organisation of the contents of the message while avoiding irrelevant details and unnecessary repetitions.

(3) Consideration

The principle of consideration holds 'considering the receiver's viewpoint while preparing the message'. A communicator should be empathetic while handling the subject matter – he must not loose sight of receiver's emotions, circumstances, attitudes, problems, and particular reactions to various situations. The message must convey the interest and concern for receiver's feelings. Derogatory, offending or negative remarks should be avoided in the message. Communicator must try to include positive, pleasant, and motivational facts to show true consideration for the receiver. Simple rule for effective communication is to follow 'You' approach instead of emphasizing 'I' and 'We'. A communicator should try to develop true interest in the receiver/ audience.

(4) Concreteness

Concreteness means clear, definite, and specific message while avoiding vague, ambiguous, and too general statements. A piece of communication must possess the essential of concreteness. The importance of this is seen from the success with which business communication fulfils its chief function, namely, its power to establish the conditions of any business transactions in such a manner as to avoid any subsequent difference of opinion or disputes. Hence, the greatest care has to be exercised in selecting those expressions which correspond best to the ideas which the writer desires to present. A concrete message does not mean using technical or expert language, rather using direct and specific language relevant for the understanding of the subject mater. Concreteness also does not mean compromising courtesy or consideration for receiver's feelings. Too much use of general statements should be avoided in the business or formal communication. Misunderstanding of words can cause unnecessary controversies and conflicts between the communicating parties.

(5) Clearness

A careful use of words is necessary so as to exclude obligations which were never intended, and to convey the complete and exact meaning which was intended. There should also be the greatest possible restriction of the use of foreign or unfamiliar words, as well as the avoidance of abbreviations and expressions which tend to distort the language. Clearness means making message clear in the mind of receivers. It requires clarity of thinking, clarity of expressions and understanding of receiver's environment and circumstances. Clarity of the objective of communication ensures effective and clear transmission of the message. Vague, ambiguous and confusing words should be avoided. Technical expressions, slangs and cryptic language should be avoided as far as possible and whenever it has to be used the required details for clarity of the meaning must also be provided.

(6) Courtesy

A polite form of language should be used, but it must not become effusive. It should be natural, fluent, free from self-consciousness; and should avoid superfluous flattery, empty phrases and personal irritation. Courtesy is not the mechanical use of 'please', 'thank you', 'welcome' words rather it is more than that; it requires a sincere considerate attitude. Courtesy in the communication is reflected through politeness, respect, and care for the receiver. While drafting the message not only the choice of words matters but the tone of expressions is also very important. The use of positive, appreciative and thoughtful expressions build the goodwill of the communicator.

(7) Correctness

The message to be communicated must be correct in all respects. Correctness of the message means use of the proper grammar, spellings, and punctuations etc. Not only the language and words used in the message must transmit the same meaning, which the sender has in his mind, but also the right use of words and expressions in the right place and in the appropriate format and style. The message should adequately serve the intended purpose, must be to the point, and should manifest a thorough knowledge of the subject with which it deals.

The information supplied in the message should be exact and accurate. It must be remembered that a specific but accurate message is much better than detailed but inaccurate message. Wrong information, facts, figures conveyed harms the reputation and image of the communicator, whereas, use of accurate data enhances goodwill of the firm. It is advisable that before sending the message to the receiver/ audience, the communicator should thoroughly check the accuracy of the information supplied in the message.

BUSINESS PRESENTATIONS

The ability to speak effectively is as crucial as the ability to write effectively. During office routine, employees will actually spend more time speaking than writing; using the phone; conversing informally with colleagues, subordinates, and superiors on routine topics; conducting meetings; working in groups; participating in conferences and sales presentations etc. It is also true that the higher an employee moves in an organisation, the more important speaking skills become. Moreover, most of the people will observe our ability to communicate only through our presentation skills. An oral presentation is an important part of business communications, whether it is a speech or proposal to some outside business organisation or an outline of plans to a group of colleagues. An oral presentation is inevitable in any business organisation. Not only the presentation but also its effective delivery is important.

Effective communication is becoming even more important for our survival and growth in the IT age and is now considered an essential skill in today's business. It is a widely accepted fact that the delivery or presentation of ideas and information is probably the most important factor in gaining the acceptance by the audience. Good ideas and information are rarely accepted on their own merit. Good ideas poorly presented are often discarded and not accepted. The acceptance of your ideas depends on your ability to communicate them to others.

In this IT age, widespread use of laptop computers with powerful presentation tools allows the quick development of good and effective visual aids to support a presentation. The widespread use of the modern presentation tools gives a false sense of security that we have a good presentation just because we have some pretty slides. But visual aids cannot save a poorly structured and delivered presentation. Over reliance on technology is one of the major pitfalls of presentations. No amount of fancy equipment is going to overcome a lack of content or an inability to put that across. As a presenter, you need to attract the attention of audience through contrast, novelty, and emotion. If all you are doing is reading notes from a handout or a slideshow then what value are you adding by reading it and taking everyone's time? The words should literally illustrate the notes.

Planning Presentation

The development of an effective presentation requires careful planning, preparation, and delivery. Most of the work is expended in the planning and preparation phase. The delivery phase is the shortest phase and can be the most enjoyable, if the planning and preparation phase have been done properly. This is particularly true when you see the positive audience reactions and receive their compliments. The best advice for delivering an effective presentation is to be prepared. The delivery will be very easy when you are well prepared.

Set Your Goal

The first step in planning a presentation is to determine the purpose of presentation. What decision do you want the audience to make? What outcome/conclusion do you want them to reach? What action do you want them to take? Your presentation is a success when you deliver the result that was expected. So the very first thing is to be clear about the objective of the speech. The goal of an oral presentation can be: to persuade or sell something, to impart knowledge or to teach something, to stimulate thought, to give some information. In addition, it can be for entertainment. It is a good idea to write down the objective of the speech in one sentence. It is beneficial as it clears the speaker's mind right at the start. Moreover, the selection of material can be based on fulfilling the objective and when the notes are complete the presenter can again check whether major goal is achieved.

Plan And Organise The Contents

For planning the contents of the speech, determine what information and data you need. You may also want to choose information that will appeal to the audience—particularly their attitudes, interests, biases, and prejudices about the topic. In selecting content, consider a variety of information types: statistics, testimony, cases, illustrations, history, and particularly narratives that help convey the goal you have for your presentation. Check the content for accuracy, use reliable data, check resources, and make sure your evidence supports your conclusions.

While choosing the contents of presentation it must be remembered that these are for the purpose of 'speaking' not for the purpose of 'reading'. Because listening is more difficult than reading, narratives can be particularly effective in retaining the attention of your listeners. While statistics and data are often necessary in building your argument, narratives interspersed with data provide an important change of pace needed to keep listeners attentive. In short, vary your content, but be sure that every item you include pertains to the goal of presentation. After planning the contents organise them. Your options are similar to those available for a written report. Select whichever method makes the material most manageable for you as a planner and most interesting and dynamic for the listener. It can be according to the— order of importance; chronological order; geographic order; division or classification etc.

Analyse The Audience

Just as readers determine the success of written communication, audiences determine the success of oral presentations. Writing or speaking is successful if the reader or listener responds the way communicator desires. A presenter must try to judge how the audience will respond. This judgement can be based on their educational and cultural background, knowledge of the subject, technical expertise, position in the organisation, and principal uncertainties or questions in this situation.

A presenter cannot speak effectively to people without first understanding their perspective. For most internal business presentations, it is fairly easy to assess the listeners. Most will be aware of your experience and why you are talking to them. They will be interested in your subject, since it will presumably have a bearing on the business as a whole. And, as business associates, they will be fairly homogeneous in their backgrounds or experience. But with a formal speech to outsiders, the task of assessing the audience is more difficult. The listeners are more likely to come from diverse backgrounds or occupations. It is a good idea to discuss some shared concerns they have, for example economic, political, or cultural issues. When you analyze your audience, try to focus on their professional as well as on their personal profiles. You have to keep both profiles in mind. Your analysis will suggest what you should say and what you should not say, and the tone you should use.

To be an effective speaker, you must know your audience, establish a relationship by being sincere and knowledgeable about the subject, then conform to their expectations about dress, demeanour, choice of language, and attitude toward them and the topic. All the above points will determine the material use and the approach to the speech. For example, a computer expert talking to other computer experts about the latest technology will be able to use far more technical language than would be possible when talking to a group of non-experts. You have a duty to those who listen to you to make sure your speech is pitched at the right level for them. Good rapport with the audience is the key to success.

Assess The Environment

The environment in which you have to speak can either hinder or help. The aim should be to minimize the hindrances and maximize the good points. Usually, a presenter does not get the time or opportunity to prepare or to check the room where the presentation is to take place. But if you have the access to the presentation room, make sure that the room is properly set-up and you can use the space comfortably. It is also important to ensure that you can focus on the ideas in the presentation, not on the room, its lighting, its comfort or the machinery which you are using. Check to see that any audio-visual aids you need, will be on hand and in good working order. If you have to use a microphone then find out how large the room is. It is better to have tried your voice beforehand than to make adjustments with the audience present.

Become aware of any likely distractions for you and your audience. A speaker who can see interesting things happening outside the window is likely to find it harder to concentrate on the audience. Other distractions like noise and general interruption need to be taken care of as far as possible.

Rehearsal Helps

Wandering presentations that lack focus, or those too dependent on working from notes, or long pauses to compose your thoughts are never acceptable. Rehearsing the presentation includes more than just going over what you will be saying. Rehearsing includes the entire presentation even using the same presentation tools. If you are using slides, or a projector, and have access to the room you will be presenting in, rehearse there. Moreover, do not memorize. Rehearsing is one thing, committing the presentation to memory and performing it by heart, is not the way to go. You need to present, not to recite. But use your notes very sparingly. Too much time spent reading notes may convince your audience that you are unprepared.

DELIVERING PRESENTATION

The delivery of effective presentations is one of the best ways to get your ideas accepted and to develop new opportunities. A good presentation will increase your credibility, enhance your authority as an expert, and most importantly show respect for the audience who is investing their time and effort listening to you.

Interact With Audience

Interaction and involvement with the audience is the first step in making a presentation successful. Where there are a limited number of people call them by name. Start every presentation by going around the room asking everybody to introduce him or herself. Now, you can call on people by name, which will make all the difference. Not only will you be able to associate a face and name but the audience members will likely open up because they are no longer strangers.

Besides providing their names, ask some participants to give a little background about themselves. Ask some questions. When did they start with the firm or department? What did they do previously? What would they like to get out of the presentation? As you delve into your presentation, do not let much time pass before you involve the audience.

Theme Is Important

When you have heard from them, spend a moment telling them about yourself to establish your authority on the subject at hand and the theme of the presentation. In a speech you should begin with the theme of your presentation. The theme need not be the eventual title; rather, it is a planning device, a linchpin to hold together the various facts or ideas you want to discuss. As you begin presentation, state your goal in terms of your audience's background and attitude. Announce your purpose early in the presentation to prepare audience for the main ideas to come. You may want to restate the purpose in words familiar to the audience.

Use Right Language

Using the right words is essential for both written and spoken communication. While the written words can be corrected easily, spoken words cannot. The speaker may not be aware of the slips he makes. We are talking about a serious exchange of ideas in a formal situation. For instance, a manager has to address his subordinates; an expert has to talk to the members of the production department. Using the exact word is an art and it is perfected through conscious practice. The right word for the right occasion should be the first principle. Do not use slang or informal speech for a formal topic. Fit your words to your topic. Avoid clichés. Use appropriate analogies. Avoid pompous words; never use big words to impress your audience. Use words and expressions which your audience is likely to understand. Appropriate quotations can make a noticeable impact on your audience.

Pause For Retention

Do not be afraid of pausing. You do not have to rush through it all like an express train. Give the audience time to take in and digest what you are saying. Certainly, pause after the main points of your talk. Pauses are essential to increase information retention. Verbal pauses can help an audience absorb information.

Present With A Style

A presentation may have effective content, excellent ideas, and accurate supporting statistics. However, if the style used in speaking is inappropriate to the occasion, to the audience and to the purpose, everything will be ineffective. The most effective style is usually a conversational style i.e. using short sentences, concrete language, and in a manner as if you are talking to the audience. When a speaker writes the entire speech and memorizes it, the presentation does not sound as if the speaker is talking naturally to the audience. The best delivery sounds like natural conversation. Look at people while you talk. The audience will feel that you are speaking directly to them.

Time Is A Constraint

In presentations you have limited time. Whatever the length of time allocated to your presentation, stick to it. If an audience expects a half-hour talk and you speak for only fifteen minutes, they may feel somehow cheated; especially if they have given up valuable time or paid money to attend. Taking more than the expected time is also not welcome. Even ten minutes beyond the expected length can seem like an eternity to an audience. Psychologists have suggested that most people's attention span is not longer than twenty minutes, and many people's thoughts begin to wander long before that. If your presentation is scheduled right before a meal, the audience may be even more restless. On the other hand, if it is scheduled right after a heavy meal, the audience may be sleepy. If you anticipate either of these problems, plan to counteract them by:

- Incorporating variety in your pace and voice;
- Using visual images;
- Involving the audience in the presentation such as asking a question; or
- Accentuating possible dramatic elements.

Use Latest Presentation Tools

With the development of technology, there are a great many presentation tools available such as Slides, LCD (Liquid Crystal Display) Projectors, Laptops, LCD panels, Video, Multimedia, Laser Pointers, Overheads, Photo-quality printers and Poster printers. Determine your communication needs, the presentation environment, and select the right type of tools to get your message across. We are living in a time when communication is visual and verbal. Visual aids are as important to oral communication as they are to written communication.

Visual aids help audience understand your ideas it also shows relationships among ideas; it helps the audience follow your arguments; and at the same time helps audience remember what you said. In addition, the presentation that uses visual aids effectively is more persuasive, more professional, and more interesting. Audio-visual aids help not only to clarify material and give it impact but also to keep an audience alert.

Avoid This

Avoid pointless actions such as adjusting your glasses, stepping out of your shoes, or attending to your clothes. Acts of self-maintenance distract you from your message. Avoid apologies. Never begin by stating that you do not know what you are doing, have not prepared, or know little about the topic. Avoid visuals that use too many colours—more than four on any one aid. Avoid making audience study your visual aids and other tools. If they are busy trying to decipher your visual aid, they will not be listening to you.

Conclude

Finally, simply summarize the main points of your presentation and then finish in a forceful and definitive way. The conclusion should reiterate the ideas presented and reinforce the purpose of the presentation. The conclusion to the presentation should help the audience understand the significance of your talk and remember main points. The conclusion should not be long, but it should leave the audience with a positive feeling about you and your ideas.

❑❑❑

7

COMMUNICATING NON-VERBALLY

It is true that we cannot live without communication. It is one of the basic needs of human beings. We spend more than 80 per cent of our waking time communicating our ideas, feelings, thoughts, and knowledge to others. However, we do not recognize that a great deal of our communication is of a non-verbal form as opposed to the oral and written forms. When we say 'communication', we immediately perceive of oral conversations, letters, telephones, television, books — in short, all the devices related to verbal communication. Verbal communication is organized by language; non-verbal communication is not. Non-verbal communication is independent of a formal language that is, communication takes place without the use of spoken words. No doubt, the role of verbal communication is unmatchable, but it does not tell the entire story. In face-to-face communications, our messages are sent on two levels simultaneously. If the non-verbal cues and the spoken message are incongruous, the flow of communication is hindered. Right or wrong, the receiver of the communication tends to base the intentions of the sender on the non-verbal cues he receives. Therefore, non-verbal behaviour is also important. More than an exchange of words occurs when people communicate; people's physical behaviour indicates feelings, beliefs, and attitudes as well. Such physical behaviour includes facial expressions, eye contact, gestures, movements of the whole body, and posture. The human body can produce over 700,000 unique movements that combine to create non-verbal communication. Other non-verbal factors that affect communication include the environment in which we communicate, physical appearance and dress, the distance between communicators, touch, and vocal cues. Verbal and non-verbal factors work in combination to give a total impression, and a wide range of behaviour interacting within a particular context creates the total message. Albert E. Scheflen, in *How Behaviour Means,* concludes: "This relation between behaviour and context defines a system of meaning."[1] Studies shows that approximately 70 per cent of the meaning of any message come from non-verbal channels. So the field of communication is not confined to verbal presentation and effective speaking rather it owes its origin to different disciplines such as psychology, psychiatry, anthropology, sociology, and ethnology. This combination of human-oriented fields com-

1. Albert E. Scheflen, *How Behaviour Means,* (New York: Gordon and Breach Science Publishers, 1973), p. 18.

bines to create an amalgam in which human communication is studied from psychological, physical, and cultural viewpoints at the same time.

It is very unfortunate that almost all the communication studies are foreign. So far, very less work has been done in India, almost negligible. That is why the present text heavily draws on foreign references.

Is It Useful?

Everyday we communicate, and the interesting thing is, most of our communication takes place non-verbally than by any other method. That is why it is surprising that over the thousands of years of man's evolution on the earth, the non-verbal aspects of communication have not been actively studied on any scale. It was only in the late 1960s that the public became aware when Julius Fast wrote the book 'Body Language' and it was a summary of the work done by the behavioural scientists on non-verbal communication. Charlie Chaplin and other silent movie actors can be termed as the pioneers of non-verbal communication skills. Charles Darwin's *The Expression of the Emotions* published in 1872 is also a landmark in this regard. Since then researchers have noted and discovered almost one million non-verbal cues and signals. The ancient tribal man could communicate only through non-verbal communication. In the absence of any language, they communicated through guttural sounds, gestures, drawings etc.

Experts on non-verbal communication agree that body language movements are partly instinctive, partly taught, and partly imitative. Unlike verbal interaction, however, most kinesic gestures are rarely explicitly taught, but instead learned through an implicit process.

Many people believe that non-verbal behaviour represents more true characteristics, attitudes, and feelings about people than does verbal behaviour, and that one can determine secret feelings about others from their actions. Scholars and researchers, however, disagree exactly how much one can learn from observing kinesic actions. In his book *Silent Messages*, Albert Mehrabian suggests that people communicate through media other than our words much more than we do through the words we choose. It should be noted here that no single gesture or behaviour is particularly useful in determining meaning. A number of factors influence our body movements; it is very difficult to distinguish the meaningful actions with accuracy. However, correlated groups of the behaviour for example postures, facial expressions, arm movements etc. can lead to meaningful hypothesis about a person's feelings. Moreover, many gestures have widely understood meanings. This seems to be more realistic. For many people, foot shaking and finger tapping signify nervousness, impatience, or boredom. A clenched fist typically indicates hostility or anger. Opening one's hands to another typically suggests openness, sincerity, and acceptance. Scratching, digging, or picking at one's own hands or body often conveys nervousness, hostility, or conflict. It is emphasized again that no single gesture carries meaning in and of itself. Also, the gestures do not always mean the same thing.

Gestures are not always culture-proof, that means, in different cultures one particular gesture may convey different and opposite meanings. For example, if you nod by moving your head up and down vertically, in India it means a 'yes,' whereas the same gesture in, say, Kuwait would mean the exact opposite, a 'no.' In India, a woman sometimes uses the gesture of touching her forefinger to her nose to express astonishment. In the Middle East, the same gesture stands for 'at your service,' and can be employed by either sex, but is used predominantly by men. In Iran the gesture that stands for 'at your service' is to put the palm of one's right hand over one's right eye.

On the other hand certain gestures are universally applicable. They are performed by cultures all around the world; the most famous examples include smiling, frowning and crying. Therefore, to understand a person's meaning, we must acknowledge all the cues they are emitting, not just isolated gestures, and the context in which these cues are occurring. It is the aggregate of all the gestures, movements, and the context that will decide the accurate interpretation of a person's feelings. Not only for independent judgement, non-verbal cues are also important for supporting verbal messages. This way, non-verbal signals can play many roles in the total communication process. At times it may be subordinate to the verbal function. At times it may be supplementary to the verbal function. At times non-verbal communication can be the primary communication function. Albert Mehrabian[1] found in his research that only about 7 per cent of the emotional meaning of a message is communicated through explicit verbal channels. About 38 per cent is communicated by paralanguage, which is basically the use of the voice. About 55 per cent comes through non-verbal, which includes such things as gesture, posture, facial expression, etc. Miller[2] also suggests the same thing "only 7% of a message is sent through words with the remaining 93% sent through facial expressions (55%) and vocal intonation (38%)." While this empirical percentage seems somewhat difficult to believe, it surely points out trends about the meaning we place on non-verbal communication.

Miller explains why humans use non-verbal communication to such a degree:

(1) Words have their own limitations. It is easier to explain the shape and design of something or give instructions using arm and hand gestures or head nods.

(2) Non-verbal signals are very effective. They primarily express inner feelings and evoke immediate action or response.

(3) Non-verbal messages are taken as more genuine. Non-verbal behaviour cannot be easily controlled as we control our verbal communication.

(4) Non-verbal signals can express even those feelings which are, otherwise, difficult to convey. These are the feelings of superiority or dislike or the feelings that etiquette or rules may prevent from being stated verbally. There is also other advantage of being able to change one's mind since a verbal commitment has not been made.

FEATURES OF NON-VERBAL COMMUNICATION

Communicate Emotions

As we have mentioned, it forms the bulk of our communication. Most of that communication is about emotional information, which in turn is a powerful motivator in human behaviour. We base our feelings and emotional responses not so much upon what another person says, but upon what another person does.

More Reliable

There is an old saying: actions speak louder than words. When verbal and non-verbal contradict, we tend to believe the non-verbal. For one thing, it is seen as being more difficult to

1. Albert Mehrabian, *Non-verbal Communication,* Chicago, Aldine-Atherton, 1972.
2. Patrick W. Miller, *Non-verbal Communication*, Washington, DC, National Education Association, 1981.

fake. An experiment reported by Zuckerman, DePaulo, and Rosenthal[3] showed that virtually everything we use to discern if someone else is lying comes from the non-verbal realm or the paralanguage realm, with the bulk falling in non-verbal.

Difficult To Mask

Verbal messages can be easily controlled by not saying anything but it is very difficult to mask one's non-verbal communication. Whatever a person is thinking silently will be conveyed through his gestures, postures, facial expressions etc.

It Speaks

As noted earlier also the principle, 'you cannot *not* communicate,' signifies the role of non-verbal communication. We can stop speaking but we cannot stop emitting non-verbal cues. Sometimes, we do not need words to communicate, for instance, if someone asks us which way the restroom is, we may simply point down the hall. In the same way if someone asks what time it is, one can show him the wristwatch without saying anything. We regulate our conversations non-verbally by raising an index finger, nodding and leaning forward, raising eyebrows, and/or changing eye contact.

INTERPRETING NON VERBAL CUES

Mehrabian[4] identified three primary dimensions for interpreting non-verbal cues.

Immediacy

The metaphor 'immediacy' is related with proxemics (explained in the following pages). Immediacy cues communicate liking and pleasure. It is based on the principle that people are attracted to things they like and repulsed by things they do not. Thus, Mehrabian holds that we make gestures intended to symbolically or literally bring the things we like closer to us. We move toward persons and things we like and avoid or move away from those we dislike. Generally, we instinctively decide whether we like someone or not and then later find reasons to back up our feelings. We can summarize the non-verbal behaviours then by saying that cues that move or lean or otherwise open up or go toward the other person communicate liking. This includes grasping gestures, body lean, open posture and other similar movements.

Animation

A person will be more animated while communicating if he/she has some motivation and interest in the other person. On the other hand, a flat tone of voice and very little movement indicate a lack of interest. Non-verbal cues that fall in this dimension include eye contact, varied vocal cues, animated facial expressions, leaning forward and movement in general.

Dominance

This metaphor is concerned with showing power and dominance in communication. They communicate information about relative or perceived status, position, and importance. These types of gestures establish dominance over others. For instance, a person of high status

---

3. Zuckerman, DePaulo, and Rosenthal, "Verbal and Non-verbal Communication of Deception," *Advances in Experimental Social Psychology* 14 (1981), pp. 1-59.
4. *Ibid.*

tends to have a relaxed body posture when interacting with a person of lower status. High-status people tend to have more space around them, big offices, and more barriers such as more gatekeepers, secretaries etc. Furniture, clothing, and location also tend to communicate in this dimension.

The above list shows that non-verbal cues transmit important information from the sender to the receiver. Let us review these non-linguistic ways of exchanging messages in more detail.

MEDIA OF NON-VERBAL COMMUNICATION

Media or tools or channels of non-verbal communication are those particular ways through which this form of communication takes place. These channels are explained below in length.

(1) Kinesics (Body Language)

Kinesics, or body language, is one of the most powerful ways that humans can communicate non-verbally. It is used to portray moods and emotions and to emphasize or contradict what is being said. It is an important component of human communication, in fact, according to psychologists 55% of the impact we make on someone is from non-verbal language, with 38% attributed to the way we say it and a mere 7% to the words we actually use.

Kinesics encompasses body movement, posture, gestures, facial expression, and eye behaviour. If we watch a baby too young to talk, we can see through the baby's use of hands, feet, mouth, and eyebrows what the infant enjoys, fears, and wants. We can notice when the child is feeling eager, confused, hungry, or sleepy. In the same way, behaviour of an adult can be assessed by observing his or her facial expressions, posture, or hand gestures. One difference might appear — adults frequently give mixed messages, whereas babies usually do not. A mixed message occurs when a person's words and body language contradict each other. For example your friend says to you, "I have plenty of time for your problem, you can tell in detail," but at the same time he is tapping his fingers and looking at his watch. What is he conveying? Here, verbal meaning and non-verbal behaviour both are incongruent.

Awareness of body language helps you find out whether you are being understood, how other people react to you, and what impact you are having on others. Body language is natural and normal but its importance is often not recognised. People who are skilled in body language search for its signals. Many people are able to give the right impression by the body language they use. They deliberately use it to convey friendly, understanding, intelligent, or sympathetic impressions to other people.

Some of the movements and gestures are as follows:

While talking the movements like extending a hand straightforward or leaning forward, are considered positive and good. If you take a lot of space while talking by moving your arms about, you are a good informer and good listener.

Our hands and arms are very strong communicators and they indicate our mood, feelings, and attitude. Pointing and arm motions can add emphasis to our thoughts and words. But too much movement can distract the listener from the verbal message. Typically, closed hands, crossed arms, clenched fists, closed hands in the lap send a negative message that shows defensive or closed attitude.

It is believed that there is a relationship between positioning of the body and facial expressions. Mostly, we communicate our emotions through our facial expressions. Studies show that certain facial areas reveal our emotional state better than others. For example, the eyes tend to reveal happiness or sadness, and even surprise. The lower face also can reveal happiness or surprise; the smile, for example, can communicate friendliness and cooperation. The lower face, brows, and forehead can also reveal anger. Raised eyebrows can show concern, confusion, and surprise or indicate the person is engaged in deep thought. A red face can indicate embarrassment or anger.

Smiling is generally a positive form of body language, but can have a negative effect if used at a wrong time and a wrong place. In Hindi movies, we usually see a villain smiling at the heroine when she is alone. Now, with the smile of the villain, heroine does not feel secure rather she feels threatened. That is why smiling is, basically, considered as a negative gesture.

A nod is a positive gesture to show interest in the speaker or in the subject area being discussed. It can show agreement without verbally interrupting the speaker. Nodding also shows that you are in fact listening and understanding what the speaker is saying. Because it acts to keep conversation going, head nodding is a gesture of special importance. It serves two functions: to reinforce the speaker and to control the flow of speech. Occasional nods signal the other person to keep talking, while rapid nodding indicates that the one nodding wishes to speak. Rapid nodding with the combination of certain facial expressions also conveys threat to other person.

(2) Oculesics (Eye Contact)

Use of the eyes in communication is known as 'Oculesics'. Eye contact also communicates certain emotions. Eye contact is taken positively but direct eye contact should not be so much that the other person feels embarrassed. In most of the Western countries, the use of direct eye contact is considered as a symbol of good listening and attention. On the opposite, some Asian countries including India see direct eye contact as unfavourable. Eye contact is perceived as aggression when used for too long, and when it is too short it is considered as uninterested. Usually, avoidance of direct eye contact is taken as a sign of dishonesty, or uneasiness to the subject being discussed. Rapidly shifting eye movements shows nervousness or a sign of uneasiness or discomfort. The boss or superior in the organisation generally maintains eye contact longer than the subordinate. In India, the subordinates use downward glances while talking to their superiors. It is generally associated with modesty.

(3) Haptics (Tactile Communication)

Touch is also a media of non-verbal communication. A human touch in communication can substitute for words, thus creating meanings that surpass the spoken language. If it is used properly it can convey more than the words ever can. On the other hand, used improperly it can build barriers and cause mistrust. Studies have shown that touching can create both positive and negative feelings. Your feelings are positive when the touch is perceived to be natural. A person gets the opposite feeling when the touch is perceived to be manipulative or insincere. Touch is experienced in many ways. Handshakes, pats, and kisses are just a few of the ways one can communicate by touching. You can easily invade someone's space through this type of communication. If it is used reciprocally, it indicates solidarity; if not used reciprocally, it tends to indicate differences in status. Touch not only facilitates the sending of the message, but the emotional impact of the message as well. In our Indian context, touch in formal communications is used very cautiously. Even gender differences also restrict touch in communication. The degree of touching easily communicates to the spectators whether it is an intimate relationship or a formal relation.

(4) Proxemics (Personal Space)

The word 'Proxemics' is concerned with the use of space in communication. It is the personal space between communicating persons. This invisible boundary becomes apparent only when someone, either talks from a distance or tries to enter in your personal zone. A deliberate and wide physical distance conveys dislike. Taking a position relatively close to the other person conveys warmth and liking. Social communication, greetings, whispers and business conversations take place within prescribed distances, making the use of cues for the type of talk in which a person wishes to engage. Degree of personal distance affects our level of comfort, and the level of comfort of those talking to us.

Space in communicators can be divided in different zones depending upon the level of intimacy among communicating people. Space up to eighteen inches is termed as personal territory; it is generally accepted norm for intimate contacts i.e. for a very friendly and close conversation. Husband-wife, father-son, close friends, lovers etc. would stand within eighteen inches for communication. Casual communication occurs at a distance of from one and a half to four feet. In casual distance we communicate with our co-workers, superiors, subordinates and the people in our close contact. Social and other formal transactions are carried on at a range of four to twelve feet. Beyond twelve feet communication becomes more formal but some times talking from such a distance gives a sign of emergency or trouble also.

Ignoring these distances in communication means violating social norms. If a man talks to a woman other than his wife or close friend at a distance of less than eighteen inches, he is trying to be intimate and he may receive hostility for this. On the same lines, communicators seated less than four feet apart are free to discuss personal matters. If they become separated by more than four feet in a social setting, talking privately could be difficult. In our Hindi movies we can usually see, while resolving their interpersonal issues, the hero talks to the heroine from a very wide distance, that is why, to us that becomes a comedy.

Goldhaber[5] says there are three basic principles that summarize the use of personal space in an organisation: The higher your position (status) in the organisation,

(a) the more and better space you will have,

(b) the better protected your territory will be, and

(c) the easier it will be to invade the territory of lower-status personnel.

The impact of use of space on the communication process is related directly to the environment in which the space is maintained.

(5) Artifacts (Environment)

In communication, 'Artifacts' means 'the environmental setting' or 'the context'. Artifacts play a vital role in communication. The environmental setting in which communication is taking

5. Goldhaber, G.M; (1993). *Organisational Communication*, 6th ed. Dubuque, IA: Brown and Benchmark.

place adds meaning to a dialogue, by adding a message of its own. The environment provides significant cues for behaviours that are expected, supported, or allowed. The design of our offices, according to researchers, can greatly affect the communications within it. How we arrange the objects like desks, chairs, tables, books etc. also influence communication. Some managers divide their offices into personal and impersonal areas. This can improve the communication process if the areas are used for the purposes intended. Such things frequently determine your power of communication in the organisation as the size of your desk, number of windows in the office, quality of the carpet, and the type of paintings on the wall. Industrialists have long realized the importance of colour, noise, and music as they relate to efficiency in industrial organisations. It is obvious that personal space and environment affect the level of comfort and status and facilitate or hinder the communication process. These are only a few of the factors involved in the effect of environment and space on non-verbal communication.

(6) Chronemics (Time Language)

Chronemics or Time language refers to the value we attach to time and the way we use time. We all move by our perception of time which is naturally culture bound. This perception is termed as 'biological clocks.' The way we use time affects our work culture, lifestyle, daily agendas etc. Time value varies from culture to culture and from region to region. In developed countries people are, generally, more particular about timings. When a person is on time it conveys positive about his/her personality. Similarly, a person who is usually late forms a bad impression about his attitude. In the business world, Americans are very punctual. On the other hand, they arrive late to parties and dances. In England time for dinner is 8 p. m. after this they consider bad manners if the person invited for dinner comes late. In Greece and Germany this is 9 p. m. in India it is even late than this. In India, we do not attach much importance to time. In govt. offices, when the employees have to work the clocks are very slow and when they have to sit idle or to rush home the clocks are very fast. So time is the inheritance common to us all. How we value time conveys either positively or negatively about us. How we are sensitive to time becomes a gauge of our social sensitivity.

(7) Paralanguage

Paralanguage, the way we say something rather than what we say, is another non-verbal code. In the process of communication, paralanguage involves inflection, emphasis, or other additions to language that enhance or alter meanings. Paralanguage, usually, includes Vocal Qualities such as characteristics of the voice like pitch, Vocalizations or special sounds like groans or sighs etc., Vocal Segregates, for example, pauses, fillers, and other hesitation phenomena. Although the judgments we make on the basis of voice are not necessarily accurate, we think they are.

Researchers have found that the tone, pitch, quality of voice, and rate of speaking convey emotions that can be accurately judged regardless of the content of the message.

Voice tone accounts for about 38 per cent of how people respond to what we say, that is why many people experience problems in written communication because there is no voice tone to give the expressions. Many people can form accurate judgments about others simply from the sound of their voices, especially in determining factors such as sex, age, birthplace, occupation etc. Trained observers can even make judgments about education, caste, status, weight, height etc. Listeners form the judgement from the speaker's voice as to his or her personality, emotional state, familiarity with the subject, persuasiveness, and confidence. Thus, listeners distinguish between verbal and vocal messages, between what is said and how it is said. As a communicator one should be sensitive to the influence of tone, pitch, and quality of voice for the accurate interpretation of message.

Silence is an overlooked aspect of paralanguage that carries meaning, now we discuss the role of silence in communication.

(8) Silence

In the process of communication, we not only speak but we also give certain pauses or the gap in words to make the meaning more clear. Silence properly used between words strengthens audibility and attracts attention of the listeners. Silence also shows that the communicator is contemplating. But long duration of silence shows forgetfulness and lack of knowledge. Therefore, silence can influence the communication process in both the directions — positive as well as negative. Silence can be used to create tension and uneasiness. For example, a communicator may withhold a piece of information which is important for the listener. On the opposite, during hot arguments silence can create a peaceful environment.

BARRIERS OF NON-VERBAL COMMUNICATION

All of us sometimes feel that others receive our communication differently from the way we intend or mean it. Our interactions have a different effect on our relationships than what we expected or wanted. All this simply means that we are creating non-verbal barriers that send mixed messages. Our words may not show our true feelings, but our body and voice conveys, even the innermost feelings. Non-verbal barriers to effective communication are as below:

It Can Be Ambiguous

Non-verbal cues cannot be classified specifically. In fact, no dictionary can classify and describe them accurately. Their meaning varies not only by culture but by the context also. A random gesture may be assumed to have a meaning when none at all was intended. Moreover, some people who may feel emotion strongly nevertheless find that their bodies simply do not respond appropriately, i.e., someone who is feeling happy may not necessarily smile.

Incongruent Words And Body Language

The biggest barrier in non-verbal communication is the use of incongruent words and body movements. That means, if the words are conveying an opposite meaning to what we are communicating non-verbally, that would block the communication. For example, a boss is praising someone for a job well done, but he is not making eye contact or smiling. So we can think, what message the receiver will have. Therefore, to be most effective, your voice tone, body posture, gestures, and movements should be in alignment with your words. Make your gestures and facial expressions congruent with your message.

Voice Tone

We all have, no doubt, experienced anger not so much from what someone else said as how they said it. Voice tone accounts for about 38 per cent of how people respond to what we say or how you respond to them. Sometimes, in a moment of hurry or anger our tone of voice gets changed which clearly shows our feelings to the listener. In those situations, even the softest words may not prevent the harm because it is the tone of the voice which matters not the words.

It Is Continuous

It is possible to stop talking, but it is generally not possible to stop emitting non-verbal cues. Also, spoken language has a structure that makes it easier to tell when a subject has changed, for instance, or to analyze its grammar. Non-verbal cues do not lend itself to this kind of analysis.

Mixed Signals

One should be careful not to send mixed signals through the body language. For example, others might perceive you to be angry with them because you have a frown on your face when speaking. You may not be angry at all, but simply concentrating on what the person is saying. Be mindful of your body language.

It Is Multi Dimensional

While watching someone's eyes, we may miss something significant in a hand gesture. Everything is happening at once, and therefore it may be confusing to try to keep up with everything. Most of us simply do not do so, at least not consciously. This has both advantages and disadvantages. Because we interpret non-verbal cues subconsciously and in a holistic manner, it can happen quickly and accurately. So, therefore, non-verbal cues are sometimes multidimensional, not easy to interpret.

Re-Acting Instead Of Responding.

Mostly, we do not act rather re-act, that means our actions are influenced by other's actions. We often 're-act' to another person based on something that has happened to us before. Responding rather than re-acting requires self-knowledge and discipline, but it's critical.

It Is Not Culture Proof

Humans of all cultures smile when happy and frown when unhappy.[6] A few other gestures seem to be universal. However, most non-verbal symbols seem to be even further disconnected from any essential meaning than verbal symbols. Gestures seen as positive in one culture (like the thumbs-up gesture) may be seen as obscene in another culture.

Gender Differences In Non-verbal Cues

There is a growing body of evidence that suggests men and women use and interpret non-verbal communication differently. Women generally have an innate ability to pick up and decipher non-verbal signals as well as they have an accurate eye for small details. That is why a few husbands can lie to their wives and get away with it. Mother, for the first few years relies solely on the non-verbal channel to communicate with the child that is why they often become more perceptive negotiators than men. Following are some points that make clear the role of gender difference in understanding non-verbal cues.

Women usually maintain a gaze longer than men. However, women are less likely to stare at someone; the research shows that they break eye contact more frequently than men.

---

6. M. Argyle, *Bodily Communication*, New York, Methuen and Company, 1988.

Edward Hall's[7] spatial zones generally are drawn closer for women than for men. Women approach more closely, and seem to prefer side-by-side conversations. The latter may explain differences in use of space; men prefer more face-to-face conversations, and people are generally more aware of space to the front than to the side.

Women are more skilled at both sending and interpreting facial expression than are men. Also, women use more facial expression in general and smile more in particular. Although women use more facial expression, they appear to use fewer and more restrained gestures than men.

IMPROVING NON-VERBAL COMMUNICATION

Excellent communication skills are the key to success in our personal and professional life. Research shows that non-verbal communication is actually more important than verbal communication. It is believed that effective communication is not always what we say, but what our body says, that makes the difference. Non-verbal communication can be maximized through the awareness and use of the following components:

Face The Receiver

A communicator should always face the listener. This signifies interest and integrity. At the same time, one should be aware of his/her expressions, which send out a multitude of signals.

Focus On Speaker

During conversations our eyes keep on wandering. One should focus on the speaker and convey interest non-verbally. Also, maintaining eye contact shows interest in the speaker/listener. Many people stop using eye contact when they are speaking about their successes due to fear or embarrassment.

Check Context

In communication, meaning depends upon context also. One should not interpret non-verbal cues isolated from other such cues, from the verbal communication, or from the physical or emotional context. It is also possible that someone's arms being crossed may indicate nothing more than physical discomfort from a cold room instead of a defensive gesture.

Body Positioning

The way we sit and lean will provide certain signals. For example, leaning forward with arms open and on the table may convey intense interest.

Consider Past Experience

We can more accurately interpret the behaviour of people we know. For one thing, we notice changes in behaviour more than the behaviour itself. Unless we know someone, we cannot know that something has changed. For another thing, we interpret patterns of behaviour. Your mother may always cry when you come home from school with an A, and so you learn that this represent happiness in that particular situation.

---

7. Edward Hall, *The Hidden Dimension,* Garden City, NY, Doubleday and Company, 1966.

Tone

This refers to our tone of voice. We should attempt to modulate our tone to appropriate levels in order to convey our message. One should try to use the tonality of voice the way that a musician uses an instrument. When you are expressing love you can speak in soft, lilting tones. When someone is crying you can speak with a crying sound in your voice. When you are setting limits on a toddler's behaviour you can use a tone of authority and firmness.

Clarify From Time To Time

Clarification of doubts removes the hindrances of understanding in communication. Stop and ask the other person what their non-verbal behaviour means if you are uncertain about it.

Use Positive Gestures To Avoid Confrontation

When you are confronting someone who is in a close relationship with you, try to use positive gestures to avoid confrontation. A caring gesture during a confrontation can assist the other person in hearing you instead of defending him/herself.

Eliminate Pseudoaffective Communication

Pseudoaffective communication occurs when words and actions disagree. For example, the patient who claims to feel fine, but looks terrible; or conversely, feels terrible, but looks fine. Communication research indicates that, in most instances, non-verbal messages (body language) are more reliable than verbal messages.

We can understand this with the help of an illustration. In movies, we usually see a surgeon coming out of an operating room. As he approaches the anxiously awaiting family, with the help of expressions on his face, we immediately conclude whether or not the patient survived the operation. So ideally, words and actions should agree. Pseudoaffective communication occurs when words and actions contradict one another. We, above all others, must make a concerted effort to verbally support the hands that deliver the adjustment. Freud said it best: "He that has eyes to see and ears to hear may convince himself that no mortal can keep a secret. If his lips are silent, he chatters with his fingertips; betrayal oozes out of him at every pore." We cannot see ourselves like others can see us; they cannot see themselves like we can see them. Only by pooling our mutual perceptions can the incidence of pseudoaffective communication be eliminated.

❑❑❑

8

Communication Barriers

To say that communication is difficult is to say nothing unusual. In every age, communication has its own peculiar problems; and our present age i.e. IT age, possessing amazing resources for increasing and amplifying communication means, facing both greater potentials and greater problems in communication. All these problems are barriers to effective communication. A barrier is any obstacle or difficulty that impede the process of communication. There cannot be such a thing as 'Perfect Communication', which is free of all barriers. The barriers may be physical, mechanical, psychological, cultural, or linguistic in nature.

In business communication, the major communication problems arise due to the structure of the organisation. The size of an organisation, authority levels, filtering, resistance to change, and status differences are the main organisational barriers. Language barrier arises in the organisation where people are of different educational backgrounds and hail from different regions. Then, there are the barriers, raised by interpersonal relationships between individual and groups, the perception and prejudices of individuals and groups, the difference in interpretation of message, emotional attitude, distrust and the channels they use to communicate. Besides there can be physical and mechanical problems in the process of communication, all these barriers whatever their nature are known as 'noise.'

There cannot be a limited list of potential and possible barriers to communication. Following is the detail of major barriers to communication:

Personality

The word personality is derived from the Latin word 'persona' which means "to speak through." Thus, it is the personality of the person through which we communicate with the outer world. Personality of a person plays an important role in the communication. Sometimes, we are so strongly influenced by the personality of an individual that we may either accept or reject what is said without any valid reason. Personality of the individual affects communication in the way that how the listener/receiver of the message interprets the personality of the communicator. It means depending upon the interpretation by the communicatee the message will be affected either positively or negatively. Personality is also not confined to an individual rather it is also a group concept. For example, people gathered in a group behave as if they are one person. And one can easily tell whether the group is friendly, sympathetic, or hostile. The journey of good communication starts with the examination of our own personality. It is a difficult task and requires making changes that improve understanding.

Self-Concept

Self can be described as the innermost personality of an individual. It is the conscious agent within every human being which perceives, interprets, and guides the individual. Every individual has his/her own self-concept, that is, every individual perceives and sees things in his/her own way. That is why people see things differently, for example, words like god, beauty, nature, respect, satisfaction, truth, honesty etc. have different meanings for different people. Every person has a self-concept, which can act to shut out information or opinion that is not in line with it. If we think of ourselves as important, then behaviour that indicates that the other person does not see us in this way can cause anger. If, on the contrary, someone acts towards us in a way that indicates they see us as very important (when we know we are not), we may see such behaviour as mockery. Thus, we listen to only those messages which are favourable to us, and ignore those which are contrary to our self-concept.

So self-perceived values can result into different viewpoints of the same thing resulting into confusion and barrier in communication.

Appearance

In this world in which we are living, we take things on their face values. It is true that the people judge people by their appearances, by the clothes they wear etc. We may not like this kind of typecasting by appearance, but practically it is true. The first impact on the audience/listener is created by the personal appearance of the speaker. Even before the speaker opens his mouth we try to form an image and opinion about him. Needless to say, that image and opinion will entirely be based on the appearance of the communicator.

In every culture, for different occasions, conventions are there, in regard to the use of dress, hairstyle, make-up etc. For example, at the time of interviews, one should be properly formally dressed whereas in informal group gatherings one's appearance can be casual. Ignoring these standards may affect the image of the person which can further distort the communication.

Poor Organisation

Another barrier in communication can be the poor organisation of the message. Ideas and thoughts may be logical but it is also important to assimilate them. The meaning of the message gets totally distorted when thoughts are presented in a confused manner. Proper organisation of the message is fundamental to communication. And proper organisation requires thorough preparation and planning. Even a two-minute oral speech or one-page presentation may require several hours of labour on the part of communicator.

Polarization

Polarization is the act of being at extremes. As a pole has two ends or two extremes, in the same way some people behave in extremes. For them there cannot be more than two alternatives. So they may think their employee as fully devoted and honest or totally corrupt, in the same way their company will this year break the past sales record or it will go bankrupt.

They do not look for middle paths. Polarization is basically an attitude and this attitude badly affects communication. Communication requires more words than merely using these 'either this-or that' extremes.

Biased Attitude And Closed Mind

An unreasonable bias and prejudice can also seriously impede the transmission of ideas. Biased attitude cause us to reject ideas without consideration. Although we usually relate prejudice to race, religion, and colour, most of us encounter it in a dozen other ways. It may be a simple but strongly held viewpoint (or perception) on the part of the superior, or it may be the negative attitude of the employee: "I've been working here for the last thirty years; although I have not tried it before but I know it won't work." Similarly, a person with a closed mind is very difficult to communicate with. A closed minded person never listens to others. He is full of prejudices and he is not prepared to reconsider his opinions. Such a person is not open to conviction and persuasion and cannot learn any thing new with this attitude.

Emotions

We all experience emotions, such as jealousy, anger, love, fear and so on. We have all been in situations in which either the sender or the receiver of the message became so emotionally charged that communication broke down. In the frenzy of emotions no communication is possible. If the sender is emotionally charged he will not be able to think and organise his message properly. Rather, all his emotions will be conveyed through the message which will distort the real meaning of the intended message. In the same way, if the receiver is emotional, it will also affect the communication process. The receiver will not be able to understand and analyze the message properly or he may misinterpret the message. Patience and coolness is the only remedy for this problem.

Age As A Barrier

Age can be a barrier in communication. People having different ages, while communicating, feel this gap in understanding of things. In certain communication situations, people say 'the problem is generation gap.' What is this generation gap? Simply, it is the age gap between communicators. The term generation gap reflects the fact that a difference in age can cause people to see things differently. Mostly, youngsters face this problem in communicating with their parents or elders.

Stereotyping

Stereotyping is the tendency to place individuals into categories. It is a psychological phenomenon which causes generalization of the persons depending upon one's perception and experiences. But it is true that all the individuals are not same, so all the individuals may not fit a common pattern. Stereotyping affects our communication also. There are so many words which may have different meanings for different people depending upon their interpretations. These words are known as 'class words.' For example, if I say that I own a 'four wheeler.' Now, the word four-wheeler does not make clear about the type of vehicle, its price, its standard etc. In the same way, the word 'house' can include anything from a hut to a villa. Of course using such words simplifies our communication. But using the words having different meanings tend to cause a lot of problems in understanding the message clearly. Stereotyping causes us to ignore the differences that exist among the things that have been clubbed together. So when we view and interpret all the things on the same lines, it is called stereotyping which is a serious barrier in communication.

Distrust

The real meaning of the word 'communication' is the 'sharing of ideas in common'. In communication, we try to establish commonness but it is possible only when there is a free transfer of information and proper understanding between the sender and the receiver. And this is possible only when there is mutual trust between the two. When there is a lack of mutual trust between the communicator and the communicatee, the message is not followed in the intended sense. In the situation of distrust, communicators do not rely on each other and they do not take the message as it is, rather a component of suspicion is added in the message which totally distorts the understanding. In business organisations, the distrust originates when one feels less competent or lacks self-confidence in his delegated position. One's judgements frequently go wrong and he/she makes illogical decisions. Repeated experience of this kind makes others to lose faith and trust in that person. All this makes his communication ineffective. Inconsistency in saying and doing also causes lack of mutual trust which acts as a barrier to communication.

Inattention

Listening is only possible if the listener is paying full attention to the message being communicated, otherwise it remains only mechanical hearing which, ultimately gives no understanding to the listener. Lack of attention on the part of the listener may be due to many reasons such as preoccupied mind, tension, overwork, lack of interest etc. Whatever may be the reason, inattention blocks the process of communication and in the absence of attention there cannot be any transfer of understanding and meaning. In schools and colleges this habit of students is quite common. Usually, when the message is not of interest to us we start losing our attention. We want to listen only those things which are of some interest to us or which are directly or indirectly beneficial to us. In the long run what seems a temporary phenomenon (inattention) becomes a permanent habit and a major blockade in communication.

No Interest

Lack of interest can be another major barrier in the process of communication. Lack of interest can be in the subject matter or on the part of either the speaker or the listener. If the listener finds contents of the message boring he will turn a deaf ear to what the speaker is saying. Similarly, a speaker may be boring for the audience. Lack of interest can be a barrier from speaker's perspective also; when the communicator finds that the audience lacks fundamental knowledge in understanding the message.

Differences In Perception

Technically, perception is the reception of incoming signals from the environment and interpreting those signals to make an understanding. Perception is a psychological process of recognizing something from the environment and it affects our senses. Any object or thing, which do not have effect on our perception, brings no effect on behaviour. We see the external world through our perception. So, it means we do not see the world, as it is rather what we see is our perception about the world. And there is always a difference in the perceptions of the people. Why? Because the formation of perception is dependent upon a number of factors such as, past experiences, education, moral values, beliefs, culture, customs etc. That is why different people, simply because of differences in perception, view one object differently. This difference in perceptions causes problems in communication. Our past experiences largely determine how we respond to a specific situation. We use our experiences, knowledge, cultural backgrounds etc. to interpret what we see. So, therefore, we have different interpretations of the same thing. When we hear something we also interpret that on the basis of our perception. Problems in communication arise when each of us perceives something very different. It does not imply that everybody should perceive every thing as the other person does, but it requires an effort to appreciate other's point of view. Only then, we can cover the differences in perception and achieve effective communication.

Past Judgements

We make our judgements on the basis of past experiences and perceptions and we carry these judgements in the future without making any changes in them. It implies that once made, our judgements and evaluations become static and we do not feel any need of modification in the future also. But our past evaluations and judgements may not be true in the present context. This rigid pattern of thinking becomes a barrier in communication. For example, say Mr. X is transferred from one branch to another in a big organisation. His previous supervisor comments to his new superior that "He is a poor worker." Now, here occur communication errors. A poor worker is a vague term and does not make clear under what conditions and circumstances Mr. X can be called poor. It also implies that in the future also he will remain same or there are no chances of improvement with the changed circumstances and conditions. The new superior of Mr. X is bound to take the negative impression based on the past judgements.

Communication Overload

With the advancement in technology, today a manager has easy access to data and information, which can be processed speedily and presented in the desired format. But possessing high volumes of information leads to the problems of organising, storing, disseminating, and interpreting. This problem is known as communication overload. Too much information and communication impairs the communication ability of the people because they are confronted with more information than they can deal with effectively. Communication overload can result in the loss or distortion of information.

Following may be the results of communication overload:

(1) Important communications may be ignored.

(2) Information gathering, processing and then communicating takes time and cost.

(3) Faulty communications or errors in messages may go uncorrected.

(4) Communication overload may give birth to data duplication.

(5) Incomplete information may lead to wrong decisions.

According to Miller,[1] for an employee burdened with information following can be the outcomes:

1. I. G. Miller, *Information Input, Overload and Psychopathology*, quoted in Jerry C. Wofford, Edwin A. Gerloff, and Robert C. Cummins, Organizational Communication, McGraw-Hill, New York, 1977, p. 273.

(1) Omission-failing to process some of the information

(2) Error-processing information incorrectly

(3) Queuing-levelling the peak loads by delaying until a lull occurs

(4) Filtering-separating out supposedly less significant information

(5) Approximation—categorizing input and using a blanket response

(6) Employing multiple channels-altering the flow by introducing additional channels

(7) Escaping — avoiding the information.

All of the above mentioned problems can bring disastrous results for a business organisation.

There can be many solutions for the problem of information overload. One solution is a well-designed information system which will provide specific data and information depending upon the requirements of the users. The other solution is 'filtering the messages' so that the important ones, those requiring immediate action, get to the decision-maker first. Another technique involves delegating and decentralizing the decision-making process so that messages do not go to a single executive. Still another technique involves carefully selecting information sources and eliminating those proven inaccurate or unreliable.

Noise

Any element that restricts one's ability to concentrate on the communication task hinders effective communication. Such distractions are called noise. Or in other words anything, which interferes with the transmission or reception of the message accurately, is noise. Noise can prove to be a major disturbing factor in communication. Clattering printers, noisy punch presses, loud speakers, noise of machines may be deterrents to the communication. In factories and industries due to the noise of machines, oral communication is almost impossible. The word 'noise' is also used to refer to all kinds of physical interference like illegible handwriting, illegible photocopies, inadequate illumination, hissing ventilation, poor acoustics, uncomfortable seating, body odour, poor telephone connections, and, uncomfortable room temperature etc.

Distance

Distance between the communicator and the communicatee also causes breakdown in communication. Wrong environmental settings or wrong seating arrangement in the room can also create problems in communication. With the availability of sound equipments communication with a very large audience is easily possible. Therefore, distance is not a very major problem; it requires a little care to overcome this barrier.

Barriers Of Transmission And Retention

There is one thing about the communication process, more the channels of communication lesser is the accuracy of the message. Why? Because different transmissions at different levels change the contents of the message. In the same way, when communication passes through various levels in an organisation, the meaning of the message gets changed. At every level a part of the information is lost. All this applies to oral communication in particular. In oral communication, when a person communicates a message to another and from another person the message passes to some other person, the original message gets changed. Either there will be some addition or deletion in the contents and quality of the message. Studies show that successive transmissions of the same message are decreasingly accurate. This happens because of many reasons such as differences in perceptions, personal biases, loss in retention of the message mentally etc. Sometimes, the message is translated in simple language so that it may be easily understandable. But translation also affects the meaning of the message, as translation can never be perfect. In the process of interpretation, simplification, and translation, a part of the message gets lost or distorted. All this acts as a major barrier in the process of communication.

Selective Communication

With the information overload in our present age, we all have become selective in listening and reading. With a countless communication media bombarding us all the day, we have become selective in choosing what to read or what to listen to. Our present information age is the age of sounds and printed words. Let us take one simple example, the newspaper which we read in the morning, usually, carries thirty to fifty pages and an average reader requires eight to ten hours to completely read the newspaper. Now, no working person can devote that much time to a newspaper. Hence, selectivity in communication has become our necessity. Then there are weekly and monthly news magazines, technical journals, brochures, and dozens of reports that must be read by an executive. At the same time meetings, seminars and presentations cannot be ignored. Then there are other things requiring attention and time such as, a person's social and private life, friends, radio, television, movies etc. The end result is selective communication. Selective communication helps us a lot but it is a barrier which may prevent us from receiving useful information.

Organisational Barriers

Organisational structure also affects the flow of information and communication. The complex structure of an organisation having different authority levels causes the breakdown in communication. Different levels of management slows down the flow of information, also at every level a part of the information is deducted or added which changes the meaning of the message. Rigid rules and regulations also restrict the free flow of communication and this causes delay in the decision-making process and action. In many organisations, sometimes, employees have undue reliance on written communication. Everything is formal and procedural. Employees hesitate in communicating something important orally. Such excessive reliance also acts as a barrier in free communication. In such an environment, people lack initiative and they follow only written policies of the organisation.

Status Consciousness

Status or position in the hierarchy of an organisation is also a major barrier in communication. Status barrier arises due to the superior-subordinate relationship in the organisation. Due to this status consciousness there remains, always, a distance between the superior and a subordinate. This distance due to the positions of authority, inhibit free flow of information, exchange of ideas, suggestions, and grievances. A superior may pass only filtered and selected information to maintain his prestige in the eyes of his juniors. Moreover, a superior due to his position may not consult his subordinates. The superior may act as a very competent person and may not invite communications from juniors. Similarly, the juniors may not discuss certain matters due to their inhibitions or they may feel less competent in advising their superior. Mostly, subordinates would communicate only those things, which the superior would appreciate. For free flow of communication, there is a great need on the part of the managers to rise above status consciousness and motivate their employees to communicate freely.

Filtering

When something is either added to or deducted from the contents of a message it is known as filtering of the message. As discussed earlier also, when certain information passes through various levels of management the meaning gets completely changed. Information is filtered by the communicator so that it will be taken more favourable by the listener. Usually, filtering is done when juniors communicate with their superiors. For example, an employee will tell only those things which his boss wants to hear. Ideally, information filtering should be done to reduce the communication overload of senior executives. It means, only relevant information should be passed on to the top management in a condensed and synthesized form to reduce the information overload. That is the true purpose of filtering; otherwise used it becomes an impediment in the process of true understanding.

Resistance To Change

We all are afraid of change which can bring uncertainty about the future patterns. In other words we resist to any change in our present routine and pattern of thinking because any change will certainly bring inconvenience, insecurity and uncertainty. Moreover, a change demands changes in behaviour and habits which is very difficult. Following the same routine and habits is very easy and smooth. So, we welcome all such communications which are consistent with our present behaviour and attitude. Thus, any information attempting to change or communicating a new idea is not taken in the right spirit. This mental block becomes a barrier in communication.

Actually, It's Your Problem

By saying these magic words anybody identifies himself or herself as someone who would avoid taking responsibility unless things turned out well, at which point he or she would be the first to take the credit. In any workplace, no one wants to hear these words. This is the wrong behaviour model for a working group. In difficult situations one of many possible correct responses can be "I understand the problem. Let us brainstorm and find the alternatives we have for this problem."

Premature Evaluation

Sometimes, people try to evaluate the message or the communicator even before the entire message is communicated. Premature evaluation is a tendency to evaluate a communication prematurely which may lead to wrong and hasty conclusions. Right judgement and evaluation requires time and patience. Premature evaluation shows impatience and lack of right judgement on the part of the receiver. Only active and empathetic listening can overcome this barrier of premature evaluation.

Poor Listening

When we think about communication, we only consider reading, writing, and speaking as parts of the communication process and simply, we forget listening which is such a major component of the communication process that without it communication is never complete. In oral communication, more than fifty per cent of our time is spent on listening. When we do not speak, we listen to others. But listening is the most neglected side of the communication process.

Poor listening is one of the most serious barriers to the communication. Why listening is so difficult? One simple reason is the difference between speaker's speaking speed and our listening speed. An average person speaks at the rate of about 150 words a minute, but the listening power of an average person is more than 500 words a minute. Therefore, in the excess time the listener's mind tends to wander here and there. Usually, a listener tries to judge the message even before it is verbally said or tries to evaluate the message/communicator or the listener may get lost in his own thoughts and problems. Listening skills are the most ignored aspect of good communication skills. More problems occur due to the poor listening than to mis-statements. To be a good listener, one should suspend the urge to speak while others are speaking. Also, a listener should not try to prepare what he will say next.

Cultural Diversity

Cultural diversity can also cause breakdowns in communication. Different cultural values, beliefs, and attitudes can cause interference in communication. People from different and diverse cultures see the things differently and this can affect the reception of a message. Moreover, many non-verbal gestures also vary from culture to culture. Interpretation of the same gesture is done variedly in different cultures. One gesture or signal appropriate in one culture may not be appropriate in another. The difference in interpretations is a big barrier in communication.

Gender Difference

In different cultures different roles are attached to the role of men and women. Sometimes these expected roles and values create problems in communication. These perceived gender roles causes a breakdown in the communication process. Cultural patterns of socialization affect the way men and women communicate with each other. In India, for example, females may not feel at ease when males pass open comments or crack jokes.

Language Barriers

Language is the basis for most of the communications. Business communication in the absence of a language is almost impossible. But, it is also true that language itself is probably the most common barrier to effective communication. Words have different meanings to different people. Language which is the basis for any communication give birth to a lot of problems for example, use of complex and technical words, idioms and adjectives and vocabulary problems. Other problems arise due to the differences in the interpretation of statements and words. People interpret and understand words and sentences according to their own experiences and perceptions. Use of any language requires clarity and precision on the part of the communicator.

Bypassing

Bypassing occurs when the same word means different things to different people. The common words and symbols, which we use, carry different meaning for different people causing problems in communication. This problem occurs due to the different educational backgrounds, experiences, and perceptions of the people. Bypassing occurs when different words are used to describe the same object and/or when a speaker uses a word that has a different meaning to the listener. In English language, for example, for one word there are many different meanings, say the word bonnet, in England and India, usually refer to the hood of a four-wheeler whereas most Americans would think of a 'head' when they hear bonnet. The words or symbols used in communication must be those that are selected from an area common to the frames of reference of the people communicating. Communicating a message using words and symbols outside the frame of reference of a receiver prevents the transmission of understanding at all.

Inadequate Knowledge

Lack of adequate knowledge can be another barrier to the effective communication of ideas. We cannot intelligently discuss a problem with those who do not have the background to understand the subject matter. For example, there will be no communication if a nuclear scientist attempts to explain radioactivity mechanics to a matric qualified person. In the same way, superficial knowledge of the subject is also a barrier in the understanding. Sometimes, the speaker's knowledge about the subject matter is so vast that the listeners do not follow despite their efforts. To overcome this problem, the speaker should first try to understand the mental and educational level of the listeners and then he should communicate accordingly. In certain cases, a communicator deliberately uses technical words and jargons pertaining to a specialised area. The listeners without fundamental knowledge of the subject cannot understand and communicate.

Mixed Communication

Mixed communication is also a barrier to effective communication. Mixed communication occurs when two messages are transmitted simultaneously — one verbal message and the other non-verbal. If both convey the same message, communication takes place; but in case there is contradiction between the two, it causes a breakdown in the communication. For example, someone may say to a visitor expressly: "Welcome! Come in"; but on the face there are expressions of boredom on seeing the visitor. Now, what does this convey? Whenever the meaning of the non-verbal message conflicts with that of the verbal one, the receiver is most likely to find the non-verbal more believable. Why? Simply, because non-verbal gestures and signals are more difficult to manipulate than verbal messages. Therefore, for a problem free communication, non-verbal messages should be consistent with the verbal messages.

Other Barriers

The list of barriers to communication can be infinite. There may be many other barriers, such as wrong assumptions, lack of ability to communicate, mirage of too much knowledge, shortage of time, failure to communicate etc., which cause distortion or obstruction in the free flow of communication and thus make it ineffective. In business organisations, people fail to communicate at the right time. There are many reasons for this, one is the laziness, and other can be the inability of the people to select what to communicate. Moreover, lack of trust among people in the organisation also blocks communication.

All these barriers to communication show that inter-personal communication is very difficult. Mere good speaking or writing skills are not enough to ensure complete understanding. The sender injects his attitudes and perceptions into the message; determines who should receive it; and the channels through which it should flow, i.e., upward, downward, laterally, or a combination of these. The attitudes and perceptions of the recipient, of course, influence the message translation, as well as the feedback he/she provides.

Following are the gateways to communication which helps in overcoming most of the barriers:

GATEWAYS TO COMMUNICATION

Effectiveness in communication greatly contributes to the success of a business organisation. In fact, one of the main problems in any organisation is promoting effective communication between its members. In communication between the communicator and the listener, the path appears to be straight. However, this is rarely the case. There are many different ways to distort the message or to filter it (both in delivering the message and in receiving the message). All of the distortions can occur for both the communicator and the listener.

Practically, we cannot eliminate all the problems and barriers to communication. 'Communication without any problem' or 'perfect communication' is a theoretical concept only. Improving communication require that we understand that communication is rarely perfect or clear in and of itself. Therefore, the first step to effective communication starts with the awareness about the existence of some barrier or distortion in the communication process. We must learn to listen better and speak more clearly. We must also check whether our message is delivered correctly and whether we have heard a message clearly.

In this section, we will discuss what are the gateways to effective communication. The important approaches and methods that can be used to minimize distortion of information are as follows:

Plan The Message

The message to be conveyed must be properly planned by the communicator. A clear and planned idea is very easy to communicate. The message should be relevant and adequate for the purpose of communication. Whether the basic outline of our message is jotted down roughly on a paper or it is formally and carefully typed, we should not attempt to communicate without knowing precisely what we have to communicate. Even a two-minute informal presentation requires time for organising and planning the message.

Use Proper Language

The message should be communicated in the simple and appropriate language to avoid semantic distortions. What is appropriate language? The answer is, that language which is easily understandable by the listeners/readers. Use of specialised and technical terms should be minimum. And whenever technical and difficult terms have to be used, communicator should also make the meaning clear. If the readers or listeners are not able to understand the language, the purpose of communication is lost.

Don't Be Evaluative

Listening with full attention to what is being said, without premature evaluation and judgement is the fundamental requirement for effective communication. Communication is often distorted when the manager uses his status and starts giving his own viewpoints and suggestions in the course of his face-to-face discussion with the subordinate without listening him fully. A manager should evaluate the information only when it has fully been communicated. Without non-evaluative listening, free and frank response cannot be expected.

Proper Orientation

All the employees should be given proper orientation towards the organisation and the work culture. They should be provided with all the necessary information relating to the objectives, policies, procedures, organisational structure etc. Authorities and responsibilities should be clearly demarked. When the employees are provided with complete information relating to the company's objectives, policies, procedures and authority relations, many possible conflicts and misunderstandings may be avoided. An employee who knows about the company's working environment is able to understand problems of other people also.

Active Listening

Listening with full attention and interest is termed as active listening. Active listening is an energetic attempt to really understand what the speaker is saying and to reflect back to him or her what this is. One should always remember that listening is not the same as hearing. Hearing is using the ears to acknowledge the sound of something. Listening means understanding from the perspective of the speaker. When people are listened to actively, they listen to themselves more closely. Sensitive, active listening actually brings about changes in the speaker and in the listener. Such active listening overcomes many of the barriers to communication.

Unbiased Attitude

Personal bias and prejudice are probably the most difficult barriers to overcome. Although education, counselling and open discussions can eliminate this problem but it is a lengthy process. The other way to overcome bias is to show people how they will benefit by following a particular course of action. People understand things very fast when they see some personal interest. Strongly biased people can be encouraged to state their reasons for rejecting a message or opinion etc. This way, then they may themselves reveal hidden prejudices, biases, and strong emotions. Once they reveal it, they can try to overcome this attitude.

Interpersonal Relations

Today, no business can survive for a long period of time in the absence of good interpersonal relations. All the business plans and activities require joint efforts for accomplishing its goals. The need is, therefore, to develop proper relations between different people working in the organisation. A senior executive should respect the dignity and authority of his subordinates and be kind and sympathetic to them. Subordinates should also trust their superior and keep him informed about their dealings with other departments and progress of their work. Superior and subordinate should develop a feeling of mutual trust and confidence. Wherever possible, the manager should communicate through personal contacts and emphasize that communication is a two-way process.

Congruence

Communication can be effective only when it is acted upon. Any information or message communicated without calling for any action or decision, distorts the image of the communicator and his position. Future communications from the same person loses weightage. Reason is that action and deeds often speak louder and clearer than words. If acts of the manager differ from what he says, subordinates will gradually become used to listen to what he does and not what he says.

Use The Grapevine

The existence of grapevine is inevitable for any organisation. Since, the grapevine is inevitably present, it should be used as a communication tool. The grapevine can be used to test some contemplated change and the results of which are unpredictable. For example, the management' s decision of 'no bonus this year' may cause strikes and lockouts. So, through grapevine the reaction of employees can be judged without announcing any formal decision by the management. It is easier to back down, if necessary, because the management was not official about it. There are occasions when due to personal and other reasons, information should not be transmitted through the official channels of communication. For example, resignation of managing director may be communicated through the grapevine. Thus, the proper and controlled use of the grapevine helps in improving the effectiveness of communication in an organisation.

Communicate In Pieces

When you have a lengthy and complicated message, communicate it in pieces so that the receiver can understand it easily. This approach will simplify matters and avoid omissions also. For a manager, this is more relevant when giving orders to subordinates. If you, as a manager, give everything at once, the only message that gets across may be the enormity of the job. The average employee might stop right then. The size of the communication you give depends on the capacity of the receiver. It is the prudence of the communicator to judge as to how much the receiver can take at one time.

Feedback

Feedback is the most important component of communication. Without feedback the process of communication is incomplete. Proper and timely feedback ensures effective communication. The problems and misunderstandings in communication are a result of lack of feedback. Meaningful communication occurs when it is received as it was intended. A simple way to ensure that communication has resulted in mutual understanding is to observe the behaviour of the receiver and notice how far his/her actions conform to the requirements of the message. In face-to-face communications the feedback is instantly available. Performance reports, question clarifications, suggestions, and empathetic listening are also very useful in providing the necessary feedback. Fallacious statements or erroneous conclusions are made because of lack of confirmation through feedback and discrepancy between the message transmitted and understood.

Overcome Bypassing

Bypassing can be overcome if the communicator tries to understand the receiver. Awareness of the background and interests of the receiver will help the communicator choose the proper words and language. Feedback from the receiver also reduces the chances of bypassing. With the help of feedback, the communicator can alter or repeat his message.

Semantic Accuracy

Proper care should be taken to avoid errors in speaking and writing. Whether it is a spelling mistake or a grammar mistake, or a wrong pronunciation; any mistake committed by the communicator attracts attention of the receiver. Even the minor errors in communication cannot be tolerated.

Add Some Eloquence

Sometimes, even the true facts and figurers do not solve the problem. Why? Because the listener is not interested or motivated. Or in other words, the communicator could not persuade or motivate the listener through his communication. Facts will do the job only when presented eloquently and in terms of listeners' emotional interests. And practically, do we care to add eloquence to our messages and other verbal activities? Perhaps no, in the sense that eloquence and persuasiveness comes from a deep understanding of the purpose and from a strong desire to do better and to persuade others to do better. The art of persuasion comes naturally when one has a clear purpose and strong desire.

Proper Attention

Listening with half attention is common to almost all of us. Often, we spend our time evaluating the communicator and the message before we have heard or read all of it. Also, we may be thinking of what we will say in response. As a listener, we should try to understand a message properly before we draw conclusions or give a reply. This is required not only for obtaining a clear understanding of the explicit verbal message, but also looking for non-verbal, implicit meanings that are related to the feelings of the communicator. Providing timely feedback to the sender is also an aid in the process of effective communication.

Also, because of our busy life styles, communicators must realise that they are, in fact, competing for the attention of listeners or readers. So, the message must be so interesting and so clear that the listeners or readers will want to understand and incorporate it immediately. This will overcome the barrier of communication selectivity.

Improve Environmental Factors

The effectiveness of communication is profoundly affected by all those factors, such as characteristics of the physical and social environment in which the message is transmitted and received by the receiver. The physical environment can facilitate or hinder communication. Social and informal interactions are affected by the physical setting such as the design of the office building. The amount of informal communication will be more if the offices or cubicles of employees are closest to one another. In the same way, if cubicles or offices are very apart it will hinder free flow of communication.

Use Proper Etiquette

To be successful in the business world, a person must use proper verbal etiquette. One important aspect of verbal etiquette is a proper introduction. Every day we encounter people in a variety of business and social situations. The way we meet and greet them creates lasting impressions and paves the way for a productive encounter. Introductions project information. Besides the obvious elements of name, title and affiliation, an introduction conveys a level of respect and reflects how the person making the introduction views the other person's status. Another aspect of business etiquette is proper telephone communication. Since much of today's business is done over the phone, using correct telephone etiquette is more important than ever. Lasting impressions may be formed during and after telephone conversations, and business people, in order to be successful, must maintain a positive impression. This dictates that people use proper telephone etiquette.

Communication can be made effective by following the above discussed simple and basic steps. Learning the basics, and they are not very difficult, is the first step in barrier-free communication.

❑❑❑

9

GROUP BEHAVIOUR AND COMMUNICATION

Understanding husman communication adequately without paying attention to the groups in the organisation is very much difficult, if not impossible. Manpower in the organisations are not non-living resources, rather they are viewed by managers and supervisors as unified groups who exchange and communicate views and ideas about work culture, HRM policies, incentives, promotions and so on. The manpower or the people in the organisations work in groups to achieve certain pre-defined goals. But the question arises what is a group? How we can define a group? Well, a group may be defined as two or more people interacting in a unified manner toward the achievement of some common goal. The members in a group interact interdependently in such a manner that each influences the others. People waiting in a room or passengers on a bus are not a group. The physical proximity does not constitute a group. On the same lines, people waiting in a queue for petrol are not a group, even though they are physically close to each other. If, there arises a serious problem and they start communicating and interacting in pursuit of a common objective, this would then become a group. In the absence of a common goal and interaction, people in proximity to one another can be referred to as a 'collection' not as a group. A group of people working in the same room, or even on a common project, does not necessarily make a group. Also, if the group is managed in a totally autocratic manner, there will be a little opportunity for interaction; hence, there will be no group formation. In the same way, if there is friction within the members, this cannot be termed as a group. On the other hand, the group may be formed by distant individuals working on different projects. In essence, the group formation leads to a spirit of cooperation, coordination and commonly understood procedures and norms. If this is present within a group of people, then their performance will be enhanced by their mutual support and cooperation.

We can find groups everywhere — in the home, at work and at play. All of us belong to one group or the other for different reasons. We join some groups for fun and some for profit. We join some groups to increase our prestige, and others simply because we are forced to. Some help us fulfill personal or professional goals, and others meet our moral and ethical needs. Groups help us define who we are and what we want to be? The groups to which we belong or aspire to belong tell others about our own preferences and goals. The groups we refuse to join tell about our dislikes, fears and values. Groups have a great impact on our daily life and all of us need to belong to a number of them to survive in today's world.

There are numerous reasons for joining groups. Some of the more common reasons are as below:

Affiliation Needs

Humans are by nature social. People have strong needs to belong and affiliate. They form informal groups to satisfy their affiliation needs. Groups provide a natural way for people to gather in order to satisfy their social needs.

Goal Achievement

A collective effort for goal achievement is also a major reason for forming a group. Common problems and objectives tend to give groups an advantage over individuals. There is more information in a group than anyone of its members may provide. Moreover, groups tend to provide a greater number of approaches to solving any particular problem. In an organisation, departments are organised around functions such as sales, production, accounting, marketing etc. If people in these groups also have similar characteristics, the basis for group formation and cohesion may even be strengthened.

Interpersonal Needs

Individuals join a group to meet their interpersonal needs. In this, the major needs are termed as inclusion, control, and affection. Inclusion is the need to establish identity with others. Control is the need to exercise leadership and prove one's abilities. Affection is the need to develop relationships with others. Groups provide outlets for these needs.

Power

Individuals gain power in groups. Employees form unions for their rights in an organisation. Consumer protection groups or human rights groups fighting against big organisations, confer power on the members that these members would not have as individuals.

Group Synergy

Group synergy refers to the idea that two plus two equals five. Or in other words, it means, 'the whole is greater than the sum of its parts'. Groups are considered to be capable of producing better results than an individual can produce working alone. From the group member's point of view, each member can participate in achievements well beyond his/her own individual potential. In an effective group, objectives are identified, strategies created and problems are recognised and solved. This leads to collaborations and the formation of partnership targeted towards a common goal. This can allow the maximisation of resources leading to greater efficiency. The productivity of the group becomes greater than the sum of its parts.

Common Traits

Individuals form groups with those who share their beliefs, values and attitudes. It is very easy to communicate with those who have common interests, likings and feelings. This commonness confirms our beliefs and ideas with less fear of contradiction. It is a common saying that birds of a feather do flock together.

Free Communication And Interaction

Opportunity for free communication and open interaction can be another reason for joining a group. Groups are easily formed where the physical proximity and interaction is more. In organisations, the basis of friendships and group formation is usually frequent interaction and communication. It is also true that people form groups with others in their vicinity.

For Gaining Support

Another reason is recognition of the worth of the individual which is often considered as the basis for delegating the responsibility to groups of subordinates. A group with its collective efforts can take big projects or tasks. A group with its increased ability to perform better can provide motivation and support to its members while working on a big project. In other words, the individual's talents are better utilized in a group.

Self-Esteem

Self-esteem is a big motivator for people. The group provides an environment where the individual's self-perceived level of responsibility and authority is enhanced and where accountability is shared, thus, providing a perfect motivator through enhanced self-esteem coupled with low stress. If an individual belongs to an exclusive group, the self-esteem of all members may be boosted. In other words, membership in a successful group also raises an individual's self-esteem.

Security

Security and safety are also a common reason for joining a group. Individuals need protection from other groups or from some external powerful people. A group being united gives strength to its members. Employees belonging to a minority may form their own group for their protection in an organisation. Likewise, in a locality, neighbours may form a group to ensure the security and protection of their neighbourhood.

TYPES OF GROUP LEADERS

As a self-managing unit, a group has to undertake most of the functions of a group leader collectively. For instance, meetings must be organised, budgets decided, strategic planning undertaken, goals set, performance monitored, reviews scheduled, etc. It has been recognized that it is wrong to expect an individual to suddenly assume managerial responsibility without assistance of the group members. Even if there are practiced managers in the group, they must first agree on a method, and then convince and train the remainder of the group.

The group leader has the responsibility to ensure that the group operates effectively. In some circumstances, the group is unable to fulfill this role — there may be conflicts between individuals in the group, poor leadership and unfulfilled roles. Group facilitation by group leader can provide a solution to these problems. Facilitation increases productivity by increasing group motivation, confidence and commitment. It provides a better climate for radical change and optimises group dynamics.

The role of leadership in management is largely determined by the organisational culture of the company. It has been argued that manager's beliefs, values and assumptions are of significant importance to the overall style of leadership that they adopt.

There are several leadership styles a leader can adopt. Each technique has its own set of characteristics, and each uses leadership in a different way. Based on their leadership styles following can be the types of a leader:

The Autocratic Leader

The autocratic leader dominates team-members, using unilateralism to achieve a singular objective. This approach to leadership generally results in passive resistance from team-members and requires continual pressure and direction from the leader in order to get things done. Generally, an authoritarian approach is not a good way to get the best performance from a team.

There are, however, some instances where an autocratic style of leadership may be appropriate. Usually, where the subordinates are totally unskilled and unqualified this approach is suitable. Some situations may call for urgent action, and in these cases an autocratic style of leadership may be the best. In addition, most people are familiar with autocratic leadership and therefore have less trouble adopting that style. Furthermore, in some situations, subordinates may actually prefer an autocratic style.

The *Laissez-Faire* Leader

The *laissez-faire* manager exercises little control over his group, leaving them to sort out their roles and tackle their work, without participating in this process himself. In general, this approach leaves the team floundering with little direction or motivation.

Again, there are situations where the *laissez-faire* approach can be effective. The *laissez-faire* technique is usually only appropriate when leading a team of highly motivated and skilled people, who have produced excellent work in the past. Once a leader has established that his team is confident, capable and motivated, it is often best to step back and let them get on with the task, since interfering can generate resentment and detract from their effectiveness.

The Democratic Leader

Under the leadership of democratic leader the members of the group enjoys a voting right for any decision. Or in other words the democratic leader makes every important decision after consulting his team, while still maintaining control of the group. The democratic leader allows his team to decide how the task will be tackled and who will perform which task.

A good democratic leader encourages participation and delegates wisely, but never loses sight of the fact that he bears the crucial responsibility of leadership. He values group discussion and input from his team and can be seen as drawing from a pool of his team members' strong points in order to obtain the best performance from his team. He motivates his team by empowering them to direct themselves and guides them with a loose reign. However, sometimes the democrat is also seen as being so unsure of himself that everything becomes a matter for group discussion and collective participation.

TYPES OF GROUPS

Every group has its own characteristics that differ from those of the members of the group. Every group, in fact, has its own attitude, style and character. Groups are formed to accomplish some objective. The objective may be to complete some kind of task or it may be to promote the interpersonal relationships between the group members. Many groups, however, fulfill both of these functions. Further all the groups are not alike; rather they differ on the basis of its size, position of members etc. We can classify different types of groups as follows:

Social And Task Group

Social groups are voluntary groups that exist basically to provide entertainment or relaxation outlets for members. Work is always secondary to social groups. Social groups are formed in organisations during lunch or break hours. It is true that all the groups have both social and task aspects, but these groups are predominantly informal and social in their orientation. Examples of social groups are families and social clubs.

Task or work groups exist primarily to accomplish some sort of work or assignment. The basic purpose of formation of these task groups is the accomplishment of some pre-defined work goals and the social or informal dimension may be very less or may even be absent. In an organisation, departments, committees, project teams etc. are the examples of task groups. Some task groups are relatively permanent and others are temporarily made for a particular project or assignment. These groups are of greatest concern to managers and to organisation effectiveness.

Reference Group

A reference group is that most aspired group where people want to belong to. A reference group is capable enough to shape the acts, beliefs, and attitudes of the people. A reference group serves as a benchmark against which people can compare their own actions and behaviour. In other words, a reference group is seen as an influential and prestigious group by others. People try to follow the standards set by this group.

Primary And Secondary Group

A primary group is a small group of people in which they have open and direct face-to-face contact with each other. In a primary group, the members have frequent interaction and they also exert influence on each other. The examples of a primary group can be close associations among work colleagues or close friends.

Secondary groups on the other hand are more impersonal and large groups. The face-to-face contact of members in these groups may be very less. Members in these groups are on formal terms and usually membership in secondary groups is for earning a living or for a professional motive. The professional associations, group of residents in locality, religious group are examples of secondary groups. Sometimes the term reference group is used for a secondary group also.

Formal And Informal Group

Formal groups, as the name suggests, are groups formally designed by the organisational hierarchy. The membership in these groups is not voluntary rather it is determined by a host of factors such as member's position on the organisation chart, place in the work flow, and appointment to various committees and task forces. Formal groups are purposely designed by the management to get the organisational work done.

In contrast to this, informal groups are formed without any formal and deliberate design or a place on the organisation chart. The basis of these groups is common values, interests, hobbies, friendship, or social needs. A tea club or a lunch table is an example of informal group. Informal groups emerge spontaneously, without formal design or a place on the organisation chart.

Informal groups are independent of the organisational hierarchy and structure. That is why any strong informal group in an organisation is seen with doubt and suspicion.

VARIABLES IN GROUP COMMUNICATION

Group Cohesiveness

Group cohesiveness refers to the degree to which the members desire to remain in the group. It is the degree of cohesiveness that depicts how tightly or loosely the members are held together in a group. Members of a highly cohesive group are motivated to the continuance of the group, to advance the group and to be active in the group. In a highly cohesive group, the members are more likely to stick together, cooperate and participate in common goals. In other words, cohesiveness is the extent to which members find the group attractive.

Group cohesion has a relation with the size of the group. Usually, a small group is more cohesive as compared to a large group. There are several reasons for this. In a small group the interaction among members decreases. Moreover, when the number of members is more the difference in attitudes, perceptions and interests is also more. This difference decreases cohesive potential. Also, in a larger group it is difficult to reach on a consensus easily.

Communication in the group is influenced by group cohesiveness. A cohesive group will have open and effective communication. Similarly, in a low cohesive group, communication itself will be a problem. It is also true that group communication and group cohesiveness are positively correlated. Group members will communicate more in highly cohesive group and less in a low cohesive group.

Roles In Groups

Every member of a group plays a certain role within that group. Some roles relate to the task aspect of the group, while others promote social interaction. Other types of roles are self-centred and can be destructive for the group.

Role expectation: A role is a set of shared expectations about who should do what under a particular situation. Role expectation is concerned with those duties and acts which are expected from a group member in a specific position. These are defined as how others believe a person should act in a given situation.

Role ambiguity: Role ambiguity occurs when a member is not clear about his or her role and duties. It also covers the circumstances when the member is not sure about the scope of his or her authority. Usually, the main reason for role ambiguity is the complex nature of the job. The other reason may be incompetence or incapability of the group member.

Role conflict: Role conflict occurs when there are contradictory or conflicting roles a member has to play. The roles assigned to a group member to achieve certain goals may be conflicting. For example, a manager has to increase the profitability by conserving the cash flows and at the same time he is to distribute bonus to employees. So the role conflict occurs when an individual is assigned simultaneous role with conflicting expectation.

Group Size

A small group can be defined as a group having at least three and no more than twelve or fifteen members. For a group formation there should be atleast three members, otherwise it would simply be a dyad (a group of two people). It is believed that with three members, coalitions can be formed and some kind of organisation is present. But when the number of members exceeds more than twelve or fifteen, it inhibits the members' ability to communicate with everyone else in the group. Two to seven members seem to be the most appropriate size range for most effective work groups. Smaller groups often do not have enough diversity of skills and interests to function effectively.

Group Communication

The members of a group must be able to communicate freely and openly with all other members of the group. Groups develop norms about inter-personal interaction and group members will develop roles which will affect the group's communication.

Group Consensus

Consensus means when all the members agree on a particular issue or solution. In other words, consensus reflects the thinking of all the members of a group. It is reaching on a decision that is acceptable to all the members and without any member actively against it. The group members all agree on the final decision through discussion and debate. Consensus is different from a majority vote in the sense that in a consensus all the members are convinced on the decision and finally, there remains no minority who is against the decision.

Group Goals

A group must have a common purpose or goal and they must work together to achieve that goal. The goal brings the group together and holds it together through conflict and tension. Initially when the group is newly formed and it is difficult for members to work together as a team as they all are new and do not know one another well. But with constant interactions and free communication they start becoming aware of each member's nature, habits, strengths, weaknesses, styles of working, attitudes etc. this relationship building in the group helps the members in achieving the group's goals effectively.

Power And Authority In The Group

Power cannot exist without relationships or communication, but power is evident in all relationships, so power is always a part of group dynamics. The concept of power is broader than the formal authority a person has due to his position in the organisation. Power comes from the individual's qualification, expertise, behaviour, actions, attraction etc. whereas the origin of authority is the organisational position of the individual. Power is a force that gives the communicator the ability to influence the receiver to take an action which would not otherwise be taken. Just as a leader cannot lead without followers, individuals and groups cannot exercise power independent of context and relationships. Power functions within specific contexts and relationships, the people who exercise power and the occasions when they do so change as time passes and contexts change.

In simple words, authority can be defined as the legitimate power to make decisions in the context of a formal organisation. It is the power that has been validated by formal cultural, societal, small group and organisational rules and practices. Authority is vested in a particular position or role. For example, appointed group leaders are granted a certain degree of power based on their leadership role. Members of a group, organisation, society, or culture develop an understanding that power should be distributed in a certain way.

Group Conflicts

Conflict is considered as a struggle between two or more members who perceive conflicting goals and feel interference from the other member(s) in achieving their goals. Conflict is the most misunderstood dimension of group communication. Group leaders always try to avoid conflicts in the groups because they consider conflict as a barrier to group's effectiveness. In fact, conflict is the most common and unavoidable part of every interpersonal relationship. It is, therefore, important to manage conflict, if the relationship is to be long lasting and rewarding. Group interactions and discussions should be encouraged to ensure that various ideas and viewpoints are heard so that the group can reach on a consensus. Conflict in the group can be used productively to generate and test new ideas, alternatives, solutions etc. and then they can be implemented with group agreement.

Group Norms

Every group has its own acceptable standards of members' behaviour. Group norms are expected behaviours developed among the group members. Basically, norms are unspoken rules and are agreed upon informal roles that guide all members' behaviour in the group. A group develops norms for almost all the areas of its functioning for example, this can be formal (work) and informal (social) behaviour, communication, work ethics, performance standards, quality of work etc. That is why, the character of a group is judged by the norms that are followed by the members.

Norms differ from Rules in the sense that they are not formal and expressed. Most of the time members of the group are unaware that norms even exist because they are so subtle and implied. So, norms if written down or expressed becomes formal rules of proper conduct. However, in most instances, norms are adopted implicitly as people align their behaviours during the group formation process until consensus in actions emerge.

❑❑❑

10

CROSS-CULTURAL COMMUNICATION

INTRODUCTION

In today's changing business world, it is very common to see multinational-multicultural offices and workforces. Rather, with more and more companies going global this has become the norm of the day. Earlier, developing cross-cultural communication skills were relevant only to those managers and executives who had to go for cross-border business assignments. But now even in your own country you have to communicate with those who have different cultural backgrounds. This way, it has become essential for business executives to develop effective cross-cultural communication skills.

Many organisations have learned that the key to successful international business relationship lies in a real understanding of the values and cultural practices of the counterparts in the host nation. For example, Indians attach a great importance to religion and hospitality. Mexican people attach importance to personal relationships. Every country and its people have different values and patterns of behaviour. So, if you want to do business in any country you need to develop an understanding of their culture and personal preferences. Any business organisation is certain to fail if it operates in a foreign country without understanding the culture and values of that country.

Surveys says that an individual should have the following qualities for effective cross cultural interactions:

(1) An open minded and receptive individual with a flexible family

(2) Outgoing, warm and interested in developing relationships

(3) Genuinely curious to know about the target country, its culture, values etc.

(4) Good communication skills and interest in learning the target language

(5) Open and broad perspective about the home country, its culture, values etc.

These qualities are the key to success and they enable managers to overcome most of the hurdles caused by differences in culture. Crossing the national borders and interacting with the people of different culture requires thorough preparation. Learning things about culture and language helps the managers in getting love and respect in that country.

Culture Defined

We all grow in a culture that provides us a particular set of attitudes and behaviour. Sometimes, we are even not aware of the most basic features of our own culture and its values until we come into contact with people from other cultures. Before we delve further into the subject of cross-cultural communication, let us first take a look at what we mean by culture. Iris Varner and Linda Beamer in *Intercultural Communication In The Global Workplace*, define culture as "the coherent, learned, shared view a group of people has about life's concerns that ranks what is important, instills attitudes about what things are appropriate, and prescribes behaviour, given that some things have more significance than others."[1]

So, about culture we can conclude:

- An individual is not born with a culture, rather it is learned and imparted through upbringing and exposure to the practices and rules of conduct of that particular culture.
- Culture is shared by the members of a society or a community. People in the same culture agree about the meanings of things, values and beliefs.
- Culture decides what is good or what is bad. It means, culture teaches values or priorities. And all this shapes our attitude and behaviour.

Our values, priorities, and practices are shaped by the culture in which we grow up. We usually behave in ways that we think are appropriate or acceptable in our culture. Any deviation from what is thought of as appropriate may in fact invite opposition from members of that culture. Therefore, it is important for us to remember that what may be deemed as appropriate in one culture may be unacceptable in another culture.

We can see people operating and interpreting situations differently using different mental representations shaped by different experiences, different belief systems and different cultures. People coming from a different culture may view what is viewed as appropriate in one culture as inappropriate or even strange. Because people of different cultures differ in the way they do things, in the way they view things and in the way they communicate. It is important for us to develop an awareness of what it means to come from our own culture and make the effort to achieve a better understanding of how things may operate differently in other cultures. This is the first important step to help us achieve effective interpersonal communication across cultures.

Determinants Of Cross-Cultural Communication

Communication plays a crucial role in developing, maintaining, and changing culture. We represent and perform culture with others through language and non-verbal messages. The symbols we use, both verbal and non-verbal, arise from the culture into which we are born. Culture is about commonality and differences. Cultural norms and rules affect the way individuals interact.

1. Varner, Iris and Linda Beamer, *Intercultural Communication in the Global Workplace*, USA, Richard D, Irwin, 1995.

Cultures can be categorized as high context or low context. In high context cultures, the context of a message is more important than words. Latin American, Japanese, and Arabic cultures are high context cultures. On the opposite, in low context cultures, explicit message is more important than the context. North American, German, and our Indian culture are low context cultures. As David Victor[2] in *International Business Communication*, points out, high and low context cultures value different kinds of communication and have different attitudes toward oral and written channels. For example, in a low context culture written word is seen as more important than oral statements, so contracts are binding but promises may be broken.

The subject of cross-cultural communication is very broad and fairly complex. Following are the major determinants of cross-cultural communication:

Religious Values And Beliefs

A culture is always influenced by religious values and beliefs of its members. Let us discuss. Christianity co-exists with a view of the individual as proactive. In some Asian countries like in India, however it is seen as presumptuous to predict the future by promising action by a certain date. In other Christian cultures, a simpler life style is considered to be closer to God. Religion also affects what foods may be eaten and on what days businesses are open; for example Hindus do not eat beef, orthodox Jews eat only Kosher meats.

Addressing

In some companies, employees address their bosses by their first names. In some other companies, this would be totally inappropriate. Bosses have to be addressed as Mr./Mrs./Ms. etc. This type of address will be in a culture with a high degree of formality. If the level of formality is seen as a continuum, then most Asian cultures will be on the high end of this continuum. In contrast, the North American culture will be one of those on the low end of this continuum. Clearly then, to avoid misunderstandings and feelings of animosities, it is important for us to develop an understanding of how things may operate differently in other cultures.

Communication Style

How we communicate also depends upon our cultural values. For example, in the United States when people are working they will be quiet. So silence is a sign of work but in Japan people talk to get work done. Depending on the culture we come from, some people may appear very direct and explicit in their communication or very indirect and vague. Again the level of directness and explicitness we display in our communication is determined to a large extent by culture.

Most people from the Asian and Middle Eastern cultures place a high reliance on shared experience, non-verbal cues and the context in which the communication takes place in their communication with others. Consequently, they can appear as rather indirect and vague in their verbal communication. However in some countries, like the United States, Switzerland, and Germany, people are very direct, precise, and explicit in their communication because they rely heavily on the spoken word for meaning. Reliance on context here is low; so is reliance on non-verbal cues. Because of their style of communication, they may appear as too direct and overly talkative.

---

2. David Victor, *International Business Communication*, Harper Collins, N. Y. 1992, p. 148.

Normally, the indirectness that characterizes the communication in some cultures is to a large extent a strategy to avoid causing another person to lose face. It can be viewed as consideration for another person's sense of dignity. However, in cultures that are direct and explicit in their communication, this indirectness may be seen as dishonesty, suggesting that the speaker may have something to hide. Therefore, if you are communicating with people who come from a culture that is on the low end of the directness and explicitness scale, you need to exercise extra care in what you say and how you say something so as not to unintentionally offend them by being too direct. You also need to pay very careful attention to non-verbal cues, shared experience, and the circumstances within which the communication takes place as the true or more accurate meanings of messages may actually reside in some of those factors rather than in the words uttered. On the other hand, if you are communicating with people who come from a culture that is on the high end of the directness and explicitness scale, say exactly what you mean. Also, do not be easily offended when your ideas or opinions are attacked with a degree of directness you are not used to. Bear in mind that in some cultures, this directness is a technique members use to achieve clarity in what they mean. So, just be objective in hearing what they have to say and remember that attacks on ideas are not personal and are not voiced to deliberately embarrass you. Also, remember that in such cultures, reliance on context is low, so be especially attentive to the spoken word as this would usually serve as your main source of information in your communication with them.

Time Perception

Perception of time also differs in different cultures. In some cultures, people place a high emphasis on schedules, a precise reckoning of time and promptness. In such cultures, schedules take precedence over interpersonal relations. Also, because of this urgency to keep to schedules, members try to get to the point quickly when communicating and as such may appear rather rude or brash. Most Western countries and quite a number of European countries follow this perception of time. This type of culture is known as monochronic-time culture. Then, there are other cultures, where timing of events is taken very lightly and people do not observe strict schedules. In such cultures, preset schedules are subordinate to interpersonal relations. This type of culture is known as polychronic-time culture. Most Asian countries, and some Latin American and Middle Eastern countries come under this. In India, we can easily see, social functions and ceremonies, for example, marriages – people do not follow preset schedules. Guests and relatives come late and nobody minds. This is taken as normal.

If we know how cultures view time, it will help us to adapt better to the global business environment. If you are someone from a monochronic-time culture, you must learn patience when communicating with people from a polychronic-time culture. If they fail to turn up for an appointment at a scheduled time, this should not be immediately interpreted as rudeness or callousness on their part. Conversely, if you are someone from a polychronic-time culture and are dealing with people from a monochronic-time culture, try to stick to schedules as much as you possibly can.

Individual Perception Versus Group Perception

Now, we look at how the individual and the group are viewed in different cultures. Cultures can be characterized as either more individualist or collectivist in orientation. Geert Hofstede, a prominent researcher, defines the individualist culture as one in which "the ties between individuals are loose: everyone is expected to look after himself or herself and his or her immediate family. In a collectivist culture, people from birth onwards are integrated into strong, cohesive groups, which throughout their lifetime continue to protect them in exchange for unquestioning loyalty."[3] In an individualist culture, the individual takes centre stage and independence is highly valued. In a collectivist culture, an individual is regarded as a part of the group and a high degree of interdependence among individuals prevails in the same group.

Many people in the United States value individualism. In traditional classrooms, US students are expected to do their assignments individually, so, if they get help from someone else it is treated as cheating. In contrast to this, in Japan people work in groups together to solve the problems.[4]

Iris Varner and Linda Beamer point out that in an individualist culture, "a single person can earn credit or blame for the success or failure of an organizational project." In a collectivist culture, however, "credit or blame goes to the group." In such a culture, "individuals do not seek recognition and are uncomfortable if it is given."[5]

Expression Of Emotion

Expression of emotion also varies in different cultures. North Americans see eye contact as a sign of honesty. In Korea, prolonged eye contact is considered rude. While communicating, Japanese look at neck. Americans have the tendency to smile at strangers but that conveys no meaning. In Germany, smile is a gesture for friends only. The Japanese smile to convey happiness, they also smile to communicate, 'that is none of your concern.'

Fons Trompenaars, in *Riding The Waves Of Culture*, notes that members of some cultures tend to be more expressive with their emotions and 'show their feelings plainly by laughing, grimacing and scowling.' However, in some cultures, members tend to be more repressive and do not show their feelings openly but rather keep them, "carefully controlled and subdued."[6] All these differences can lead to miscommunication in the multicultural workplace. In workplaces where people from different cultures are in contact, misunderstandings can easily occur. People from the more expressive culture may view people from the repressive culture as cold or unfeeling. On the other hand, people from the repressive culture may view their more expressive colleagues as immature and eccentric.

PROBLEMS WITH CROSS-CULTURAL COMMUNICATION

William B. Gudykunst and Stella Ting-Toomey describe three ways in which culture interferes with effective cross-cultural understanding. According to them there are three types of problems in cross-cultural communication[7].

---

3. Hofstede, Geert, 1991, *Cultures and Organizations* London: Harper Collins.
4. Christina Haas and Jeffery L. Funk, "Shared Information: Some Observation of Communication in Japanese Technical Settings", *Technical Communication* 36, no. 4 (Nov. 1989): p. 365.
5. Varner, Iris and Linda Beamer, 1995, *Intercultural Communication in the Global Workplace*, USA: Richard D. Irwin.
6. Trompenaars, Fons, 1993, *Riding the Waves of Culture: Understanding Cultural Diversity in Business.* London: Economist Books.
7. Gudykunst, William B., and Stella Ting-Toomey, *Culture and Interpersonal Communication,* Interpersonal Communication, Vol. 8. Newbury Park, Calif.: Sage, 1988.

(1) Cognitive
(2) Behavioural
(3) Emotional

(1) Cognitive

The word cognitive is used in the broadest sense, including perception, memory and judgment. Cognitive problems are the problems concerned with the frames of reference or worldviews that provide a backdrop that all new information is compared to or inserted into.

(2) Behavioural

A particular culture has its own acceptable behaviour. The norms regarding acceptable behaviour affect verbal and non-verbal communication in that culture. Whether one looks the other person in the eye-or not; whether one says what one means overtly or talks around the issue; how close the people stand to each other when they are talking—all of these and many more are rules of politeness which differ from culture to culture.

(3) Emotional

Different cultures regulate the display of emotion differently. In some cultures, people get very emotional when they are debating an issue. In Japan, people are taught to control their emotions. Even in strong situations, it is acceptable to laugh but not to cry. In case of US, it is acceptable to frown, swear and yell, but not to cry. In some cultures people try to keep their emotions hidden, exhibiting only the rational or factual aspects of the situation.

All these differences on cognitive, behavioural and emotional levels lead to communication barriers. If the people involved are not aware of the potential for such problems, they are even more likely to fall victim to them, although it takes more than awareness to overcome these problems and communicate effectively across cultures.

Now, let us discuss other barriers in cross-cultural communication.

Language As A Barrier

In language also, different patterns are followed from culture to culture. North American and European printing moves from top to bottom and from left to right. Arabic reads from right to left, but still from to top bottom. Japanese reads from right to left and from bottom to top, so Japanese and English books start at opposite ends. Even every day practices differ from culture to culture. An American carpenter pushes a saw; a Japanese pulls it. Light switches and doorknobs turn the opposite way in Japan and in the United States.[8] Therefore, effective communication with people of different cultures is especially challenging. Cultures provide people with ways of thinking, ways of seeing, hearing and interpreting the meaning. Thus, the same words can mean different things to people from different cultures, even when they talk the same language. When the languages are different and translation has to be used to communicate, the potential for misunderstandings increase.

8. William Ruch, "Corporate Communication, *A Comparison of Japanese and American Practices*, (Westport, CT: Quorum Books, 1984) pp. 5-6.

When we discuss the subject of communication across cultures, language is something that we cannot ignore because language is so much a part of culture and for most of us is the main medium we use to transmit messages. However, because of its central importance, factors pertaining to language can also be the source of many misunderstandings in cross-cultural communication.

Now, we will look at some of the problems that could arise when we communicate with one another cross-culturally that are caused by language-related factors. More specifically, we will look at the problems with translation, the problems with pronunciation, the problems with word choice and meaning and the problems with slang and idiomatic expressions. Hopefully, with a greater awareness of these potential problems, we could take some steps to use language more effectively for improved communication across cultures.

Problems With Translation

When we communicate with people of a different culture, it is always good to be able to utter a few words or phrases in their language to establish affinity. However, when we are not proficient in the target language, there is a strong tendency for us to translate messages from our native language to the target language. Sometimes this technique works very well. Unfortunately, at other times, we may land ourselves in some very embarrassing situations. In Brazil, where Portuguese is spoken, one airline company advertised that its Boeing 747s had 'rendezvous lounges' without realizing that *rendezvous* in Portuguese implies prostitution. In China, Kentucky Fried Chicken's slogan 'Finger-licking good' was translated as 'it is so good that you suck your fingers.' In Thailand, the slogan 'Come alive with Pepsi' was translated 'Bring your ancestors back from the dead with Pepsi.' In Puerto Rico, General Motors had difficulties advertising Chevrolet's Nova model because the name sounds like the Spanish phrase No *va,* which means 'It does not go.' When the CIA used a machine translation system to translate Russian, the Bible verse 'The spirit is willing, but the flesh is weak' became 'The vodka is good, but the beef is rotten.'[9]

So, translation from one language to another can altogether change the meaning of the message. Only in a perfect world, all business people would know the language of each culture with which they deal. It is generally said in terms of international business, that you can buy in your native language anywhere in the world, but you can sell only in the language of the local community. If we think problems can only arise when two cultures are using different languages, we are wrong. Even when two cultures are using the same language for communication, problems may still be encountered when communicating with one another cross culturally. We can just take the English language as an example.

Problems With Pronunciation

English is such a language which is widely used throughout the world, even then the problems exist due to the differences in pronunciation. Speakers of the English language from two different countries face problems in understanding each other. For example, take the case of Singapore, many of the people use the English language without any problem. But when they communicate with a foreigner, the latter face a problem in understanding them. The reason is the difference in pronunciation. One other reason is that most of the Singapore people do not

---

9. Scott Ober, *Contemporary Business Communication*, 3rd edition, Houghton Mifflin Company, USA, 1999.

make a distinction between the certain words, for example, 'airport' and 'airpot', 'tree' and 'three', 'pen' and 'pan' etc. We can imagine how these pronunciation differences can lead to miscommunication when communicating across cultures.

Ambiguous And Unfamiliar Words

There are so many words which may have different meanings for different people depending upon their interpretations. These words are known as 'class words.' For example, if I say that I own a 'four wheeler.' Now, the word four wheeler does not make clear about the type of vehicle, its price, its standard etc. In the same way, the word 'house' can include anything from a hut to a villa. Of course using such words simplifies our communication. But using the words having different meanings tend to cause a lot of problems in understanding the message clearly.

So, these types of problems are not unusual in international business. What can we do to solve the problem? The answer is simple, always take 'feedback', and correct the other, if he or she is getting different meaning. Also, try to use simple and clear words to avoid confusion later on.

OVERCOMING CROSS-CULTURAL COMMUNICATION BARRIERS

The world, in which we are living is culturally diverse. We all encounter individuals from different races, religions and nationalities in our daily interactions. There is often anxiety surrounding unfamiliar cultures. What manners are acceptable? What will offend a person from a very different background? It can be paralyzing to deal with other people if we do not know what to expect. We can find many similarities between cultures, but usually the differences are what may look like barriers to us. When this happens, we talk about communication gap, culture shock, language difficulties and other labels we learned to associate with these matters. However, we should think of cultures and languages as bridges rather than gaps, as gates and links rather than barriers. After all, diversity is here to stay and we need bridges and gates. The good news is that bridging the differences is not that hard to do. The following suggestions are applicable to people in a variety of settings.

Desire To Communicate

The desire to communicate is the first step in removing cultural anxiety. The desire to connect with another human being is the bond that will express itself clearly. A genuine effort to understand another person goes a long way in the path to communication. First of all, be aware of what it is to be from your own culture. Then learn all you possibly can about the culture of the people with whom you want to communicate. Knowing about other cultures will help you develop your own skills.

Recognize Dissimilarities

Being different should not always be seen as negative. Be proactive when approaching a new culture. This is a learned skill which means it will require research, practice and growth. People from different backgrounds may have varied approaches to conflict management, learning styles, family structure, religion and most other aspects of life. It is impossible to know the varied systems of all cultures, so approach this process one culture at a time as you meet and deal with new people.

Appreciating The Dissimilarities

There is a common saying "to know me is to love me." This is also true in case of a culture — the more we know about other cultures and societies, the more we appreciate them. This knowledge comes as we go beyond the superficial. Since many of us were socialized to judge very quickly what comes through our senses, we are either attracted to or repelled from surface elements in a culture, such as those that first meet our senses: the smell and taste of the food, the sound of the music, the look of the people and their attire, the styles of greeting and personal touch. However, when we make the time and effort to get close enough to observe the detail, things begin to take on a different colour and we begin to enjoy them. For appreciation to happen, then we must postpone criticism and try to keep an open mind. As we absorb the new information, learning takes place. And the 'foreign' culture ceases to be foreign.

Something Is Always Similar

When dealing with diverse people, we should look for similarities. Our goals, dreams, and aspirations may be more alike than our skin colour. Parenting approaches may differ, but the common bond of a mother and a child crosses many barriers. Most people have basic needs in common, like Maslow's hierarchy of needs that suggest all people have physiological, safety, acceptance, self-esteem and self-actualization needs. Considering these things it is easy to see our essential common ground. And this is where we can begin our comprehension of others.

Do Away With Ethnocentrism

Ethnocentrism is the emotional attitude that one's own ethnic group, nation, or culture is superior or in other words it is an excessive or inappropriate concern for racial matters. Usually, people have the tendency to judge all other groups according to their own group's standards, behaviours and customs and to see other groups as inferior by comparison. This is because different cultures have different ways of behaving and interpreting behaviours. When communicating with people across cultures, one should give up any sentiments of ethnocentrism.

Use Information

Right and the relevant information is the only key for survival in the information age. A person having information about what is happening around him can break all the communication barriers. Information and knowledge about the other cultures, values, customs etc. helps in removing ignorance and one's own biases in accepting new ideas.

Learn To Adapt

Be flexible and ready to adapt and adjust your behaviour, but do not overdo your adjustment as then you risk being perceived as insincere. Just try to act in a way appropriate to the target culture, be yourself and show sincerity.

Beware Of Generalizations

There is a difference between culture and personality. You will find people who are friendly, shy, rude, or polite in all cultures. For example, not all Americans are informal, not all are rich and concerned with efficiency, and in the same way not all Indians are poor. Keep in mind the great diversity of values, attitudes and personalities within a culture.

Don't Be A Stereotype

It is important as you become a promoter of cross-cultural communications that you reach beyond stereotypes. It is necessary to evaluate people on an individual basis. Stereotypes often reflect the differences in socio-economic status, religion, or dialect. These differences are apparent in all races and cannot identify one specific group of people. It is important to suspend judgment, avoid misconceptions, narrow perspectives and immature reactions. Stereotypes often contain a granule of truth, but this tiny truth cannot characterize an entire culture. Getting the whole picture is being active and thinking critically about people and their behaviour.

Be More Tolerant

Because people of different cultures do things differently from one another, you must be tolerant of deviations from the norms — what you are used to in your own culture. Remember that what may be the norm for you may not be the norm for other people coming from a different culture.

Overcoming Language Barrier

Language problems are the most common problems in the cross-cultural communication.

Language problems can be solved by speaking slowly and clearly, ensuring accurate pronunciation, using simple and common words. We should also use the basic principle for effective communication, that is, 'feedback.' If feedback is employed properly we can overcome more than ninety per cent of our communication problems.

Finally, the barriers that exist between cultures are weak. All we need is desire, information, and the willingness to take initiative to break them. An individual's ability to be open to new ideas and new people will go a long way in the process of cross-cultural communication.

❑❑❑

11

Listen Please

Almost every job requires excellent communication skills. Worse yet, in every job there remain problems of communication. They say: Improve communication skills. Now what to do? Communication skills do not require a MBA degree, just some common sense and a better understanding of the role communication plays in everything you listen. Do not assume that better communication skills mean you have to speak like Amitabh Bachhan. Listening skills are the most ignored aspect of good communication skills. More misunderstandings occur due to poor listening than to mis-statements.

Almost all of us have experienced at one point of time that during a meeting or a lecture we were not listening to the speaker. Why? Because we were not there or in other words we were mentally absent. This is a failure in communication or to be more precise failure in listening. Why there is failure in listening? Possible reason could be perhaps conversation was beyond bearable time limits or it might also be possible that the speaker was not speaking clearly or the subject was not interesting or the speaker himself was boring or he was not well prepared or we had our problems to think about than to listen to the speaker. The reasons and excuses for not listening are infinite but one thing is clear that a failure in listening means a complete breakdown in communication.

Most of us know that listening is not just an inborn virtue but a skill that can be learned. To improve your listening, consider the following:

- Listen, do not speak, while the other is speaking.
- Do not try to prepare what you will say next.
- Sit straight and listen intently with full attention.
- Give feedback, from time to time, whether you are following, or not what is being said.

Why to listen?

The average manager spends about 80 per cent of his time in communication and almost half of that time goes in listening. Another thing that shows the importance of listening is that we listen more than we read for acquiring knowledge, ideas and concepts. Following are the chief reasons for 'why we listen?'

Listening To Understand Others

As listening is the lifeblood of communication so it is with a relationship. If you want to test it, do not listen to your friend/relative while he is conveying something important for him. Show him you are not listening. You will get the results, that is, the importance of listening. When the speaker speaks he expects the others to listen properly. Not listening may be taken as personal insult and may cause problems in personal relationships. In the same way, proper and patient listening shows interest and respect for the speaker. So, listening to others strengthens our relations with them.

Listening For Information

It is true that only a true listener can gather some information and knowledge. Mostly, we listen to understand some information, instruction, problem, or some facts. A person who knows 'speaking' only restricts his knowledge by not listening to others. We all read the newspaper daily, magazines, journals, books etc. but most of the information we collect is through listening. We listen to our colleagues, friends, radio, television, and people around us. All these sources make up our most of the daily knowledge and information.

Listening To Motivate

Listening is critical to every relationship, for knowing the speaker is interested in what he is saying, makes listener feel cared about and emotionally connected. Listening provides encouraging input to the speaker's response which helps him carrying his ideas one step forward. This is especially important in sales management, customer service and advertising situations. All speakers look for feedback that encourages them to take their ideas to the next level. Since research shows that feeling connected is pre requisite to motivation, showing that we listen is important not only as a matter of kindness, but also as a motivational strategy.

Listening For Entertainment

We listen through ears and the sound waves goes in the mind to derive the meaning and then it stimulates a body response which gives pleasure or pain depending upon the perception of meaning. Everything that is heart soothing we all enjoy listening. So, we often listen for the sake of pleasure, enjoyment and entertainment. We pass several hours with our friends conversing and discussing different matters. Why? Because we derive pleasure in listening to those things which are of interest or benefit to us. We listen to music and watch television for entertainment and relaxation. We view movies, songs, plays and games for pleasure. Therefore, entertainment is one of the main reasons for listening.

Listening For Communication

Communication is possible only if listening is there. Without a listener who will speak? At least not a sane person in normal circumstances. A communicator as a speaker requires at least one listener to complete the process of communication. Not only listening facilitates communication, it improves communication skills also. Through observation we can improve our communication. We sometimes attend meetings or public speaking sessions partly to observe the skills of the participants. How the speaker conforms to the standards of effective oral communication, how the speaker presents his ideas, how he responds to different questions, how he defends his points and how he concludes. All this can be appreciated only through listening.

BARRIERS TO LISTENING

Perhaps the most difficult question to answer is 'Why people fail to listen?' Simply, because there is no single reason that can be attributed to failure in listening, there can be numerous reasons that breakdown in listening. Some of the major barriers in listening are as follows:

Don't Hear, Listen Please

An important distinction is made between active listening and just hearing. Active listening is a mental process in which the listener tries hard to understand both the content and the feelings of the speaker. On the opposite, hearing is only a physical activity which involves only ears and excludes mind and heart. It means, in hearing there is no understanding of the message. Only when the mind and the heart are applied to understand the message and the context, hearing becomes listening. But unfortunately many people, in a conversation, appear to be listening when in fact all they are doing is waiting for their turn to speak. Carl Rogers says "Active listening is an important way to bring about changes in people ...clinical and research evidence clearly shows that sensitive listening is a most effective agent for individual personality change and group development." He also says that when people are listened to in this way, they listen to themselves more acutely and that active listening reduces barriers and differences between people. So, one of the major barriers in listening is, hearing the words alone without actually drawing the meaning.

Biased Attitude

Personal bias can be another barrier to listening. Depending upon the first impression a listener has got from the appearance of the speaker, he or she makes judgement about the speaker. The listener may conclude even before listening to the speaker that speaker has nothing useful to contribute. This is a biased attitude on the part of the listener that causes breakdown in active listening. Sometimes the speaker uses certain words or sentences that we just stop listening. For example, the speaker says, "We've got to change the system..." Now, you are biased about such statements, so, you call him a hypocrite and stop listening.

Premature Evaluation

Sometimes, people try to evaluate the message or the communicator even before the entire message is communicated. Premature evaluation is a tendency to evaluate a communication prematurely which may lead to wrong and hasty conclusions. Usually, a listener tries to judge the message and tries to evaluate the message/speaker before listening to the speaker completely. Right judgement and evaluation requires time and patience. Premature evaluation shows impatience and lack of right judgement on the part of the receiver. Only active and empathetic listening can overcome this barrier of premature evaluation.

Advising

Everybody has certain advises for certain situations. But uninvited advice cannot draw respect from others. Moreover, in some communication situations this becomes a barrier in listening. When the speaker is saying something and without listening to him first, the listener starts giving certain advises or suggestions as per his experience; that proves fatal for the communication. Rather than advising the speaker, one should try to listen first then after understanding the speaker, his communication and context, the listener should suggest some solution etc.

Listen Completely

Whenever you are listening, listen to those words and phrases that have not been uttered by the speaker even, that is complete listening. Most of us are partial or logical listeners that means we listen to the contents only. In logical listening, listener fails to respond verbally and non-verbally to the speaker's feelings. As a result, the speaker fails to feel listened to empathically. The emotions and feelings which the speaker is trying to communicate verbally and non-verbally, the listener should try to understand that also.

Lack Of Attention

Listening requires a desire and an effort to listen. It is only possible if the listener is paying full attention to the message being communicated, otherwise it becomes a mechanical process which, ultimately gives no understanding to the listener. Lack of attention on the part of the listener may be due to many reasons such as preoccupied mind, tension, overwork, lack of interest etc. Whatever may be the reason inattention blocks the process of communication and in the absence of attention there cannot be any transfer of understanding and meaning.

Competing

It is a usual practice we all do that is to compete with the speaker. Whenever a person is communicating something we all have a natural tendency to show that 'my style of doing things is better than yours' or 'what you are saying, I already knew it.'

Insincere Sincerity

Insincerity, posing as sincerity, is a tough act to pull off long-term. People show fake sincerity towards the speaker that they are fully mesmerized and listening to the speaker.

But engrossed in the process of acting they forget to concentrate on the matter. On the opposite, far from being won over by such responses the speaker notes the listener's insincerity.

Boredom

An average person's thinking speed is, roughly, four or five times his speed of speech. And if we are not interested, the subject is boring, or if the speaker is not speaking well, all this will put a stop on listening. Boredom is the most common reason for failure in listening. We listen to those things only which are of some interest to us or which directly or indirectly benefit us. Otherwise, the lack of motivation for listening causes a breakdown.

I Am Listening

Our normal response to every conversation is, 'I am listening'. And most of the times even if we are not listening, we utter the same words. All of us try to show, whenever we are listening, that we are very much interested in the speaker or the subject matter. This permanent gesture of 'I am listening' is a major obstacle in effective listening. Among the more damaging forms of non-listening is pretended listening. We may fool the speaker by nodding and saying 'I am listening' from time to time, but we cannot fool ourselves. One should always try to listen the speaker/conversation with interest. Even under some social pressure if we have to listen to, we should try to listen actively.

LISTENING STYLES / TYPES

All the listeners do not belong to the same club. In fact people use different types or styles of listening. Following are some of the common styles or types of listening:

Passive Listening

Passive listening means listening without giving a response or feedback. A passive listener does not make any effort to motivate the speaker for further talk. He shows that he is not interested in the conversation and does not care for the speaker. He just listens mechanically without even trying to understand the message.

Active Listening

Active or reflective listening, on the opposite, involves live interaction between the speaker and the listener. The listener restates or paraphrases his understanding of the message and reflects it back to the sender for verification. This verification or feedback process is what distinguishes active listening and makes it effective. Listener gives constant feedback to the speaker and in a way direct the conversation. Through active listening, the listener offers the speaker a chance to express his feelings and ideas openly. Listener shows full interest in the conversation and tries to understand the things from speaker's viewpoint. That is why, it is also known as emphatic listening. Active listening helps in establishing a warm and honest relationship between the speaker and the listener. Active listening is the most ideal form of listening and difficult to achieve.

Fake Listening

Silence of the receiver should not be taken as efficient listening. It can be fake. The fake listener is full of polite smiles and other facial expressions. In fake listening, the listener pretends that he is actively listening to the speaker. The problem for the faker is that most speakers can detect the difference between the non-verbal responses of one who is truly listening and of one who is not. The faker's non-verbal responses lack sincerity.

Such lack of sincerity also holds true for the 'Janus listener'. Janus was a Roman god with two faces. Janus listeners wear two faces. They wear one face while listening to people they look up to and another while listening to people they look down on. With the former they wear masks that hide their real faces. The masks come off whenever they are speaking with anyone they look down on. Like the faker, the Janus listener lacks sincerity.

Critical Listening

In this type of listening, the listener acts as a critic. He does not listen properly and whatever the comments and questions he asks they are also posed critically. In fact, critical listener has a biased and negative attitude. He always tries to find out problems and weak spots in the message/speaker. He is so intent on finding problems or weaknesses that he does not listen to what is being said. This type of listening usually results in distortion and misunderstanding. The critical listening causes breakdown in listening and is a major barrier in communication.

Selective Listening

In selective listening the message is not taken as it is, rather something is added or deducted as per the interest and perception of the listener. All this is psychological, which means the listener's mind does not receive that sound stimulus in which it has no interest. This leads to strengthen one's own beliefs and restrains further learning.

Evaluative Listening

Research has proved that a speaker cannot talk as fast as listener's brain can process the information. There remains a lot of extra time for a listener to evaluate the speaker, contents of speech, the environment and context etc. This extra time is used by listener in making a judgment and perception about all the concerned factors, some of which are mentioned above. And we should also not forget that this is the time when a listener can be easily distracted (if he is not evaluating). The listener, then, either daydreams or thinks about his or her own problems. This way, the habit of evaluating while listening is a major barrier to effective listening.

ARE YOU A BAD LISTENER?

Most people think they are good listeners, just as they think they are good speakers. But in reality, listening is the most neglected aspect of communication. Listening is a difficult task and most of us do not know how to listen. Yet effective communication, to a large extent depends upon our listening habits. In schools, students learn how to read, speak and write. But nowhere they are taught how to listen.

Dr. Ralph Nichols[1] of University of Minnesota and an authority on communication, after reviewing several experiments in listening gives a test to measure bad listening habits. With the help of following questionnaire, he suggests, we can analyze our listening habits:

(1) Science says you think four times faster than a person usually talks to you. Do you use this excess time to turn your thoughts elsewhere while you are keeping general track of a conversation?

(2) Do you listen primarily for facts, rather than ideas, when someone is speaking?

(3) Do certain words, phrases, or ideas so prejudice you against the speaker that you cannot listen objectively to what is being said?

(4) When you are puzzled or annoyed by what someone says, do you try to get the question straightened out immediately either in your own mind or by interrupting the speaker?

(5) If you feel that it would take too much time and effort to understand something, do you go out of your way to avoid hearing about it?

(6) Do you deliberately turn your thoughts to other subjects when you believe a speaker will have nothing particularly interesting to say?

(7) Can you tell by a person's appearance and delivery that he will not have anything worthwhile to say?

(8) When someone is talking to you, do you try to make him think you are paying attention when you are not?

1. Ralph G. Nichols, "Do We Know How to Listen? Practical Helps in a Modern Age," *The Speech Teacher* 10, no.2, March 1961.

(9) When you are listening to someone, are you easily distracted by outside sights and sounds?

(10) If you want to remember what someone is saying, do you think it is a good idea to write it down as he goes along?

Now, if your answers to all the above mentioned questions are 'NO' that mean you are perfect in listening (but that is unlikely). On the other hand, every 'YES' answer point out some bad listening habit. So, with the help of this checklist, we can analyse our poor listening habits. But, what is the solution for poor listening habits? Or how to be a good listener?

HOW TO BE A GOOD LISTENER?

Listening is an active process and requires effort. You cannot just relax on your seat and listen, rather you will have to sit erect in order to listen and understand the message. Moreover, in communication, both speaking and listening are not unilateral activities. It is not like that speakers would only speak and listeners would only listen. Rather, in any conversation both parties alternately speak and listen. When we use the word speaker, we are referring to the one who initiates the conversation; when we use the word listener, we are referring to the one who listens to the speaker's words. Sooner or later the listener responds. The listener's responses then trigger the speaker's own responses. This way the cycle of oral communication moves. It is also clear from this that the listener (like speaker) owns half of the responsibility for the effectiveness of communication.

Following are the guidelines which helps in becoming a good listener:

Listen Actively

Being a good listener requires active participation. In any discussion, it is necessary to make sure that one understands what the other person is saying. Active listening keeps both parties in alignment. Often a listener needs to reflect back to what he or she has heard. Words have different meanings to different people and one word, interpreted differently, can change the understanding of the thought. To reflect back to the speaker what you have heard, without giving advice, keeps you and your partner in tune and on the same level.

Concentrate On The Speaker

For better listening, concentrate on the speaker. Focus your attention on what the person is saying. Do not try to prepare what you will say in response.

Do Not Interrupt

Do not interrupt the speaker in between and suspend that urge to speak intermittently. If the speaker is taking much time getting to the point, be patient and listen. Give full time to the speaker to complete his talking.

Watch Non-Verbal Cues

Sit attentively while listening to the speaker. Maintain eye contact with the speaker to show that you are listening with attention. Show through non-verbal cues also that you are listening. Also watch speaker's body language and gestures to have the full meaning of his message.

Listen Without Prejudice

Do not be biased about the speaker or the contents of the message. Listen with open mind and then evaluate patiently. After the speaker is through, give your view or opinion and then discuss it without any prejudice.

Feedback And Paraphrasing

The listener's feedback can be either verbal or non-verbal. Verbal feedback can be in the shape of questions and comments. Non-verbally, the listener can respond through his eyes, facial expressions, gestures and body language to show that whether he is following or not. To paraphrase means to summarize the speaker's main points for clear understanding of the message. For example, the listener after listening to the speaker may say, "So by saying this you mean..." The reason for paraphrasing is to understand the other person's perspective. We all have different past experiences and perceptions, and that is why we interpret things differently. These methods help in removing the barriers in understanding.

Practical Tips For Effective Listening

The following are the guidelines that can help in improving your listening skills.

- Look at the person, and suspend other things you are doing. Analyze the speaker's words and ideas while you are listening, but do not become so engrossed in your own analysis that you miss important points.
- Listen not merely to the words, but the feeling content also.
- Develop a positive attitude towards the speaker.
- Be sincerely interested in what the other person is talking about.
- Do not be distracted by a speaker's personality or speaking style rather, respond thoughtfully to the speaker's words and avoid making judgments too quickly,.
- Restate what the speaker said.
- Ask clarification questions once in a while.
- Be aware of your own feelings and strong opinions.
- If you have to state your views, say them only after you have listened.
- Take notes. Being a good listener sometimes means being a good note-taker. You may wish to record your own thoughts and question as you are listening, so that you will remember to verify or ask them after the speaker is finished.

When you are not taking notes, look at the speaker. This is not only a courtesy but an aid to concentration and comprehension.

❑❑❑

PART C

INFORMATION TECHNOLOGY

12

Information Technology: What And Why?

Broadly defined, Information Technology is concerned with all forms of tools, techniques, and technology applied for transmitting, storing, processing and disseminating information. It refers to any combination of equipments and procedures that facilitate the acquisition, creation, retrieval, storage, searching, viewing, updating and transmission of information using electronic means. Usually, information technology is viewed as a synthesis of developments in the field of computer science and the developments in telecommunication technology. The developments in the telecommunication technology in the first half of 20th century led to installation of worldwide telephone systems, radio and television networks and later development of satellite-based telecommunication. The continuous research and development efforts in telecommunication made communication more efficient, reliable, cost effective and also increased the coverage as the technology matured.

The developments in the area of computer technology are also not of recent origin; computer owes its roots to the ancient machines which could perform simple calculations. The oldest perhaps is the adding machine developed by French scientist Pascal in 1642, then the calculating machine of German scientist Liebnitz around 1700, after that the difference and analytical engines of Charles Babbage in early 1800, and then the tabulating machines developed by Dr. H. Hollerith around 1880 to process the U.S. census data. After that within a short span of time the technology progressed remarkably from the so called First Generation computers that were bulky, unreliable, expensive and very difficult to operate, to the Fourth Generation computers that are 'miniaturized', with a very high speed and huge storage capacity, very economical, reliable and simple to use. The real thrust to the development of computers came during the second half of the 20th century with limited use of computer for data processing. The rapid developments in all technologies making up different components of the computers led to unprecedented growth in computer industry. This development led to mass scale spread of powerful computing resources at a very affordable price to the users and trend in use of computers shifted from users approaching central computers for data processing to computers moving to the users desk for all the activities like word processing and note preparing, data processing, data analysis, trend and pattern analysis as well as scenario building.

Thus, information technology is a logical development arising out of confluence of these two technologies which has narrowed down the difference between collecting, storing and processing information and transporting the information elsewhere thereby driving the geographical distances to irrelevance.

Broadly the areas under IT are:

- Computer hardware and software
- Software development and the tools used for developing applications
- Various information systems
- Data communication systems.

All the above-mentioned components of information technology are discussed in the subsequent chapters in detail.

INFORMATION TECHNOLOGY IN INDIA

Across the last 50 years, the application of information technology to society has gone through distinct stages. First it was in a few areas of military affairs and science. Then it spread to financial institutions and large businesses. Now it is spreading throughout society. The spread is not even, and how it occurs depends increasingly on institutional and social factors instead of technical factors. The development in the area of information technology has a profound impact in Indian economy and also on the quality of human life. In a period when slow growth is haunting the Indian economy, the IT sector stands as a shining example of an industry that has continued to grow belying all expectations. In 1997-98, the total turnover of the industry was more than Rs. 10,000 crores. This represented an increase of 58 % over the 1996-97 turnover of Rs. 6,000 crores. The IT industry in India has maintained a growth rate of around 50 % over the last seven years. In the stock market also, only the IT stocks have proved to be star performers consistently outperforming the Sensex.

Indian IT industry has an interesting history. The pre-1977 period was dominated by large mainframe computer manufactured by global giants like IBM. The exit of the multinational giants saw a host of home grown companies making their mark. These Indian companies included HCL, CMC, ECIL, ICIM, and Wipro.

The period of 1980s witnessed a boom in PCs. In this period there was a tremendous growth in the number of players manufacturing indigenous computers. The real boom however came in the 90s following the liberalization of the economy, several multinationals ventured into the Indian market. Computers invaded the homes and offices of many Indians. The Indian software industry began to make inroads into the software market and began to provide software services and solutions.

The achievements of the Indian IT industry so far have been quite noteworthy (as also explained in the introductory chapter). On the software front, more and more Organisations all over the world are outsourcing their software requirements from India. This is because of technical skills of Indian software professionals and high quality software development coupled with lower costs. Indian software companies have acquired a worldwide reputation of providing software solutions with cost and quality advantage and strengths to handle large projects.

Services and solutions provided by the Indian IT industry are of two types – On-site, where services are provided right on site by software professionals stationed there and off-site where using high speed data communications line, programmers in India are able to develop software on any computer anywhere in the world. With countries like the United States, where there is a 12-hour time difference, a virtual 24-hour office can be provided to the client.

On the hardware front, the sale of PCs and other peripherals has been gradually increasing. Besides the government and the corporate, the penetration of PCs in the home segment has improved tremendously over the years. The number of PCs sold is supposed to have touched the million mark per annum.

Despite this progress there is a lot to be done. Even the high profile Indian software industry has several weak points. Most of the Indian software professionals are devoted to making customized software solutions where the profit margins are low. The real molar comes from product software where companies like Microsoft and Oracle make a killing. For example, Windows the most popular brand of Microsoft has a near monopoly in the market of PC operating systems. On the other hand, in India, except for financial applications, the Indian software industry has hardly any product software. The Indian IT industry is facing a lot of challenges. The cost advantages that Indian software industry enjoyed are being threatened by countries like China, Mexico, Philippines and East European countries. The industry is also facing a problem of shortage of trained software professionals. No major investment has been made on IT education over the last two decades. IT education has been cornered by teaching shops who have taken it up as business with an eye more on numbers and profits. Moreover, the awareness of information technology in India is very low. The usefulness of IT has not percolated down to the masses. Use of IT in government and public sector including banks is very limited. The service level of many IT companies has not reached desirable levels. Lack of funds has always been a major problem area for entrepreneurs, funds are difficult to come either in the form of venture capital or loans from banks.

The problems are many but not entirely insurmountable. Experts agree that the key for the success of the Indian IT industry is in the development of intellectual property. Special attention needs to be paid to the development of R&D.

As explained in the introductory chapter, Indian government is encouraging both software development and hardware manufacturing in the country by creating an appropriate environment. Various measures are being taken from time to time in this regard so that there is stimulation for creation of wealth and economic growth leading to better employment opportunities within the country.

Government-wide Electronic Information Infrastructure will be appropriately created to simplify service delivery, reduce duplication and improve the level and speed of service to the public. Telecommunication linkages through optical fibre cable and VSAT systems will be installed to form a communication backbone.

The Government also recognizes the importance and scope of e-Governance and will promote the use of necessary technologies for efficiency and transparency in its functions. The Government is identifying areas which require introduction of IT in the overall functional framework of the Government. Towards this end IT literacy and training will be encouraged within the Government along with the suitable infrastructure. Attention will be paid to models, network design and overall systems management. For a better citizen interface the following will be emphasized for computerization, viz., vehicle registration, land records, birth and death registrations, employment exchanges, payment of excise duty, sales tax and local tax, electronic bill payment of water and electricity, computerization of health records, relevant education through internet, work of police and police stations, Criminal Justice etc. government departments and organizations will have E-mail communication. All important Government Policies, Acts, Rules, Regulations, Notifications which have a direct bearing on the members of the public would be made available through internet or other suitable networks. The government has also recommended that each ministry must allocate 2-3 percent of its Budget on **IT** promotion. This is a step for development of domestic software industry and a move towards integrating **IT** with government functioning and e-governance.

ROLE OF INFORMATION TECHNOLOGY

The **IT** has improved ability of human beings to process routine data, analyse the results and communicate the results as well as information. Collection, processing and analysis of data to form the judgment on the information is essence of human thinking process; and communicating ideas and information with others for a common goal is the core of any social activity. As **IT** is essentially about these activities, there can hardly be any sector of social activity where the importance of **IT** has not been felt.

Information Technology In Education And R & D

The **IT** has a more pronounce impact in the field of educational, scientific and technological research. The introduction of Educational & Research Network (ERNET) has enabled linking of computers of academic institutions like universities, educational and research institutions with each other thereby giving information on research activities undertaken around the world.

The computer based training packages are being used in educational fields as diverse as pre-school education to research. These tools combine the audio as well as video like Multimedia for developing computer based training packages which are very user friendly and give personnel touch to the process of learning with animation and graphics. The computer based training packages have potential to revolutionizing the concept of distant learning and on the job training for those who cannot attend regular educational courses.

IT is used in wide ranging research activities ranging from astrophysics and space travel to nuclear science and microbiology for complex calculations, simulations and studying the patterns. Similarly, **IT** is also used in research activities such as weather forecasting, remote sensing of biomass, minerals and hydrology which has direct bearing on the society due to accurate forecasting. The **IT** is used for collecting data using the satellite cameras, analysing the images using computers and predict the weather conditions and availability of natural resources on the earth and also under sea in the field of oceanography. This has led to significant reduction of damage to life and property in natural calamities like cyclones and floods.

IT has enabled the scientists to emulate conditions and situations in the laboratory which are either difficult or expensive to create or impossible to create. A separate branch of **IT** called 'Virtual Reality' is being developed which not only simulates these conditions but allows the scientists to study impact of different situations and actions on these simulated conditions e.g. training of commercial and armforce air craft pilots.

Information Technology In Production And Manufacturing

The **IT** is used in manufacturing industry for designing and process control besides other management related activities like inventory control, financial analysis, project management, development of MIS, etc.

IT has altered the techniques of engineering by its tools called Computer Aided Designing. The CAD tools enable the engineers to automating the design and drafting process and build different graphics. The tools is used for designing, modelling and proto typing of new products, graphics and architectural designs, studying impact of design changes on overall design of product, material and cost estimation for new products, etc. This helps the design of most suitable engineering product with minimum manual efforts thereby maximize the human ingenuity in product development.

The **IT** also has played a great role in the area of manufacturing activity viz. the production and process control. This is known as Computer Aided Manufacturing or CAM. The microprocessor chips are used in wide ranging gadgets such as microwave ovens, automobiles, power plants, security systems and chemical industries for controlling the process. The abnormal behaviour or occurrence can be detected and pre-programmed decisions like switching off the plants can be taken with the help of these microprocessors based process controllers. Occurrence of an event like reaching particular temperature, next activity can be triggered automatically. The use of programmed devices like industrial robots have been used in hazardous industries where prolonged exposure of any human being is not advisable. There is increasing trend towards automation of such processes which would improve the working conditions as well as reduce the cost of production.

Information Technology In Nation's Security

IT is extensively used to gather geographical information, analyse the data, carry out operations research for the purpose of logistic support and plan the movements. IT provides very essential navigational support for the aircrafts and the naval ships. The images processing capabilities of **IT** along with satellite telecommunication are used for gathering information on geographical details and terrestrial movements such that almost all man made products like aircrafts, missiles, guns, ships can be identified by the surveillance system with their possible trajectories and paths.

The role of **IT** has been instrumental in the development of powerful guided missiles which have completely altered the concept of defence and security. The missiles like Patriot, Agni or Trishul could only be developed using **IT** which enables the missiles to sense and lock their targets, scan the territory and change trajectory so as to hit the targets.

The **IT** is also used for encrypting and decrypting the strategic information for secured communication between defence agencies. **IT** also plays a very important role in training of the defence personnel with specialised simulators which can simulate the conditions in the sea or air. It can also simulate different war games so as to train the soldiers for actual combat conditions.

IT is also used for storing data on the crime events and the modus operandi used in various crimes, processing the images of the criminals, the fingerprints, and handwriting so as to match the available records.

Information Technology In Administration And Social Services

Today, the governments of the world are expected to provide a welfare state to their citizens and have a wide-ranging responsibility towards their citizens. The states have responsibility towards the health, education, employment, security and welfare of their citizens. For discharging these duties, the governments need huge data on their citizens for planning for health service, education, transport facilities, etc. Weather forecast and early warning systems for calamities such as cyclones, floods etc., are some of the essential social services which are heavily dependent on IT support.

The census data is the largest data which has direct bearing on the society and impact on IT, this is too evident. Today, the government and social services sector are the largest users of IT. Even where the IT is not widely used in government sector, there is pressure on the authorities to use IT for their activities and welfare schemes to improve the governance.

Taxes being the main revenue, the government requires huge data about the taxpayers, as well as need to watch the tax compliance. Similarly, governments are largest spenders in any country with expenditures on wide ranging activities. These activities of the government are distributed all over the country requiring a good network of computers for speedy data compilation.

Information Technology In Medical Science

IT is extensively used in medical research for developing new combinations of drugs. Genetic engineering and information technology are two tools which are set to bring very important changes in medical technology in the coming decades.

IT is increasingly used in hospital administration to keep information on patient's health record for the doctors to trace case history. Similarly, the data on health symptoms and possible diseases is also stored so that the computer can identify the health conditions with the different symptoms in the database and help the doctor with possible cause and also suggest the treatment. Computers are also used for on line systems for monitoring patient's health for any medical emergency. The microprocessor controlled devices are used for heart patients to control the working of heart and trigger timely action. Similarly, such devices are also used in the artificial limbs provided to physically handicapped persons.

Information Technology in Financial Sector

As the Internet and the information technology revolution sweeps across the old economy, financial institutions (FIs) in our country are increasingly realising the need to adapt to the changes taking place. Customer loyalty can no longer be taken for granted, and that forces banks to constantly seek innovative ways to attract and retain customers. To adapt to the new business environment, Indian banks need to proactively harness technology to handle distributed operations, high-volume transactions and data management. This will allow banks to enhance profitability through tighter fiscal and operational control, and achieve customer delight-a critical requirement in today's Internet driven market.

Financial institutions today face competition from several fronts. New, non-traditional financial players are entering the market, often with huge cost advantages and wider delivery channel options. Traditional banks are therefore, facing increased pressure on margins. Customers have a huge variety of options in terms of vendors, products, services and delivery channels. This means that banks need to bring down transactional and operational costs to retain customers, which has proven to be five times less expensive than getting new customers. The most effective way of doing this is by strategically investing in **IT**. Foreign and new private sector banks in the country have led the way in automating the financial services industry. Indian public sector banks, however, have been slow in following. The situation, however, is changing and the initial resistance to technology is fading as top management of several Indian banks are viewing **IT** as a business enabler and a vital part of their strategy. Various banks are now committing to substantial **IT** investments in core and Internet technologies.

In the financial sector, other services such as insurance, leasing companies, mortgage companies, investment consultancy, stock exchanges, share registry and custodial services like depositories process large volume of data. These services have got a big boost with the advent of Information Technology. The banking and insurance companies use the **IT** to keep track of their customers, transactions and financial needs, stock markets use **IT** for on-line trading with the help of computer based terminals connected to 'trading servers', depositories and custodial services maintain computerised records of shares and securities held by them on behalf of their customers and investment consultancy services use computer based systems for analysis of the financial positions, investment opportunities available to their customers, risk factors involved and so on. The organisation such as Reuters has effectively utilized **IT** for providing the on-line data on various needs of the financial sectors.

The impact of **IT** on financial services has been most significant in payment services wherein ATM, Credit cards, Debit cards, Smart cards and other modes of payment have revolutionised the payment mechanism. This has been made possible by making cash available anytime during twenty-four hours of the day at any place in the world and has also obviated the need for physical cash. The IT is changing the very concept of cash and credit throughout the world.

TECHNOLOGICAL ADVANCEMENTS IN BUSINESS PAYMENTS

(i) Electronic Fund Transfer (EFT)

Electronic Fund Transfer sometimes wrongly described as a 'paperless payment' is a system of transferring funds on request using a wide area network. Electronic funds transfer covers a wide range of transaction services, such as:

- Banking services.
- Funds transfer between accounts at the same bank or at different banks.
- Stock brokerage services like placement of orders for stocks.
- Retail ATM services.
- Business transactions involving funds transfer between accounts, investments and overdraft arrangements.
- EFT provides various advantages.
- Immediate or overnight transfer of funds from the consumer's bank account to the service provider's bank account.

- Online credit authorization, hence reducing bad-debt and cheque problems.
- Reduced need for customers to carry cash or cheque.

(ii) Automatic Teller Machine (ATM)

Banking organisations have been very quick to take the advantage of the EFT (Electronic Funds Transfer) environment, as evidenced from a growing number of ATM networks. The wide spread acceptance of ATMs by the public as a means of doing banking transactions provides a major indicator of what customers want. The success of EFT depends heavily on networks to provide reliable and efficient interconnections. ATMs are specialized terminals that dispense cash and require wide area network communication with the central banking computer. The volume of information flow is small; typically 20 to 40 characters are required to verify a customer's identity and debit the account. ATM terminals are often connected to a concentrator which in turn is connected to the central banking computer. All these interconnections require a highly and secure data network.

(iii) Electronic Cash

This is another form of automation of cash into electronic form. It addresses circumstances in which the payer is not present at the point of sale or service, but has electronic communication facilities available, e.g. is connected to the Internet, or to some other form of global information infrastructure, such as a cable-TV installation with enhanced capabilities. Electronic Cash or the Digital Cash is a system of transferring funds through a network such as Internet. The digital equivalent form of cash is known as E-cash. In a digital cash system, cash exists in the form of validated tokens represented by a string of digits. E-cash can be purchased from on-line currency server usually a Bank or Financial Institution (FI). This Bank or FI uses a digital signature algorithm for its clients or customers. Clients or customers can use this e-cash to purchase items over the Internet.

(iv) Credit and Debit Cards

Credit cards in their present form emerged in the United States in 1960s. However, it was not until more recently that credit card usage has expanded significantly throughout the world. Debit cards have been introduced more recently and together they represent the most rapidly growing method of payments in many countries.

Credit and debit cards are rapidly growing in significance as the preferred method of settling small value payments associated with the purchase of specific goods and services. Separate electronic clearing and settlement systems have been established by the major credit card companies. Both MasterCard and Visa have established their own networks which are used for verifying transactions world-wide. Electronic point of sale terminals permit card details to be verified in less than 15 seconds with networks linking the merchant, the credit card processor and the card issuer worldwide. These networks are growing rapidly as the trend for consumers to make payments by credit card in place of writing a cheque continues to grow.

Credit cards are distinguished from debit cards by having access to a line of credit made available to the cardholder by the card issuer. They generally require four separate parties to each transaction, the cardholder, the merchant selling the goods or services, the merchant acquirer processing the credit card payment and the card issuer. In certain cases the merchant acquirer and credit card issuer will be the same company although generally trading under a different legal entity.

(v) Smart Cards

Smart cards are just like credit cards, same size and shape, and can be carried in a pocket or in a wallet but they serve different purpose. A smart card contains a chip which has a processor and memory unit. A smart card generates encrypted random numbers with a lifetime of around one minute. The user enables the card by entering a PIN and then it generates a response or one time password. The response or password is calculated using data encryption which is stored in the card. This provides a means for storing passwords, private keys or digital cash on the card. These cards have become popular due to the limitations of pure password-based systems. This is indicative of the move away from passwords (what the user can remember) to tokens (what the user can carry). These cards are also known as PCMCIA cards as they are also designed to fit in the PCMCIA slots of a computer.

(vi) Electronic Data Interchange (EDI)

Electronic Data Interchange (EDI) is the exchange of structured data between the computer systems of trading partners. It is predicted that this method of 'paperless' trading will change the existing pattern of doing business. So EDI or Electronic data interchange is defined as the interchange of standard formatted data between computer application systems of trading partners with minimal manual intervention. EDI communicates information relevant for business transactions between the computer systems of business organisations, government organisations, small business houses, banks and FIs. EDI covers interchange of business data like invoices, purchase orders, shipping notices, delivery instructions, and other standard business correspondence between trading partners. EDI can be used to electronically transmit documents such as purchase orders, invoices, shipping notices and other standard business correspondence between trading partners. EDI speeds up the trading cycle, enabling a faster response to customer orders and requests. In addition, by data interchange, EDI simplifies the customer's data processing task by supplying only that desired amount of data that is required by the customer. In addition EDI also facilitates transmission of financial information and payments in electronic form. When used for making payments, EDI is referred to as Financial EDI (FEDI) and Electronic Funds Transfer (EFT). EDI is a way of substituting electronic transactions for paper transactions. However, it is much more than mere substitution. It is a means to streamline procedures and improve efficiency and productivity.

Information Technology In Business Management

The **IT** with its computer based system for information processing has influenced the process of management in all the activities of the organisations like strategic planning, production planning, inventory control, finance and accounts, marketing and personnel management.

The computer systems enable the management process of planning by identifying the problems and opportunities through analysing the trends from the data stored; supporting analysis, evaluation of options and selection of alternatives. It also supports decision implementation by watching the progress and identifying possible problems. The techniques such as Programme Evaluation and Review (PERT), Critical Path Method (CPM) simulations and linear programming enable the process of decision making.

The **IT** is mainly used for keeping track of inventory of raw material, semi-finished and finished goods. It is also used for distribution and marketing logistics, keeping information on branch plants, etc. The information is made use for planning the purchases, organizing the production schedule and keeping track of the production process. The introduction of **IT** has enabled the industry to adopt management techniques like 'Just in Time Management' that can reduce cost of holding the inventory of raw material and finished goods.

The **IT** helps management in maintaining the personnel inventory for the skill levels available, training inputs imparted to the staff planning, staff career planning including retirement planning, maintaining the staff records of salary and other payments, etc.

The **IT** has an impact on organisational structure since the processing capabilities enable the data dependent activities to be either automated or delegated. At the same time, centralisation of data and communication capabilities of **IT** can help in centralising the organisational structure for improved decision making. In practice, both centralisation and decentralisation of activities are done with the help of **IT** depending on the type of organisation, nature of applications and the cost considerations involved. For example, resource and finance management can be centralised, whereas production management or process management may be decentralised.

The control activities of the management are supported by **IT** with its ability to analyse past and present data, comparing the trends and results with pre-set standards and generating exception reports.

Information Technology In Economic Development

The **IT** has led to improvement in efficiency of the business and non-business organisations which has improved the effective and economic utilisation of available resources. The increasing importance of **IT** can be judged by the increasing expenditure on **IT**. This has gone up to four per cent of Gross National Product (GDP) in developed economies and even expenditure in other economies. Even in India, it is approximately one per cent of the GDP. The **IT** has a role of better resource allocation and improvement in productivity of all the economic activities. The improved product designs and quality as a result of improvement in management process has resulted in availability of higher quality products and services. The services sector has been recording maximum growth rate as a result of increasing usage of **IT**. As already discussed, the improvements in the financial sector and the payment systems using **IT** have increased the sense of financial security to the individuals. The improvements in social security and health services have further improved the quality of life. Among other things, individuals are also benefited due to improved travel services like reservations, exchange facilities, bookings etc. The **IT** has also its impact on recreational facilities as the entertainment industry has been using **IT** in areas like computer games, animation techniques and computer graphics, etc. which aim at the comfort and recreational needs of the individuals.

Information Technology In International Business

The revolution in telecommunications is simultaneously creating the huge, global, single-market economy, while making the nations more powerful. The growth of telecommunication has increased the awareness among people regarding the availability of goods in other parts and also enabled development of services to facilitate this trade. Due to geographical uniqueness and historical developments, different parts of the world have different natural resources and manufacturing skills. The people also specialised themselves in producing certain goods, services better than that at other places at a lesser cost. Certain technologies available in some parts of the world are in demand in other parts of the world also. Further, the **IT** has helped in improving the productivity of the people.

Many organisations which have superior information and analytical capabilities using their **IT** infrastructure, have set up their ventures to exploit this opportunity for optimizing their profits. According to Michael Porter,[1] an increasingly important element in modern international competition is the amount and quality of information that is available in a nation. Information helps to overcome inertia and create a sense of urgency in companies. It is integral to the upgrading of competitive advantage in established industries. Information about markets, technologies, and competition shapes the decision-making of companies, and it also highlights new needs and opportunities while exposing threats that exist.

Different regions of the world have specialised themselves in certain products and skills. There is also cost difference in different parts of the world due to availability of economic factors such as natural resources, trained workforce, capital, etc. This creates an investment opportunity. The **IT** makes it possible to analyse the economic, social and political data and identify the risks and opportunities for such investment.

IT has enabled speedy transmission of the data as well as actions such as investment or disinvestments through the stock markets. The fund transfers using electronic media are speedy, efficient and secure. Further the development of custodial services and depositories using computer-based systems have obviated need for holding the instruments in physical form. This has changed the investment climate and increased opportunities for global investors to invest in most profitable markets around the globe thereby increased the international business. The study indicates that the investments in financial markets which make very extensive use of Information Technology are many times more than those markets where **IT** is not used extensively.

The **IT** dominated information services lead to quick dissemination of information that can affect the strength of economy and thereby the value of currency of the nation creating arbitrage opportunities. This has led to very active trading in currencies, is also to the tune of one trillion dollars per day which is made possible by the role of **IT** in this segment. This giving rise to new dimensions in financial sector such as how to measure the velocity of money, money supply, etc.

This increased international trade and commerce in itself has created demand for further services such as cross border settlement through correspondent banking, banking and insurance services to provide credit and other facilities for promotion of international trade, factoring services for credit management. The financial services with superior **IT** infrastructure and better information processing capabilities have found new market for their services in other parts of the world where they have competitive advantage in the new market.

Transport and travel services like shipping and air travel, hotel industry are in increasing demand due to increased trade and IT has a role in all these services. Providing information related services on investment climate like social, economic and political developments itself has become a tradable service.

With these developments, the traditional boundaries of nation states are being redrawn and getting blurred. In the collective forum of nations represented by World Trade Organisation, there

1. M.E. Porter, *The Competitive Advantage of Nations*, 1990, p. 639.

is persistent demand for dismantling national restrictions on movement of goods, barriers and tariffs placed by the governments and allowing free entry to goods and produce from other countries.

This way **IT** has led to increase in international business. This has in turn increased the demand for further development of information technology. The increased interaction between people of the world using information technology and trade facilitated by **IT** has turned the world into proverbial 'Global Village' wherein every one is aware of capabilities of each other and has also increased exchange of goods and services. It can be said that only those nations which have a more advanced information technology and infrastructure will enjoy the critical competitive advantage in the global economy of the next generation.

TRENDS IN INFORMATION TECHNOLOGY

Computers were invented and developed for scientific and engineering purposes. Users, for the most part, were highly trained technical experts. Subsequently, the freedom and opportunity provided by the improved generation of computers caused a significant increase in the demand for new and innovative kinds of information processing systems. Organisations soon realized the potential cost saving and productivity improvements that were possible by using computers to process the large volumes of data associated with managing their activities. However, the initial applications of computers to the business world were limited to systems analysts and programmers. The operating environment was still extremely technical and confined to batch processing often requiring hours, or even days to obtain results. This form of Information Processing Systems was still too elementary to allow direct application to the management process.

The idea soon flourished that computerized information systems could be used more effectively if the operating environment would permit use by non-technical individuals and if solutions could be obtained in real-time. Interactive systems were developed to allow each user to share the computer facility and obtain (almost) immediate results. The decreasing cost and size of computer made them more attractive and practical for a larger base of users. This in turn coupled with improvements in the way computers interacted with the users, resulted in a new brand of Information Systems that could be more readily applied to help organisations process, store and retrieve large quantities of data. For rapid processing of data into information and its dissemination to concerned branches demanded for MIS departments. Spread of Internet made dissemination of information easier and effective among geographical apart branches. To reduce overall lag time and production cost, idea of doing total business electronically came into existence. It is a welcome change if we see at the results due to E-business, despite the facts that still it is in its infant stage.

The continuous strife of businesses to increase productivity and efficiency, reduce the costs of their products and services and use technology to continually innovate in order to expand and create new markets is not new. It is just that today, competition is much more fierce than ever before. The entire range of intricate and complex activities including warehousing and transportation by sea and air, involving national check posts and international customs barriers create major bottlenecks in the efficient and cost effective movement of goods. It is clear to see that in today's world, the competitive edge comes from super-efficient management of supply chains. Technology is an enabler of change and a catalyst, but change itself has to be driven by business drivers that take advantage of the technology. The globalization of the market place and the means of accessing the same through the national and global information superhighways.

Several manufacturing organisations have already set up Just-In-Time technologies with fully automated factories, which has resulted in improved productivity and reduced costs.

Effective and innovative use of information technology to create the right kind of information from its knowledge base that is associated with technology can create significant value that will provide the competitive edge. Electronic commerce is an outstanding example of this kind of value addition for businesses in the market place.

Together, IT and business both are not only defining new organisations, products, services and ways of delivering them but also newer ways of satisfying the needs of customers. The free flow of information, which is enabled by the Internet without any geographic and national barriers, comes forth with myriad security and privacy problems. There are legal issues with respect to patents, trademarks, copyrights, responsibility of ownership of data, contracts and so on. This calls for fundamental changes in the legal, commercial and economic frameworks.

It is quite clear that in the coming years, electronic commerce will be heavily oriented toward products that can be delivered as well as ordered through Internet connections. This means anything that can be digitized, from music to news to software to pictures, while the realities of the market require ease of use for both merchant and consumer.

Current economic trends are forcing companies to re-focus on core business efficiencies, dumping IT projects that complicate the management of their core business and reconsidering plans for expansion into new businesses that cannot show concrete return. On-line businesses were the first attempt. Organisations viewed Internet technology as a quick and inexpensive way to improve business efficiencies: by automating communication and order processing with vendors and customers. However, millions had been spent on Enterprise Resource Planning (ERP) and Supply Chain Management (SCM) systems that were still being customized to meet expectations of the business. The mix of ERP and SCM deployment with business expansion projects using the Internet (e-procurement, e-marketplace, B2C stores and more) proved to be a failure.

The first of these tentative on-line businesses were order-processing systems that were separate from the rest of a company's customer information. Companies ended up with two systems: one for traditional operations and a second for their Web business. Building integration between the two systems was an afterthought. The on-line business is a good example of an unfulfilled promise because the Internet promised the opportunity for efficiencies and profitability. However, the Internet business offered such low risk that companies did not perform thorough ROI (Return on Investment) analysis, think through integration challenges, or manage the on-line business according to the traditional standards. Internet expansion projects failed and the technology providers who had promised success failed too. Failure was caused not by technology, but by the lack of focus on the business created with the new technology.

STRATEGIES FOR GAINING INFORMATION TECHNOLOGY ADVANTAGE

Following are the strategies that will ultimately win:

- Focus on their core competence
- Growth and collaboration through existing channels
- Implement and integrate with existing systems.

Focus on Core Competence

Organisations design and build products with a focus on speed-to-market. They are experts at technologies for managing the supply chain and communicating with their suppliers. They rely heavily on sales partners to take the finished product to market. Sales partners merchandise, promote and offer value-added services that leverage the product and brand. They are experts at technologies for managing product information, inventory, point-of-sale, and marketing promotions. The technology they choose for collaborative on-line selling should be selected by both the manufacturer and their selling partner, but owned by neither. Each must stay focused on the business they know.

Growth and Collaboration

There simply is not enough return in the automation of existing processes if the result is a drastic departure from the manual version that works. For this reason, e-procurement networks and e-marketplaces are being replaced with private exchanges. Private exchanges do more than automate existing business processes; with business growth comes the ability to exchange customer information and enable a feedback loop that can result in incremental revenue and margin. Private exchanges connect manufacturers with their distribution, reseller and dealer networks and their customers to ensure collaborative selling success across all related parties. The same technology adapts to give end-users the choice to research a purchase on-line and take delivery from any entity they deem adds value.

Implement and Integrate

Technologies which offer value-chain efficiency and channel expansion must synchronize with inventory control, product forecasting, customer service, materials management, resource scheduling, shop floor production, and other such technologies. Today's integration technologies must bridge the platform gaps and offer real-time data exchange and centralized data management. The technologies do not require changes to existing business processes, operations or workflows, but instead expedite their automation for streamlined efficiency.

When technology allows a business to focus on its core competence, exploit existing channels for growth and integrate front-end and back-end systems, it ensures success. Employees from every department in a company can depend on having access to the most current and accurate customer history and transaction data as they attempt to focus on top-line growth and on expense control. Even more impressive would be the ability for a company to leverage the same technology without having to own any of the infrastructures.

Companies are refocusing on core businesses and are cautious about investing in technological growth. The technologies that win will be those that allow for refocusing on business processes, while allowing for affordable growth and integration with legacy systems.

❑❑❑

13

UNDERSTANDING COMPUTERS

Probably, the first computer on the earth was the Abacus, invented about 5,000 years ago in Japan and is still in use today. This device allows users to make computations using a system of sliding beads arranged on a rack. Early merchants used the abacus to keep trading transactions. But as the use of paper and pencil spread, particularly in Europe, the abacus lost its importance. In 1642, Blaise Pascal invented a numerical wheel calculator. This brass rectangular box, also called a Pascaline, used eight movable dials to add sums up to eight figures long. Pascal's device used a base of ten to accomplish this. In 1694, Gottfried Wilhem von Leibniz a German mathematician improved the Pascaline by creating a machine that could also multiply. Like its predecessor, Leibniz's mechanical multiplier worked by a system of gears and dials. Partly by studying Pascal's original notes and drawings, Leibniz was able to refine his machine. It was not until 1820 that mechanical calculators gained widespread use. Charles Xavier Thomas de Colmar, a Frenchman, invented a machine that could perform the four basic arithmetic functions. Colmar's mechanical calculator, the arithometer could add, subtract, multiply and divide. With its more practical approach to computing, the arithometer was widely used up until the First World War.

The real beginning of computers, as we know them today, lay with an English mathematician Charles Babbage. Babbage noticed a natural harmony between machines and mathematics. Machines were able to perform tasks repeatedly without mistake; while mathematics often required the simple repetition of steps. Babbage applied the mathematics on machines in 1822 when he proposed a machine to perform differential equations, called a Difference Engine. It was large as a locomotive and powered by steam and the machine could perform calculations and print the results automatically. After working on the Difference Engine for ten years, Babbage began to work on the first general-purpose computer, which he called the Analytical Engine. Babbage's Analytical Engine outlined the basic elements of a modern computer and was a breakthrough concept. Consisting of over 50,000 components, the basic design of the Analytical Engine included input devices in the form of perforated cards containing operating instructions and a memory of 1,000 numbers of up to 50 decimal digits long. It also contained a control unit that allowed processing instructions in any sequence and output devices to produce printed results.

In 1889, an American inventor, Herman Hollerith developed the tabulating machine to process the U.S. census data. The previous census in 1880 had taken nearly seven years to count but with Hollerith's machine the census results were compiled in just six weeks time. Hollerith brought his machine into the business world, founding Tabulating Machine Company in 1896, (in 1924 it became International Business Machines (IBM)). Other companies also manufactured punch readers for business use. Both business and government used punch cards for data processing until the 1960s.

In the following years, several engineers made other significant advances. Vannevar Bush developed a calculator for solving differential equations in 1931. The machine could solve complex differential equations. The machine was cumbersome because hundreds of gears and shafts were required to represent numbers and their various relationships to each other. To eliminate this bulkiness, John V. Atanasoff, a professor at Iowa State College envisioned, an all-electronic computer that applied Boolean algebra to computer circuitry. This approach was based on the 19th century work of George Boole who clarified the binary system of algebra, which stated that any mathematical equations could be stated simply as either true or false. By extending this concept to electronic circuits in the form of on or off, Atanasoff and his student Berry had developed the first all-electronic computer by 1940. However, their work was overshadowed by similar developments by other scientists. The first modern computers were built for military purposes during World War II, and the first commercial computers were built during the 1950s. They were built with vacuum tubes, therefore they were heavy, expensive, and unreliable. Nonetheless, aerospace companies were among the first to purchase and use these bulky machines. In the late 1950s, with the invention of the integrated circuit, popularly known as the silicon 'chip'. A single chip could replace racks of bulky and heavy vacuum tubes. The first application of chips was in the guidance system of the Minuteman ballistic missile. It was followed shortly by the on-board guidance and control computer for the Apollo spacecraft that took men to the Moon. With Minuteman and Apollo as pioneers, chips became faster and cheaper. Today, consumers can buy a pocket computer far more powerful than the ones that took men to the Moon in 1969. Computers are used for a wide range of applications, including personal interactive use (word-processing, games, desktop publishing, web browsing, e-mail), real-time systems (patient care, factories, missiles), embedded systems (cash registers, wrist watches, toasters) and transaction processing (banking, reservations, e-commerce).

The word 'Computer' owes its origin to a Latin word 'compute' which means *'to calculate'*, therefore, a computer is considered to be a calculating device that can perform arithmetic and logical operations. It is not just a calculating device; rather it has the capability to process logic operations like comparisons etc. It gets the data through an input device, processes it as per the instructions given and gives the information as output. A computer has memory and can store a lot of information. The stored information can be retrieved, used and operated upon as desired. Computations are done at an extremely fast speed with complete reliability and accuracy.

Definition: A computer is an electronic device that accepts data and instructions, processes the data according to the set of instructions and produces the desired information. In fact, the computer can be understood as a data processing machine. In other words, a computer is a problem-solving machine that accepts data, stores data, processes data and presents results.

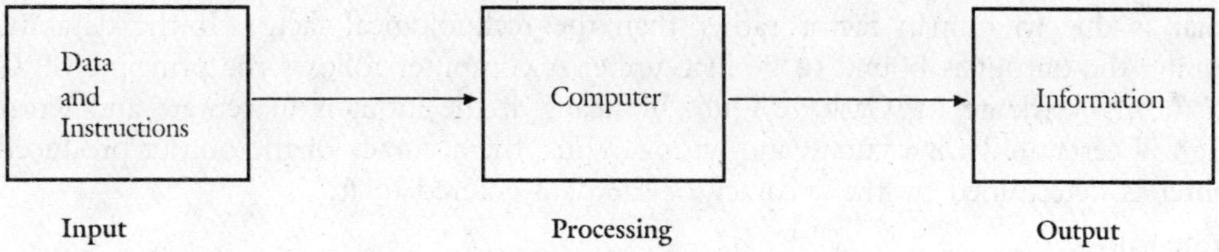

Fig. 13.1 Computer as a processing system

SOME STANDARD DEFINITIONS OF COMPUTER

Webster's Dictionary

"a device used for computing; specifically, an electronic machine which, by means of stored instructions and information, performs rapid, often complex calculations or compiles, correlates and selects data".

International Standards Organisation or ISO

"a data processor that can perform substantial computation, including numerous arithmetic and logic operations, without intervention by a human operator during the run".

U.S. Institute

"a device capable of solving problems by accepting data, performing described operations on the data and supplying the results of these operations."

CHARACTERISTICS OF A COMPUTER

After human brain, a computer is the fastest machine on the earth. Computers can perform millions of calculations at an unbelievable speed. Computers are not only fast, they are very accurate and reliable also. For us, the smallest unit of time is a second but for a computer, a second is not the smallest unit rather it can be divided into a millisecond microsecond, nanosecond and picosecond. A nanosecond is equal to one billionth or thousand-millionth of a second.

The major characteristics/features of a computer are as below:

(1) Speed

The computer is the fastest calculating machine ever invented. The performance of a computer is judged by its processing speed which is based on its 'cycle time'. A slow computer will have cycle time in the order of 300-400 nanoseconds, and presently an average desktop computer's cycle time is 900-1000 nanoseconds. In other words in one nanosecond the computer can perform 900-1000 operations.

A computer' processing speed is expressed in megahertz (MHz) which means millions of machine cycles per second. So, a computer with a speed of 900 MHz will be capable of handling roughly 900 million machine cycles per second.

(2) Accuracy

A computer is consistently highly accurate in its calculations and decisions. It performs each and every calculation with the same accuracy. A computer may produce wrong results, but that is due to human factor rather than the technological factor. If the data input is inaccurate, the output is bound to be inaccurate. A computer follows the principle of 'GIGO' which means 'Garbage In, Garbage Out'. It means, if the input is inaccurate and wrong the output will certainly be inaccurate and wrong. Thus, the accuracy of the output produced by a computer is determined by the accuracy of the data entered to it.

(3) Reliability

Reliability is the extent to which we can rely on a computer. As far as accuracy, speed and serviceable life is concerned, a computer is an extremely reliable machine.

(4) Storage Capability

Depending upon its secondary storage capacity, a computer can store and recall any amount of data. Data on the computer can be saved and retained as long as desired by the user and can be retrieved as and when needed. Time does not affect a computer's storage and retrieval capability.

(5) Diligence

Being a machine, a computer is free from any monotony, tiredness, lack of attention, etc., and therefore, can work for hours constantly with the same speed. This quality is very rare in human beings, especially, where the work is routine and requires great accuracy.

(6) Versatility

Versatility means being competent in different things or being able to turn easily from one subject to another. This is one of the biggest properties of a computer. A computer can perform several and varied functions at the same time. At a particular point of time, it may be processing the examination result and at the same it may be computing salaries of the employees and in between, it may be searching an important document from its memory.

(7) A dumb Machine

We cannot ignore the fact that a computer is a dumb machine. It can perform only those functions for which it can be programmed. A computer does not do what you want it to do; rather it does things as per the programme fed to it. A computer cannot think and it has no intelligence. A computer is instructed in detail what to do and in what sequence.

(8) Emotionless

Unlike human beings, computers do not have emotions, feelings and instincts. A computer's working is based on the instructions given by the user. That is why the computers can work for hours mutely and without boredom.

Operations Performed By A Computer

A computer can perform a variety of tasks. We use computers for programming, word-processing, spreadsheets, data management, graphics and communications. Much of the processing computers do can be separated into two operations — Arithmetic operations and logical operations. Processing is built around the computer's ability to perform arithmetic and logical operations. Software is a set of instructions written by humans and given to the computer. These instructions (programmes) tell the computer which operations to apply to the data, to ultimately produce informational output. Software directs the processing sequence and allows a computer to perform specific tasks.

(a) Arithmetic operations: Arithmetic operations are computations with numbers (addition, subtraction, division, multiplication etc.).

(b) Logical operations: Logical operations are a comparison of any two numbers to determine if one is greater than, smaller than, or equal to the other. A computer can compare numbers, letters, or special characters. The computer can then take action based on the result of the comparison.

BASIC MODEL OF A COMPUTER

A computer is termed as a data processing machine. It accepts data and then stores or processes it immediately and displays the output for the user. The basic model of a computer shows the working of a computer. All computer systems perform the following five basic operations:

(1) Input Function

The input function is the process of entering data and instructions into the computer system. The computer accepts the data and instructions from the user through various input devices like keyboard, mouse, scanner etc.

(2) Storage Function

A computer can store data and instructions for future use and processing. A computer has 'memory' and can store a large amount of data.

(3) Processing Function

A computer can process the input or stored data as per the instructions by the user. A computer performs arithmetic and logical operations on data in order to convert them into desired output. Processing is the main function of the computer.

(4) Output Function

With the help of this function, computer displays the processed results or output. The output is communicated to the user through various output devices like monitor, printer etc.

(5) Control Function

All the other functions performed by the computer are controlled by this control function. Control function guides the computer to process and give output in the right manner and proper sequence.

The following diagram shows the interaction of the components of the simple model of a computer. The arrows indicate the flow of control in the form of data and instructions. An input unit provides the input for the processing to CPU (Central Processing Unit) which, after processing, directs the processed data to output unit for display to the user. The storage unit or the memory of computer stores the data.

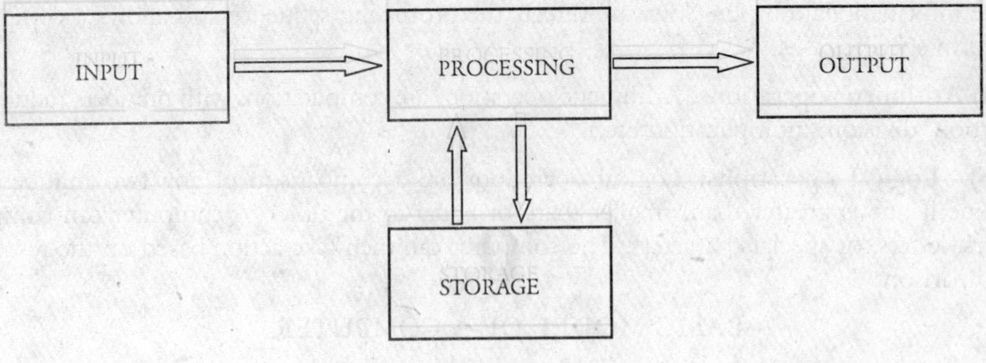

Fig. 13.2 A simple model of a computer

ORGANISATION OF A COMPUTER SYSTEM

A computer system receives data, processes it and delivers the processed input as output. The computer receives data as input, processes it into useful information and delivers information as output. The common input devices are the mouse, keyboard, light pen, touch screen, microphone, etc.

The brain of any computer system is the CPU or central processing unit. The CPU or a 'Processor,' such as Intel's Pentium or AMD's Athlon range from 100 MHz. to the latest 1,000 Mhz. The CPU contains the primary or main storage, arithmetic and logic section and control sections. The main storage or 'memory', is used for storing data as input, the programme to be used for processing, data being processed and the results of processing before they are displayed by an output device. All calculations and logic operations are performed in the arithmetic and logic section of the CPU. The control section of the CPU controls operations, maintains sequence and directs the operations of other attached units. The processing of data is not done in the control section rather it acts as a central nervous system of the computer. Output devices communicate the processed results to the user. Output devices like input devices are the communication media between computer and the user. The most common output devices are monitor screens, magnetic tapes and printers.

Almost all the computer systems today, use secondary or auxiliary storage devices to supplement the storage capacity of the main memory. The most common secondary storage devices are magnetic or hard disks, floppy disks and magnetic tapes.

A computer programme is a set of step-by-step instructions to the computer to perform specific functions and operations using some computer language. After the programme is entered through input unit; the computer processes the data according to the programme.

Main Memory Unit

The term 'memory' identifies data storage that comes in the form of chips, and the word storage is used for memory that exists on tapes or disks. Moreover, the term memory is usually used as shorthand for physical memory, which refers to the actual chips capable of holding data. The physical memory is also referred to as the main or primary memory.

The main or primary storage section of a computer has many small storage areas called locations or words. A word can store a specific number of bits or binary digits (0 or 1). The word length may vary from 8 bits for a small computer to 64 bits for a very large computer, depending on the architecture of the computer. A group of 8 bits is also called a byte. Each word is assigned an address or location – unique number that identifies the word location. A word or storage location can hold either a data item or an instruction and its identifying number remains the same regardless of its contents. A group of binary digits is used to represent alphabetic and numeric characters using a data representation coding scheme. The user does not have to bother about data representation coding schemes as coding and decoding from alphanumeric to binary and *vice-versa* is automatically handled by the computer itself. Retrieving data from a storage location is non-destructive, but entering data into a location is destructive, i.e. the previous contents of the location are automatically erased and replaced.

There are several different types of primary memory:

- **RAM (random-access memory):** It is named as random-access memory because any of the locations on a chip can be randomly selected and used to directly store and retrieve data and instructions. RAM is the same as main memory. The term RAM refers to read and write memory; that is, you can both write and read data from RAM. This is in contrast to ROM, which permits only to read data. RAM is a volatile memory, which means that it requires a steady flow of electricity to maintain its contents. As soon as the power is turned off, whatever data was in RAM is lost.
- **ROM (read-only memory):** ROM or read-only memory chips are used by manufacturers to permanently store some programmes. Computers almost always contain a small amount of read-only memory that holds instructions for starting up the computer. ROM chips have wide applications as a programme storage medium in video games and personal computers. Unlike RAM, ROM cannot be written too.
- **PROM (programmable read-only memory):** A PROM is a memory chip on which a programme can be stored. Users can store their own frequently used programmes on a programmable read-only memory (PROM) chip. Once programme have been written into a PROM chip, they are permanent and cannot be altered. Like ROMs, PROMs are also non-volatile.
- **EPROM (erasable programmable read-only memory):** An EPROM is a special type of PROM that can be erased by exposing it to ultraviolet light.
- **EEPROM (electrically erasable programmable read-only memory):** An EEPROM is a special type of PROM that can be erased by exposing it to an electrical charge.

Cache Memory

Cache memory is random access memory (random access memory that a computer microprocessor can access more quickly than it can access regular RAM). As the microprocessor processes data, it looks first in the cache memory and if it finds the data there, it does not have to do the more time-consuming reading of data from larger memory.

Some memory caches are built into the architecture of microprocessors. The Intel 80486 microprocessor, for example, contains an 8K-memory cache, and the Pentium has a 16K cache. Such internal caches are often called Level 1 (L1) caches. The Pentium III processor includes two separate 16 KB level 1 (L1) caches, one for instruction and one for data. Most modern PCs also come with external cache memory, called Level 2 (L2) caches. These caches sit between the CPU and the DRAM. Like L1 caches, L2 caches are composed of SRAM but they are much larger. Certain versions of the Pentium III processor include a Discrete, off-die level 2 (L2) cache. This L2 cache consists of a 512 KB unified, non-blocking cache that improves performance over cache-on-motherboard solutions by reducing the average memory access time and by providing fast access to recently used instructions and data. Performance is also enhanced over cache-on-motherboard implementations through a dedicated 64-bit cache bus. In such system, L1 and L2 are on chip and the off-chip cache is referred to as L3.

Disk caching works under the same principle as memory caching, but instead of using high-speed SRAM, a disk cache uses conventional main memory. The most recently accessed data from the disk (as well as adjacent sectors) is stored in a memory buffer. When a programme needs to access data from the disk, it first checks the disk cache to see if the data is there. Disk caching can dramatically improve the performance of applications, because accessing a byte of data in RAM can be thousands of times faster than accessing a byte on a hard disk. When data is found in the cache, it is called a *cache hit*, and the effectiveness of a cache is judged by its hit rate. Many cache systems use a technique known as smart caching, in which the system can recognize certain types of frequently used data. The strategies for determining which information should be kept in the cache constitute some of the more interesting problems in computer science.

Virtual Memory

Main Memory (DRAM)

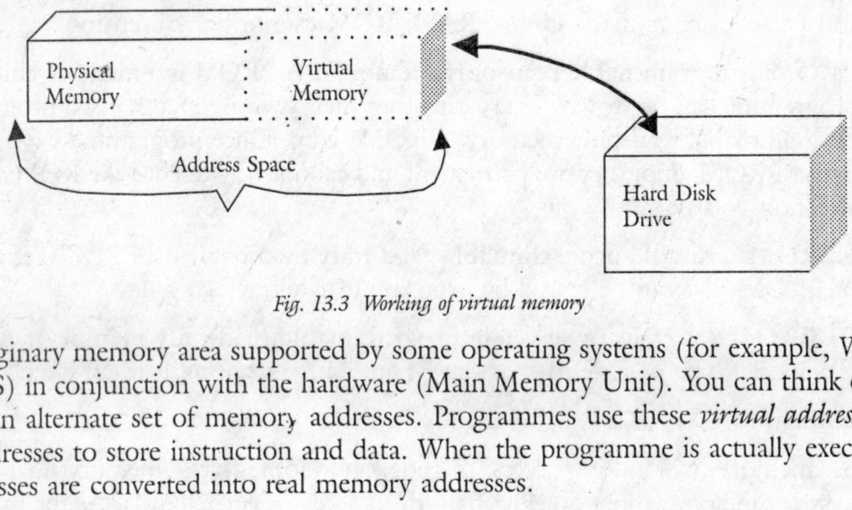

Fig. 13.3 Working of virtual memory

An imaginary memory area supported by some operating systems (for example, Windows, but not DOS) in conjunction with the hardware (Main Memory Unit). You can think of virtual memory as an alternate set of memory addresses. Programmes use these *virtual addresses* rather than real addresses to store instruction and data. When the programme is actually executed, the virtual addresses are converted into real memory addresses.

The purpose of virtual memory is to enlarge the address space, the set of addresses a programme can utilize. For example, virtual memory might contain twice as many addresses as memory. A programme using all of virtual memory, therefore, would not be able to fit in main memory all at once. Nevertheless, the computer could execute such a programme by copying into main memory those portions of the programme needed at any given point during execution. To facilitate copying virtual memory into real memory, the operating system divides virtual memory into pages, each of which contains a fixed number of addresses. Each page is stored on a disk until it is needed. When the page is needed, the operating system copies it from disk to main memory, translating the virtual addresses into real addresses. The process of translating virtual addresses into real addresses is called *mapping*. The copying of virtual pages from disk to main memory is known as paging or swapping.

Secondary Storage Devices

Magnetic disks or hard disk drives are the most popular secondary storage medium. They are typically made of thin metal plates coated on both sides with a magnetisable recording material. These disks are portable and can be shifted from one computer to another very easily. Magnetic disks are placed on a vertical shaft which rotates at a high constant speed. A space is left between the spinning disks to allow access arms with small read-write heads to move to any storage location. Data are organised into a number of concentric circles on the disk surface called 'tracks'. Each track has a designated location number. There are typically 200 to 800 tracks on the disk surface. The track is divided into 'sectors' or 'blocks' that are fixed in size. The disk's 'read-write' heads are capable of accessing the disk surface from track to track very quickly usually in milliseconds.

Flexible disks or the floppy disks are another popular and cheap storage media. Earlier they used to come in 8 inches and 5 1/4 inches diameters but now the usual size is 3 1/2 inches. A floppy disk may store about 1Mb or one million bytes of data and costs around Rs. 700 only; a hard disk may store up to 40 Gb (Gigabyte)[1] or more and costs around Rs. 5000.

CD-ROM or compact disk-read-only memory storage disks and drives are also used very commonly. Since you cannot write on these disks (unless you have a CD writer), these are used as input devices for entering the data from the disks. The access time is relatively fast. One CD-ROM disk stores about 650 megabytes and costs around Rs. 200 and a CD drive costs around Rs. 2000.

Another popular secondary storage device is the Magnetic tape. It has been used as a storage medium since the very early computers were produced. Because of its relatively fast transfer rate, magnetic tape is still a very popular input medium for large-volume data jobs. In addition to providing rapid input and output, it is the most widely used secondary off-line computer storage medium. The tapes are most suited to serial processing of large volumes of data. They are also more secure and can be accessed when they are loaded onto the computer. They are also smaller in size so they can be easily transported and less susceptible to damage than hard disks.

Central Processing Unit

The CPU, Central Processing Unit is the brains of the computer. Sometimes, referred to simply as the processor or central processor, the CPU is where most calculations take place. In terms of computing power, the CPU is the most important element of a computer system. CPU is also called the processor and has the electronic circuitry. It controls and coordinates the activities of all other components of a computer system and performs all the arithmetic and logical operations to be applied to data. In fact CPU is the brain of the computer and functions much like the brain of a human being. The CPU is made up of two basic blocks: ALU and Control Unit, which perform the arithmetic and logic operations and the controlling respectively.

---

1. A Gigabyte is a billion bytes or a thousand megabytes.

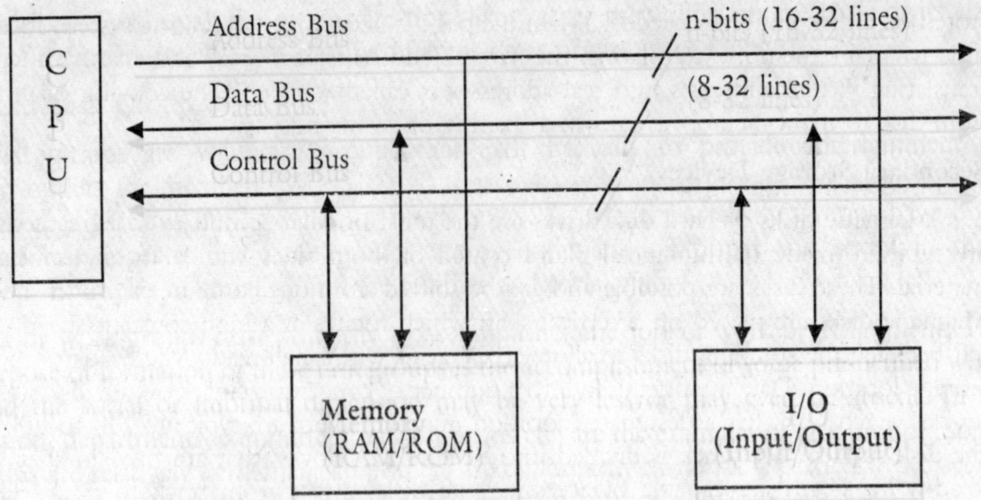

Fig. 13.4 Functional organisation of a computer system

On large machines, CPUs require one or more printed circuit boards. On personal computers and small workstations, the CPU is housed in a single chip called a microprocessor.

Two typical components of a CPU are:

- The arithmetic logic unit (ALU), which performs arithmetic and logical operations.
- The control unit, which extracts instructions from memory and decodes and executes them, calling on the ALU when necessary.

Arithmetic And Logic Unit

The arithmetic and logic unit (ALU) of a computer system is the place where the actual execution of the instructions takes place during the processing operation. To be more precise, all calculations are performed and all comparisons (decisions) are made in the ALU. The data and instructions stored in the primary storage prior to processing are transferred as and when needed to the ALU where processing takes place. No processing is done in the primary storage unit. Intermediate results generated in ALU are transferred back to the main memory until needed at a later time. Data may thus move from primary storage to ALU and back again to memory many times before the processing is over. After the processing is complete, the final results which are stored in the main memory unit are released to an output device.

Control Unit

The control unit contains electronic circuit that uses electrical signals to direct the entire computer system to carry out, or execute stored programme instructions. It does not execute programme instructions; rather it directs other parts of the system to do so. It communicates with all other devices. By selecting, interpreting and seeing to the execution of the programme instructions, the control unit is able to maintain order and direct the operation of the entire system. It manages and coordinates the entire computer system. It obtains instructions from the programme stored in main memory, interprets the instructions and issues signals that cause other units of the system to execute them.

Buses

Buses connect address, data and control instructions together. A bus is a collection of wires through which data is transmitted from one part of a computer to another. A bus can be considered as a highway on which data travels within a computer. When used in reference to personal computers, the term *bus* usually refers to *internal bus*. This is a bus that connects all the internal computer components to the CPU and main memory. There is also an expansion bus that enables expansion boards to access the CPU and memory.

All buses consist of an address bus, a data bus and a control bus. The data bus transfers actual data whereas address bus is used to identify particular locations (addresses) in the main memory and Input/Output unit. The width of the address bus (that is, the number of wires) determines how many unique memory locations can be addressed. The size of a data bus, also known as its width, is important because it determines how much data can be transmitted at one time. For example, a 16-bit data bus can transmit 16-bits of data, whereas a 32-bit data bus can transmit 32-bits of data.

The control bus is used to control flow of data, e.g. to read or write from or to memory.

Every bus has a clock speed measured in MHz. A fast bus allows data to be transferred faster, which makes applications run faster.

GENERATIONS OF COMPUTERS

Computers have changed every aspect of our lives. Today, computers do much more than simply compute. To fully understand the impact computers have on our lives and promises they hold for the future, it is important to understand their evolution. The evolution of modern computer is divided in different generations as below.

First Generation (1945-1956)

During the Second World War, governments of several nations sought to develop computers to exploit their potential strategic importance. This increased funding for computer development projects hastened technical progress. By 1941, German engineer Konrad Zuse had developed a computer, the Z3, to design airplanes and missiles. In 1943, the British developed a code-breaking computer called Colossus to decode German messages. But, Colossus was not a general-purpose computer and it was designed to decode secret messages.

Howard Aiken, an American engineer working with IBM, succeeded in producing an all-electronic calculator by 1944. The purpose of the computer was to create ballistic charts for the U.S. Navy. But it was very huge in size. The Automatic Sequence Controlled Calculator or Mark I was an electronic relay computer. It used electromagnetic signals to move mechanical parts. The machine was slow and inflexible; but it could perform basic arithmetic as well as more complex equations.

Another major development during the war was the Electronic Numerical Integrator and Computer (ENIAC), produced by a partnership between the U.S. government and the University of Pennsylvania. It consisted of 18,000 vacuum tubes, 70,000 resistors and 5 million soldered joints. This computer consumed 160 kilowatts of electrical power, enough energy to dim the lights in a small city. ENIAC was a general-purpose computer that computed at speeds 1,000 times faster than Mark I.

John Von Neumann, a professor in the University of Pennsylvania, designed the Electronic Discrete Variable Automatic Computer (EDVAC) in 1945. This computer had a memory to hold both a stored programme and data. This allowed the computer to be stopped at any point and then resumed, allowed for greater versatility in computer programming. The key element to the Von Neumann architecture was the central processing unit, which allowed all computer functions to be coordinated through a single source. In 1951, the UNIVAC I (Universal Automatic Computer), built by Remington Rand, became one of the first commercially available computers to take advantage of these advances. Both the U.S. Census Bureau and General Electric owned UNIVACs.

First generation computers were characterized by the fact that operating instructions were made for the specific task for which the computer was to be used. Each computer had a different binary-coded programme called a machine language that told it how to operate. This made the computer difficult to programme and limited its versatility and speed. Other distinctive features of first generation computers were the use of vacuum tubes and magnetic drums for data storage.

Second Generation (1956-1963)

The invention of the transistor greatly changed the computer's development. The transistor replaced the large, cumbersome vacuum tube in televisions, radios and computers. As a result, the size of electronic machinery has been shrinking ever since. The transistor was at work in the computer by 1956. Coupled with early advances in magnetic-core memory, transistors led to second generation computers that were smaller, faster, more reliable and more energy-efficient than their predecessors. The first large-scale machines to take advantage of this transistor technology were early supercomputers, Stretch by IBM and LARC (Livermore Atomic Research Computer). These computers, both developed for atomic energy laboratories, could handle an enormous amount of data, a capability much in demand by atomic scientists. The machines were costly, however, and tended to be too powerful for the business sector's computing needs, thereby limiting their attractiveness. Second generation computers replaced machine language with assembly language, allowing abbreviated programming codes to replace long, difficult binary codes. These second generation computers were also of solid-state design and contained transistors in place of vacuum tubes. They also contained all the components we associate with the modern day computer: printers, tape storage, disk storage, memory, operating systems, and stored programmes. One important example was the IBM 1401, which was universally accepted throughout the industry and is considered by many to be the Model T of the computer industry. In the end of 1965, most large business routinely processed financial information using second-generation computers.

It was the stored programme and programming language that gave computers the flexibility to be cost effective and productive for business use. The stored programme concept meant that instructions to run a computer for a specific function (known as a programme) were held inside the computer's memory and could quickly be replaced by a different set of instructions for a different function. A computer could print customer invoices and minutes later design products or calculate paychecks. More sophisticated high-level languages such as COBOL (Common Business-Oriented Language) and FORTRAN (Formula Translator) came into common use during this time. These languages replaced cryptic binary machine code with words, sentences and mathematical formulas, making it much easier to programme a computer. New types of careers (programmer, analyst and computer systems expert) and the entire software industry began with second-generation computers.

Third Generation (1964-1971)

The transistors were clearly a technological improvement but they still generated a great deal of heat, which damaged the computer's sensitive internal parts. In 1958, Jack Kilby, an engineer with Texas Instruments, developed the Integrated Circuit (IC). The IC combined three electronic components onto a small silicon disc, which was made from quartz. Scientists later managed to fit even more components on a single chip, called a semiconductor. As a result, computers became ever smaller as more components were squeezed onto the chip. Another third-generation development included the use of an operating system that allowed machines to run many different programmes at once with a central programme that monitored and coordinated the computer's memory.

Fourth Generation (1971-Present)

After the integrated circuits, the only place to go was down in size, i.e. Large scale Integration (LSI) could fit hundreds of components onto one chip. By the 1980's, very large scale integration (VLSI) squeezed hundreds of thousands of components onto a chip. Ultra-large scale integration (ULSI) increased that number into the millions. The ability to fit so much onto an area about the size of a coin helped diminish the size and price of computers. It also increased their power, efficiency and reliability. The Intel 4004 chip, developed in 1971, took the integrated circuit one step further by locating all the components of a computer (central processing unit, memory and input and output controls) on a minuscule chip. Whereas previously the integrated circuit had to be manufactured to fit a special purpose, now one microprocessor could be manufactured and then programmed to meet any number of demands. Soon, everyday household items such as microwave ovens, television sets and automobiles with electronic fuel injection incorporated microprocessors.

Such condensed power allowed everyday people to harness a computer's power. They were no longer developed exclusively for large business or government contracts. After the mid 1970's, computer manufacturers sought to bring computers to general consumers. These minicomputers came complete with user-friendly software packages that offered even non-technical users an array of applications, most popularly word processing and spreadsheet programmes. Pioneers in this field were Commodore, Radio Shack, and Apple Computers. In the early 1980s, video games and home video game systems ignited consumer interest for more sophisticated, programmable home computers.

In 1981, IBM introduced its personal computer (PC) for use in the home, office and schools. The 1980's saw an expansion in computer use in all three arenas as clones of the IBM PC made the personal computer even more affordable. The number of personal computers in use more than doubled from 2 million in 1981 to 5.5 million in 1982. Ten years later, 65 million PCs were being used. Computers continued their trend toward a smaller size, working their way down from desktop to laptop computers (which could fit inside a briefcase) to palmtop (able to fit inside a breast pocket). In direct competition with IBM's PC was Apple's Macintosh line, introduced in 1984. Notable for its user-friendly design, the Macintosh offered an operating system that allowed users to move screen icons instead of typing instructions. Users controlled the screen cursor using a mouse, a device that mimicked the movement of one's hand on the computer screen.

As computers became more widespread in the workplace, new ways to harness their potential developed. As smaller computers became more powerful, they could be linked together, or networked to share memory space, software, information and communicate with each other. As opposed to a mainframe computer, which was one powerful computer that shared time with many terminals for many applications, networked computers allowed individual computers to form electronic co-ops. Using either direct wiring, called a Local Area Network (LAN), or telephone lines, these networks could reach enormous proportions. A global web of computer circuitry, the Internet, for example, links computers worldwide into a single network of information. During the 1992 U.S. presidential election, vice-presidential candidate Al Gore promised to make the development of 'Information Superhighway' an administrative priority. Though the possibilities envisioned by Gore and others for such a large network are often years (if not decades) away from realization, the most popular use today for computer networks such as the Internet is electronic mail, or E-mail, which allows users to type in a computer address and send messages through networked terminals across the office or across the world.

Fifth Generation (Present and Beyond)

Present age and the times to come are classified as the fifth generation of computers. Using recent engineering advances, computers are able to accept spoken word instructions (voice recognition) and imitate human reasoning. The ability to translate a foreign language is also moderately possible with fifth generation computers. This feat seemed a simple objective at first, but appeared much more difficult when programmers realized that human understanding relies as much on context and meaning as it does on the simple translation of words.

Many advances in the science of computer design and technology are coming together to enable the creation of fifth-generation computers. Two such engineering advances are parallel processing, which replaces Von Neumann's single central processing unit design with a system harnessing the power of many CPUs to work as one. Another advance is superconductor technology, which allows the flow of electricity with little or no resistance, greatly improving the speed of information flow. Computers today have some attributes of fifth generation computers. For example, expert systems assist doctors in making diagnoses by applying the problem-solving steps a doctor might use in assessing a patient's needs. It will take several more years of development before expert systems are in widespread use.

COMPUTER AS A SYSTEM

A system is a group of integrated parts that have the common purpose of achieving some objective(s). A computer in this sense can be understood as a system. Computer system consists of the three following subsystems:

(1) Hardware

(2) Software

(3) Humanware

(1) Hardware

Hardware is a general term used to refer to the physical computer machinery and its tangible components i.e. those components, which can be touched and seen. Thus the monitor, the keyboard, input and output devices etc. are all hardware.

The computer hardware has progressed from huge but inefficient and expensive data processing computers to sleek, efficient and inexpensive personal computers — containing miniature Integrated circuits containing millions of hardware components — on users desktop which can be networked. Mass production is delivering the immense computing and communicating capabilities in the hands of users. At the same time increasing miniaturization has enabled introduction of powerful laptop computers at an affordable price for the high-end mobile users like executives and professionals. The advances in solid state physics have made it possible to integrate more and more components in less and less space and the speed and power of the CPU has been doubling every eighteen months.

The server market is witnessing similar development. The recent trend in computer servers indicates shift towards scaleable processor architecture, Reduced Instruction Set Computing (RISC) processors and use of parallel processors for computing (Massively parallel machines) are few examples. The internal processing capability of servers has increased to addressing 128-bits at a time as against 16-bits earlier thereby opening new opportunities for advanced computing. The Random Access Memory (RAM) of the computers is keeping pace with the trend of processor power.

The storage devices are also becoming more and more powerful with the capacity 100GB of hard disk becoming common. The advent of CD-ROM technology has made it possible to store huge data on a single compact disk and the personal computers have been provided with multimedia capabilities for reading audio and video data on CD-ROM. High density optical storage devices are being experimented for storage of very large data.

The computer peripherals such as Video Display Units (VDU) have become increasingly more versatile with very high resolution and clarity of pictures possible with their Super Video Graphic Adapter cards (SVGA). The flat screens using liquid crystals are also introduced.

The printer technology has undergone changes from dot matrix impact printers to non-impact printers such as laser jet, desk jet and ink jet printers with their high quality printing. New high-speed printers are also being introduced for desktop publishing and heavy printing. Similarly, touch screens and touch keyboards are also introduced to improve the ease of communicating with the computer.

Types Of Hardware

There are mainly following types of hardware used in the computer system:

- Hardware for input such as keyboard, mouse etc.
- Hardware for output such as printers, monitors etc.
- Hardware for processing which includes IC chip, flip-flops etc.
- Hardware for storage such as floppy disks, CD-ROMs, tapes etc.
- Hardware for communications which include equipment required for data communication in a computer network. Examples are LAN card, gateway, bridges etc.

(2) Software

It is important to note that a computer cannot do anything of its own. It must be instructed to do a desired job. Hence, it is necessary to specify a sequence of instructions that a computer must perform to solve a problem. Such a sequence of instructions written in a language that can be understood by a computer is called a computer *programme*. The term software refers to the set of computer programmes. Without software, a computer is like a car without petrol or an audio system without a song. Thus, there is a special relationship between hardware and software. Both are complementary to each other.

Historically, computers used numbers as the primary form of input data. With the advent of new computer software and hardware, the definition of data has expanded. Users can now input text (letters and special characters), audio-visual (music, video, voice, pictures) and physical (light, sound, temperature, pressure) as well as numerical data.

Although a modern computer is capable of accepting many types of input, it can only operate on digitally formatted data, just as original computers did. Human written software must be created to interface the computer with the various types of input data. Because a computer runs on electricity, data must be stored as a series of on and off patterns. Like a lightbulb, computer circuits can be in only one of two states: either on (represented by 1) or off (represented by 0). Each numeric value is known as a binary digit (bit) and unique combinations of those two bits are what binary codes, or machine language is comprised of. Different patterns in binary code could then be used to represent various input characters. Once data has been converted to binary form, computers (essentially just a switchbox) would then apply a software programme (applications or apps) to the digital input data, sequentially execute the instructions and successfully process it into information.

While this processing method is extremely functional to a computer, it is not very friendly to humans. Humans quickly realized that writing in binary code (machine language) was extremely difficult, very time consuming and highly prone to errors. Writing software programmes in numerical (or digital) format is an immense task for anyone. Therefore, developing software into a more user-friendly format was necessary in order to unleash the capabilities of this digital switching-machine.

As programmers developed existing code, new computer capabilities were imagined and the demand for even more advanced software increased which prompted programmers to develop even more software. It was and still is, a continuous circle of improvements. The early days of computing were restricted to scientific and engineering applications, but after the once-imagined possibilities became realities, the general public's appetite for computer accessibility and capability began to skyrocket. Thousands of new programmes were being written as swiftly as possible and yet the demand continued to increase. Of the thousands of programmes available, software types typically fall into 2 categories: system software and application software.

Types Of Software

Computer software is normally classified into two broad categories:

(a) Application software

(b) Systems software

(a) Application Software: Application software is a set of one or more programmes designed to carry out operations for a specified application. Application software are used to perform specialized functions or specific jobs. Specific jobs might be to create a family tree, learn basic math or quantum physics, create a plot for a novel, do payroll and accounting, draw flowcharts or a dream house. Specific purpose application packages are also available for specialised areas, such as banking, hospital administration, insurance, publishing, manufacturing, science and engineering, etc. Regardless of type of task, users can choose from thousands of applications to facilitate the job. Application software are unique in their construction and can be used only for identical jobs. The common examples of application programmes include payroll package, examination evaluation programme, and inventory programmes etc.

Four of the major categories that represent the progress of application software, made since the late 1970s, are:

- Spreadsheet
- Database management
- Word processing
- Entertainment

Spreadsheets

The first successful spreadsheet programme was VisiCalc, written for the Apple II.. Introduced by Dan Bricklin and Bob Frankston in 1979, VisiCalc gave PC users the ability to prepare detailed budgets and financial analyses. Its popularity soared because it enabled PC users to do something that a mainframe could not— enter numerical or financial data and immediately see its affect on other numbers. At a time when the PC was struggling to be taken seriously, VisiCalc changed its perception from a toy to a legitimate business tool. VisiCalc had such a strong appeal that people would go into a computer store and ask for the VisiCalc computer, not the Apple II.

Following the success of VisiCalc, in 1982 Lotus 1-2-3 was introduced and quickly became the number one spreadsheet software. One reason for its success was that it integrated three applications; spreadsheet, graph generation and database management. Many other spreadsheet programmes followed, including Microsoft Excel (1987) and WingZ for the Apple Mac (1988).

Database Management

One of the applications that initially seemed to be limited to mainframes and minicomputers was the management of large databases. When Ashton-Tate introduced dBase II for CP/M, it was the first serious database manager for PCs. Developed as a programme called Vulcan by Wayne Ratliff to manage a company football pool, dBase went on to be a powerful business tool for DOS machines. Like Lotus 1-2-3, dBase II was also an integrated software, combining database management, spreadsheet, graph generation and word processing in one software programme.

One of the major factors determining the success of any application is the programmer's ability to change and adapt the original programme to be run by newer operating systems and expand the programme's capability to meet user's needs. Ashton-Tate, the company that bought dBase from Ratliff, was unable to do this and other database managers such as Microsoft Access and Visual FoxPro ultimately overtook them.

Word Processing

A major problem for word processing software was the perception that computers calculated and generated reports full of numbers — not words. The first word processing software was a small programme called Electric Pencil, developed by Michael Shrayer in 1976. In addition to writing Altair programmes, he wanted to be able to write the user manuals that accompany each programme.

The first word processing programme that truly established the category was WordStar, introduced by Seymour Rubinstein in 1979. Throughout the 1980s, different word processors came into prominence with each new release. Magic Wand (1979), Corel's WordPerfect (1984), Microsoft Multi-Tool Word (1983), and Apple's Write captured market share as they expanded the uses for word processing programmes.

Although each release of word processing programmes expanded the capability of this software category, users still remained frustrated when they printed their documents. What they saw on the screen was not what they saw come out of the printer. In 1985, Adobe Systems, Inc. introduced PostScript page description language (PDL) and along with Apple's LaserWriter printer created an entire industry and software category called desktop publishing. Together, the PDL and the printer enabled PC users to format a document on the screen exactly as it would appear when printed and introduced a new word — WYSIWYG — What You See Is What You Get. Being able to view a document before printing augmented the creativity of many users.

Before long, word processing programmes were capable of more than just manipulating words; the ability to insert pictures, clip-art and graphs was introduced. But even as programmers continued to respond to the public's software requests, their insatiable appetite for innovation grew. The popularity of word processing software continued to escalate and more tools were continuously added. Unique tools such as spell-checker, thesaurus, font menus, grammar check and templates eventually became commonplace. Often times users would find a needed tool in one of their programmes but not another, so programmers created suites. Suites typically integrate a word processor with a database manager and a spreadsheet application, so that each programme would have the ability to share data with any other programme in the package.

(b) Systems Software: System software is a set of one or more programmes, designed to control the operation of a computer system. These programmes do not solve specific problems. They are general programmes written to assist humans in the use of the computer system. System software performs a variety of functions like file editing, memory management, resource accounting, database management, programme compilation and running etc. Its function is to compensate for the differences that exist between the user needs and the capabilities of the hardware. The systems software is an indispensable part of a total computer system. Without systems software, application packages could not be run on the computer system. A computer without some kind of systems software would be very ineffective and most likely impossible to operate.

System software controls various internal computer activities. Any software that controls such activities will fall into one of three categories: System management software (operating system), System development software (programming languages) and Utility software.

Types Of System Software

System software can be categorized into following three types:

I. System management software (operating systems)

II. System development software (programming languages)

III. Utility software

(I) Operating Systems

The operating system (OS) is a group of system programmes that help in the operation of a computer by telling the computer how to interpret commands, process the inputs and outputs and manage data. The OS is automatically loaded when the PC is started and can activate other programmes. An operating system contains the algorithms that define how the computer is to interact with the outside world and for controlling activities of the computer. Without an operating system, it is not possible to use the computer. An operating system is the software, which makes the computer ready to use. An operating system is the most essential system software that manages the operation of a computer. It is an integrated set of programmes that is used to manage the various resources and overall operations of a computer system. It is designed to support the activities of a computer installation. Its prime objective is to improve the performance and efficiency of a computer system and increase facility, the ease with which a system can be used. It makes the computer system user-friendly.

An operating system is designed to serve two basic purposes:

(1) To control the allocation and use of the computing system's resources among the various users and tasks, and

(2) To provide an interface between the computer hardware and the programmer that simplifies and makes feasible the creation, coding, debugging and maintenance of applications programmes.

The operating system binds all user programme to the hardware and the ease with which the user can interact with the machine depends on user friendliness of the operating system. The Development of user friendly, based graphic, icon driven system software with different windows to run different programmes simultaneously have facilitated much needed user friendly environment for interaction between the user and the computer. Such systems are called Graphic User Interfaces or GUI.

The most common OS for PCs is the Disk Operating System (DOS). As the founders of Microsoft, Bill Gates and Paul Allen bought Quick Operating System (Q-DOS) from Seattle Computer Products and expanded it to MS-DOS for IBM's first PC in 1981. IBM's OS/2, Apple's System 7, Microsoft's Windows 95,98,2000 and Windows NT, and AT&T's UNIX are other popular operating systems. The windows based operating system such as Windows 95, 98, 2000 and Windows-NT or any operating system providing Common Desktop Environment (CDE) has not only enabled a friendly user interface but also allowed multiple applications to run on the same machine and made free interchange between various applications possible. The software packages have been developed to make use of these features of the operating system.

The user interface between the user and the computer is sought to be further improved by introduction of natural language systems and voice activated systems where the computers can be operated giving verbal commands which are translated into computer commands by the operating system. The computers software applications which accept dictation from the user and convert it into text are also introduced. Thus, there is digitization of text, image and voice enabling users from any part of the globe to have Video-conferencing anywhere, anytime. With the technological advances, operating systems have become larger and more sophisticated in response to the capabilities of new hardware and other software.

Operating systems perform the following functions:

- Communication link between the computer system and the user.
- Interpretation of commands, instructions, and other data entered by the user.
- Management of different files on the system, by storing and transporting files from various storage devices.
- Memory management, by allocating primary memory and other storage devices to the system programmes, user programmes and data.
- Processor management, by scheduling different tasks of the processor.
- Coordination of compilers, assemblers and other software to the various users of the computer system.
- Input/Output management, by managing and coordinating various input and output devices.

(II) Programming Languages

The language which we speak, becomes the basis for understanding between human beings to facilitate the communication. In the same way, a programming language is used to communicate with the computer which understands only machine language, the language of 0 and 1 only. Programming languages are the various methods of writing computer instructions. The instructions adhere to a particular set of protocols for each language. Through the years, more than 200 languages have been developed, some of which are quite specialized. Some of the most popular languages include BASIC, COBOL, Pascal, C, C++, Visual Basic, and FORTRAN. But regardless of which language a programme was written in, a computer can only process binary code. Therefore, each language must eventually be converted back to binary code before any instructions can be followed.

The first generation of computer languages was machine language. Machine language was very difficult to use, time consuming, full of errors and limited a programmer's creativity.

The second generation of computer language, assembly language was developed in the 1950s and reduced the complexity of programme authoring by using symbols instead of 0s and 1s. However, each computer or family of computers had its own assembly language which prevented the software of one computer model from being used on a different computer model. Although programming became easier to write, it remained idiosyncratic with its lack of portability.

Third generation languages, called high-level languages, were developed for two reasons — programmers could work on different computers without having to learn a new assembly language each time, and the software written on one computer could be used on another. A compiler, or programme translator was used to help solve these problems by translating a programme into machine language and checking the programme for syntax errors (spelling or grammar mistakes unique to a specific language). The advent of the compiler greatly reduced the programmer's burden of memorizing specific code for each machine.

Fourth generation languages, called very high-level languages, use a similar language translator (called interpreters) but require fewer lines of code because they rely on objects of code that are reusable. These predefined objects have numerous strengths such as portability, easy structuring and simplified development but also make the languages less flexible.

Until 1970, IBM bundled its software with its computers, selling the hardware along with the software needed to run it. In 1970, IBM began charging a separate fee for its software, thus opening a market for independent software developers to write programmes that would run on IBM machines. By the time the first personal computer (PC), called the Altair, hit the market in the 1975, there were many well-developed computer languages and competent programmers available to write software for the new industry. Micro Instrumentation and Telemetry Systems, Inc., the manufacturers of the Altair, introduced an operating system that was a version of Beginner's All-Purpose Symbolic Instruction Code (BASIC), written by Bill Gates and Paul Allen and enabled Altair owners to write their own programmes.

Language Translators

High-level languages are easier for programmers to work with, but CPUs cannot execute them directly. Instead, another computer programme (in machine language) executes and as part of its execution either compiles or interprets high-level programmes. Such system software are called language translators.

The language translator takes as input some programme in one language, called the source code, and produces after translation the equivalent machine language programme, called the object code. The following figure shows this process.

Source Code ⟶ Translator ⟶ Object Code

(High level language) (Input) (Output) (Machine language)

Language translators can be broadly categorized into two types:

(1) Compilers

(2) Interpreters

(1) Compilers

Compilers translate a programme from high-level language to machine language. A compiler is a programme that reads as input a programme in a high-level language (the source code) and produces as output a programme in machine language (the byte code or object code). For example, a compiler will translate a programme written in a high-level language (such as C, COBOL, Pascal etc.) to its equivalent machine language code. The object code can then be executed immediately or saved and executed at a later time. A different compiler programme is needed for each combination of source language and machine language. However, a single source programme may be compiled separately to produce machine language programmes for several different platforms. For example, C++ compilers are available for many different platforms. The same source programme written in C++, can be compiled and executed on several different platforms, so long as the programme does not make any requests of the operating system (e.g., opening or saving files) that are specific to a particular platform.

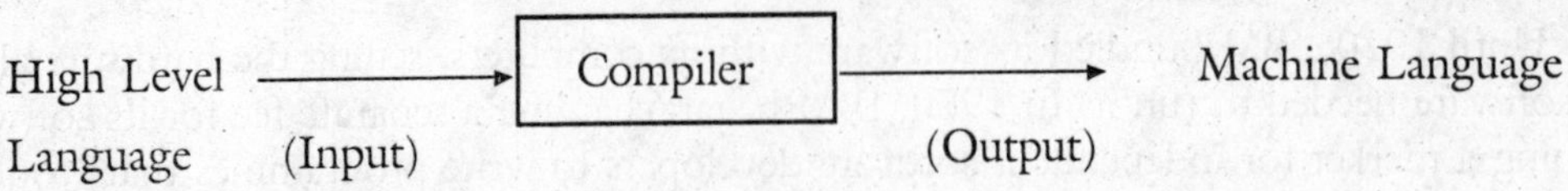

Compilers translate the entire source code in one go and produce the executable code that can be directly run on the computer. Compilers are fast and preferred for most of the applications, development.

(2) Interpreters

Like a compiler an interpreter is another language translator that converts a high-level language programme into machine code. An interpreter reads in source code and directly produces the output that the source code would produce if it were compiled and executed immediately. One way to create an interpreter is to make a compiler that immediately executes the source code that it creates, but it is often simpler to make interpreters that work more directly. An interpreter is different from a complier; the difference is that an interpreter converts the source code statement by statement into object code and does not produce any executable file. Interpreters are slow in processing and are required every time the source code is to be executed on the computer.

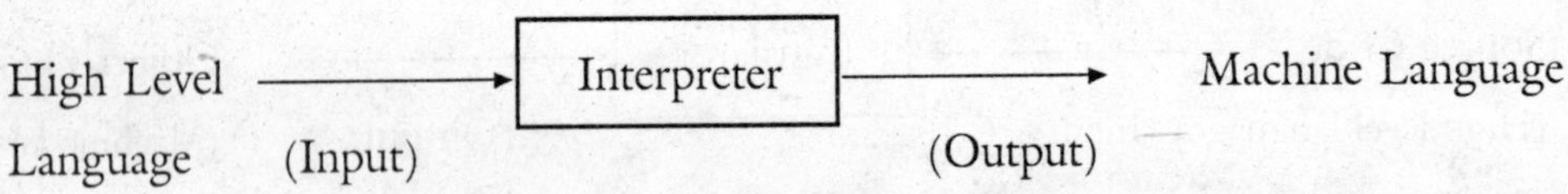

Think of an interpreter as a simulator for a virtual machine. Each high-level programming language includes some instructions that do not correspond to machine instructions of any real CPU. But imagine a virtual CPU that could directly execute an instruction such as looping 10 times. No such virtual machine exists, but an interpreter or emulator programme is a simulator for such a virtual machine. It produces the same output that the virtual machine would produce when executing a programme in the high-level language. Sometimes the interpreter programme is itself called a virtual machine, because it does exactly what a real machine would, if such a machine existed.

Any high-level language can, in principle, be either interpreted or compiled. It is easier to write interpreter programmes for some languages than others and therefore, some languages tend to be thought of as 'interpreted' languages. Among these are LISP, visual basic, and JavaScript. For example, most Web browsers have an interpreter programme for JavaScript. This makes it possible to embed a JavaScript programme in an HTML document and have it automatically executed during the display of the HTML page.

(III) Utility software

Utility software expands the performance of the operating system by adding functions that are not part of the original operating system. Utilities perform such jobs as troubleshooting hardware, inspecting diskettes for damage, file conversion, defragmenting, data compression and file spooling. Some utility programmes, such as Symantec's Norton Utilities, even retrieve data from damaged disks. Utilities can also be used to customize the operating system environment. Although, some of these utilities come as part of the standard operating system but most of the software utilities are available as independent software, which can be purchased from the vendor and used for the specific purpose they have been designed for.

(3) Humanware

Humanware is the living part of a computer system and the organisation under which it is installed. Humanware simply means the people. The people who deal with computers and its management put together are called Humanware or Peopleware. Humanware comprises of all the computer staff people who are directly or indirectly concerned with the computer system. They include systems analyst, computer programmers, database administrator, data entry operators, hardware engineers etc.

LIMITATIONS OF A COMPUTER

A computer is a dumb machine; in other words, everything we want a computer to do, we have to feed every minute detail to it in the form of a programme. Therefore, a computer will do what it is instructed to do and not what we want it to do. A computer lacks creativity and original thinking. This makes the job of a programmer difficult and challenging, as the efficiency of the computer will depend directly upon the intelligence and the efficiency of the programmer. A programmer needs the technical knowledge of programming languages and software packages to use the computer effectively.

Following are some other limitations of a computer:

Dependence Over Programmer

A computer cannot do anything of its own. From the simplest possible calculation to the most difficult one, the programmer is required to write step-by-step precise and unambiguous programme. Therefore, the utilization of a computer depends upon the efficiency of the programmer or team of programmers working for any organisation. Sometimes, a heavy investment in most advanced and sophisticated computers capable of executing billions of instructions per second could remain underutilized or even go waste because of the non-availability of good computer staff. Also short supply of good programmers and other computer professionals cost the organisations very dearly to recruit or hire computer programmers and systems analysts.

Investment And Associated Costs

Computer installation and automation requires huge investments, which only the big industrial houses can afford. Also the recurring and maintenance cost of a computer system is very high. Further, installation of computers requires the cost of associated infrastructure, for example, the air-conditioner, proper furniture to place the computer, monitor, printer etc. Also a computer requires an uninterrupted power supply, making the installation of a constant voltage stabilizer or UPS necessary. The total cost of this whole range of gadgetry sometimes becomes unaffordable, which puts limitation over its use.

Dumb Machine

A computer is a dumb machine, with no mind of its own. A computer cannot make intuitive decisions. A computer can process a job only if a clear and precise algorithm (a step by step solution to solve a problem) can be written and the computer will work strictly according to this sequence of the algorithm. A computer can only process information, but cannot understand it.

Continuous Monitoring And Upgradation

A computer system requires continuous monitoring and Upgradation as everyday new computers are coming in the market with more processing speed, more memory and better audio and video qualities. Even a latest machine bought today will become obsolete within days time. Thus, a common man cannot afford to upgrade the computer system that fast.

Desk-killing

With the introduction of computers in almost every activity of business, the job of many persons can be handled by only a single machine and with more accuracy and reliability. But this characteristic of computer has become a drastic threat to the job security of workers. Even the manual work is being handled by computers inside a factory, resulting in layoff of workers. The retrenchment of workers and reduction in vacancies in organisations because of the replacement of manual work with computers, the problem of desk killing has taken birth.

Non-portability

Programmes and software written for one type of computers may not work on other type of computers. This is called non-portability of software. The problem of non-portability of programmes sometimes render otherwise useful programmes useless on other computers. This is an added problem for professional programme developers who develop general-purpose programmes.

Security Threat

A computer and the data stored in a computer are never secure from unauthorised users unless some security mechanism such as passwords etc. is used for safety. The user is, therefore, always bothered about the security and the secrecy of his work on a computer and has to remember all the time the passwords. Passwords are required to be frequently changed to avoid any possibility of crackdown, especially when the computer is a part of some network or Internet. Sometimes, a busy user may forget his own password and may lose permanently access to his data and programmes. This is another limitation of computers.

Requires Backup

Another limitation of computers is the accidental loss of data because of some hardware problems like sudden power failure, disk crash etc. or some software problem like virus etc. Such device failure causes the entire system to stop and may result in heavy loss to the user.

Side Effects

Last but not the least, a computer has certain dangerous side effects for a human body. It is now proved that the excessive use of computers badly affects human body in several ways. The constant gaze on the screen of a coloured monitor affects human eyesight. Also, the hard disk produces certain gases which leads to many diseases and problems in human body. The longer working hours on a computer also causes psychological problems such as depression and suicidal tendencies. All this puts a limitation on the use of computers.

❒❒❒

14

THE INTERNET

The Internet is a network of thousands of computer networks connecting millions of people all over the world. In the communication perspective, the Internet can be defined as the community of people and organisations that communicate with the help of technology. The Internet is a vast information system connecting millions of computers worldwide allowing people to communicate, conduct business, research, sale, purchase, etc. Every piece of information we would ever need is available on the Internet, we just need to learn how to access it. The Internet has rapidly changed from a network connecting scientists and engineers to a network connecting everyone. E-mail addresses are as common as telephone numbers with the advent of the 'Information Superhighway.' The designers of the original Internet could not possibly have foreseen the current success of their creation or the myriad of purposes that it is being used for now and will be used in the future. Although, its original purpose was to provide researchers with access to expensive hardware resources, the Internet has demonstrated such speed and effectiveness as a communication medium that it has transcended the original purpose. It has, in recent years, grown so large and powerful that it is now an information and communication tool one cannot afford to ignore.

Today, the Internet is being used by all sorts of people and organisations—newspapers, publishers, TV stations, celebrities, teachers, librarians, hobbyists and business people—for a variety of purposes, from communicating with one another to accessing valuable services and resources. You can hardly pick up a newspaper or magazine without reading about how the Internet is playing a part in someone's life or project or discovery.

The Birth Of The Internet

The Internet is not a recent innovation; it traces its history back more than forty years to a project called ARPANET. The Internet emerged from the ARPANET (the network of the Pentagon's Advanced Research Project Agency), which was sponsored by the U.S. Department of Defence, to link the enormous number of private sector and university-based researchers working on Defence-funded projects. Instead of performing its own research, ARPA (a branch of the Department of Defence), which became DARPA (Defence Advanced Research Projects Agency) in 1972, regularly funded research projects related to technological development or military problems. At first this interconnection of experimental and production networks was called the 'DARPA Internet', but later the name was shortened to just 'The Internet.'

In the 1960s, ARPA became interested in developing a way for computers to communicate with each other and began to fund programs at universities and corporations. A network would both advance American technological development and provide a secure command and control over information during wartime. In the 1960s, the cold war between the western nations and the Warsaw Pact countries, principally the Soviet Union, almost resulted in the beginning of World War III. In 1962, the Soviet Union placed nuclear-armed missiles on the island of Cuba, just ninety miles off the coast of the United States. The U.S. military realized that a nuclear attack on major communication centres would paralyze the U.S. defence system completely. The ARPANET program was developed to devise a system of decentralized computer linkages that would reduce dependence on major communication centres to link national security sites. The result was a technology that reduced data transmitted over a network into packets that were transmitted independently from one another through connected computers throughout the country. The packets were received from all over the country by the target computer and reassembled into coherent messages.

Access to the ARPANET in the early years was limited to the military and universities doing defence research. Cooperative, decentralized networks such as UUCP, a worldwide Unix communications network, and USENET (User's Network) came into being in the late 1970s, initially serving the university community and later, commercial organisations. In the early 1980s, more-coordinated networks, such as the Computer Science Network (CSNET) and BITNET (Because It is There Network), began providing nationwide networking to the academic and research communities. These networks were not part of the Internet, but later special connections were made to allow the exchange of information between the various communities.

In the late 1980s, a coding protocol called HTML or the HyperText Markup Language was developed. HTML is composed of a set of formatting indicators that could be embedded in information. These formatting indicators could be interpreted by software called the browser. The first developed browser was called Mosaic. The formatting created the protocol called the World Wide Web or Web. The Internet is not the same thing as the WEB. The World Wide Web is the name applied to the files available on the Internet that use the HTML tags for formatting. Other types of files are travelling the Internet including FTP, Gopher, IRC, digital video and others. The WWW is a distributed hypermedia environment within the Internet which was originally developed by the European Particle Physics Laboratory (CERN). The World Wide Web allows multimedia information to be located on a network of servers around the world which are interconnected, allowing one to travel through the information by clicking on hyperlinks. Any hyperlink (text, icon or image in a document) can point to any document anywhere on the Internet.

In 1986, the National Science Foundation Network (NSFNET), which linked researchers across the country with five supercomputer centres came into existence. Soon expanded to include the mid-level and statewide academic networks that connected universities and research consortiums, the NSFNET began to replace the ARPANET for research networking. The ARPANET was honorably discharged (and dismantled) in March 1990. CSNET soon found that many of its early members (computer science departments) were connected via the NSFNET, so it ceased to exist in 1991.

Most of the growth in the WWW (World Wide Web) as an information and commerce channel has occurred since 1992. The number of connections to the WWW has been growing at an accelerating rate ever since. Although computers connected to the WWW were primarily computers at universities and at a very few businesses at first, as more and more business connected to the net, the net as a general business tool was born. The present popularity of the WWW as a commercial medium (in contrast to other networks on the Internet) is due to its ability to facilitate global sharing of information and resources, and its potential to provide an efficient channel for advertising, marketing and even direct distribution of certain goods and information services. In fairly short period of time, the movement in Net connectivity began to shift from business-to-business linkages to focus on home connections.

Therefore, initially the Internet had a humble mission, to explore experimental networking technologies that would link researchers with remote resources such as large computer systems and databases. The success of ARPANET helped cultivate numerous other networking initiatives, which grew up intertwined; years later now these have evolved into an ever expanding, complex organism comprising tens of millions of people and tens of thousands of networks.

IT'S GROWTH MEANS INTERNET'S GROWTH

It is important to understand the significance of the Internet's growth and popularity. The speed, convenience and very low cost of data transmission result in greater immediacy in human communication and has unleashed an extraordinary explosion of new ideas and services. Vast quantities of inter-personal communication are undertaken using it and large numbers of documents are accessible from servers located throughout the world. Initially, access to data on the Internet required considerable technical capability; but the days of obscure interfaces are quickly receding. Most important among the internet services are electronic mail; menu-based search capabilities to discover and access text documents anywhere in the world; and 'world-wide web' (WWW) servers, which provide access to compound documents containing several different formats (including image, voice, video etc.), whose elements may be stored on different machines scattered throughout the world.

With professional-quality services now available, the kinds of documents, which are accessible via the Internet, are no longer limited to research papers, discussions on varied topics, films and life on the net, games software and university course material. For example, university library catalogues are accessible over it; specialist collections of scientific papers and data can be located and copied using it; government committees make their discussion papers available over it; and government agencies publish reports, submissions and proceedings on servers connected to it.

The services are maturing beyond structured data and text. Sound, graphics and images can also be transmitted. Text messages can be delivered directly to fax machines. Synchronous conversations are being supported, particularly in text, but also using sound. Video transmission is being experimented in many locations, and the 'video-phone' may well become widely available on the Internet in the near future.

The Internet is commonly described as a 'network of networks.' It does not just connect one computer with another; it connects the computer with all other Internet-connected computers. The Internet is not just a bunch of computers, rather it is a perpetually expanding universe with its own geography, weather, and dynamic cultures. The Internet will continue to flourish. It is, however, in transition from a multi-national campus-based family, to a multi-purpose community which services research, educational, corporate and governmental needs quite generally. In this cyberspace, people communicate across time zones without ever seeing each other, and information is available 24 hours a day from thousands of places. The Internet is already the largest computer network in the world and, in terms of connected networks, people, and resources; it is getting larger every minute.

How Big It (Internet) Is?

Nobody really knows how many computers and networks actually make up the Internet. It is estimated that there are now as many as 30,000 networks connecting more than 5 million computers and around 70 million users logging on to it in around 90 countries. Whatever is the actual number, however, it is clear that this number is increasing day by day. In India also, the Planning Commission, in its Ninth Plan projections, has predicted a sharp increase in the use of the Internet. There will be more than 1.6 million Internet users by the end of year 2002. The number of e-mail users is 20,000 at present and they are expected to rise to 50 lakh (250 times increase) by the end of the Planning period.

The types of resources accessible via the Internet are growing at an astounding rate. The term resource describes anything you can access on the Internet, no matter where it is physically located. Examples of some Internet resources are a database of regularly updated weather information, an online magazine, a case study and an archive of daily newspaper articles. A resource can also be a mailing list or a newsgroup that brings together people from all over the world to discuss shared interests such as cricket, cooking, cinema, poetry, romance etc. In short, there are literally tens of thousands of servers, archive sites, mailing lists, newsgroups, and databases available on the Internet.

Internet Grown Up Now

It is hard to imagine how the Internet has grown so fast and been so successful without some professional organisation or individual managing the project. Yet no one has a monopoly on access to or use of the Internet. One of the reasons, the Internet is so successful is the commitment of its developers to producing open standards. The specifications or rules that computers need to communicate are publicly and freely available and published so that everyone can obtain them. Technically, the Internet is that collection of networks which are inter-connected using a particular set of standards popularly referred to as 'TCP/IP' or 'Transmission Control Protocol/Internet Protocol.' The total number of 'nodes' (computers) it connects is in the hundreds of thousands and the number of people is in the millions. Each node on the network co-operates with the remainder by acting as a switch or exchange and passing data along towards its ultimate destination. In order to do this, some of the nodes act as 'name-servers' and maintain a set of routing tables which determine where, depending on its intended recipient, each packet has to be sent next. Fundamentally, the Internet revolves around the concept of a 'packet.' All information and communication transmitted on the Internet are broken into packets, each of which is considered an independent entity. The packets are then individually routed from network to network until they reach their destination, where they are reassembled and presented to the user or computer process.

The networks on the Internet are not controlled by a central brain, such as a powerful supercomputer; rather, all the networks and computers act as peers in the exchange of information and communication. The technology that makes it happen is known as internetworking; it creates universality among disparate systems, enabling the networks and computers to communicate. This method of networking is very flexible and robust. It allows diverse computers and systems to communicate by means of networking software, not proprietary hardware. If a network goes down—meaning it is not available to transfer information—the packets can be rerouted to other networks in many cases. This dynamic alternate routing of information creates a very persistent means of communication.

While most people do not care about these standards and technical details, an understanding of the underlying infrastructure will help in learning to use the Internet properly and in taking full advantage of its powerful capabilities.

Who Is The Guardian?

No one owns the Internet. Any single person, company, university, or government did not fund it. Every person who makes a connection, every group whose local area network (LAN) becomes connected, owns a slice of the Internet. It is a global collection of networks, both big and small. These networks connect together in many different ways to form the single entity that we know as the Internet. In fact, the very name comes from this idea of interconnected networks. According to Bill Kirkman,[1] the Internet was not thought "as a unitary infrastructure but as a voluntary protocol which millions had opted to use. It was an ad hoc, flexible, bottom up, chaotic phenomenon."

Till date there is no single agency or organisation totally responsible for controlling the Internet. However, it does not mean it is not monitored and maintained in different ways. The Internet Society, a non-profit group established in 1992, oversees the formation of the policies and protocols that define how we use and interact with the Internet.

Internet Services

The primary purpose of the Internet is information sharing. About any information search, it has become a common thing to say 'it will be on the Internet.' Almost every information is available on the Internet. Besides providing information services Internet has the following capabilities and uses for the users:

- Information resources
- Free or shareware software
- Virtual colleges and classes
- Customer services and information by commercial organisations
- Customer feedback and support

1. Bill Kirkman's article, 'Governance of the Net', *The Hindu,* 23 May 1999, p. III.

- Books, papers, case studies and course materials
- Games, music and other sort of entertainment
- E-mail
- Chat
- Library catalogues
- Usenet newsgroup and electronic mailing lists
- Sale and purchase services
- Virtual payments
- Stocks monitoring
- Electronic newspapers, magazines, journals etc.
- Airline and railway reservations
- Video conferencing
- Job search, interviews etc.

The Principles Behind Internet

If we ask an Internet wizard what this network is all about, most probably we will get a long and technical lecture. Fortunately, the most important principle of all is that you do not have to fully understand how the Internet works to use it. Most of the users are pounding away at keyboards and communicating merrily, with no knowledge of how the Internet works. Now, we will discuss some of the basic principles that underlie the Internet.

The Internet is a huge collection of millions of computers, all linked together on a computer network. The network allows all of the computers to communicate with one another. A home computer is usually linked to the Internet using a normal phone line and a modem that communicates to an Internet Service Provider (ISP). A computer in a business or office has a Network Interface Card (NIC) that directly connects it to a Local Area Network (LAN) inside the business. The business then connects its LAN to an ISP using a high-speed phone line like a T1 line. A T1 line can handle approximately 1.5 million bits per second, while a normal phone line using a modem can usually handle 30,000 to 50,000 bits per second.

ISPs then connect to larger ISPs, and the largest ISPs maintain fiber-optic backbones for an entire nation or region. Backbones around the world are connected through fiber-optic lines, undersea cables or satellite links. In this way, every computer on the Internet is connected to every other computer on the Internet.

A Network Of Networks

The Internet is an incalculably massive network of networks. The Internet is made up of little Local Area Networks (LANs), citywide Metropolitan Area Networks (MANs), and huge Wide Area Networks (WANs) that connect computers for organisations all over the world. These networks are hooked together with everything from regular dial-up phone lines to high-speed dedicated leased lines, satellites, microwave links and fiber optic links. And the fact that they are on the Internet means that all these networks are interconnected. This network web extends all over the world. There are so many networks interconnected within the Internet that it is impossible to show an accurate, up-to-date picture. Everyday, new computers and links are being added. It is estimated that a new network is added every 10 minutes.

Computer's Communication

The computers on a network communicate to one another. For this they use the same communication protocols. There are lots of protocol standards such as DECnet, SNA, IPX, and AppleTalk, but to communicate, two computers are required to use the same protocols at the same time. Researchers at DARPA worked on a protocol which would be able to handle larger number of users, and resultant TCP/IP was born in the 1970s. The U.S. government in 1978 accepted this more sophisticated technology and TCP/IP became the preferred networking tool.

TCP/IP, which stands for Transmission Control Protocol/Internet Protocol, is the language of the Internet. You may speak French and I may speak Hindi, but if we both speak English, we can communicate. So, any computer that wants to communicate on the Internet must speak TCP/IP.

TCP/IP was a part of an experiment in internetworking, that is, connecting different types of networks and computer systems. First used ubiquitously on the ARPANET in 1983, it was also implemented and made available at no cost for computers running the Berkeley Software Distribution (BSD) of the Unix operating system. TCP/IP, developed with public funds, is considered an open, non-proprietary protocol and there are now implementations of it for almost every type of computer on the planet. Non-proprietary means that no one company has exclusive rights to the products needed to connect to the Internet. Any number of companies makes the hardware and software necessary for the network connection.

TCP/IP is not the only protocol suite that is considered open. Since the early 1980s, the International Organisation for Standardization (ISO) has been developing the Open Systems Interconnection (OSI) protocols. While many of the OSI protocols and applications are still evolving, a few are actually being used in some networks on the Internet and more are planned. So even though most of the computers speak TCP/IP, the Internet is officially considered a multi-protocol network.

The Tools Of Internet

Electronic mail, remote login and file transfer protocol are basically the Internet tools. These are TCP/IP applications. There are plenty of applications using variations on or combinations of these basic tools. The three basic Internet services are:

Electronic mail is the most commonly available and most frequently used service on the Internet. Through e-mail a text message can be sent to another person or to a whole group of people.

Remote login is an interactive tool that allows the user to access the programs and applications available on another computer.

File transfer protocol allows users to transfer files from one computer to another. A file can be a text document, graphics, software, sound etc.

There are quite a few applications available today that use a combination or variation of these three tools to hide details even further. These operate on a client/server model, that is, you use the client on your computer and it contacts servers for directions and information. Clients and servers do not have to be located in the same geographical area. This technology is very flexible; during one session, your client may access servers all over the world to help you find information. As the Internet has grown larger, locating the information we need has become difficult unless we are using information discovery and retrieval tools. The major resource-browsing applications, which operate on the client/server concept, include Internet Explorer, Netscape Navigator, Eudora, Gopher, World Wide Web (WWW) and Wide Area Information Servers (WAIS).

How Does TCP/IP Work ?

When you are actually using the above-mentioned tools, information of various types is being transferred from one computer to another. TCP/IP breaks this information into pieces called packets. Each packet contains a piece of the information or document plus some ID tags, such as the addresses of the sending and receiving computers.

Each packet can travel independently. Because of all the network interconnections, there are often multiple paths to a destination. The packets may travel different networks to get to the destination computer. The packets may arrive out of order, but that is not a problem, because each packet also contains sequence information about where the data it is carrying goes in the document and the receiving computer can reconstruct the whole document again. That is why, the Internet is known as a packet-switched network.

Worldwide Networking

Once all the networks are in place, the Internet, which is actually tens of thousands of networks, looks seamless to the user. By connecting networks together to enable communication and information exchange, all the details are hidden from the user: the packets, the routers, and all those interconnections. Despite of different computers and disparate networks, somehow the whole web works and any computer directly connected to the Internet can communicate to all the other computers on the Internet. So, you working on a computer in your office in New Delhi or in your spare bedroom in Punjab can communicate with a colleague in Canada or a friend in England. It is as if you are directly connected by one wire.

Internet Enables Human Communication

Every day, hundreds of thousands of people are communicating through the Internet—conversing, collaborating, working, playing and studying. Even marriages are made and broken on the Internet. Clubs are formed. Problems are solved. Jobs are found. Handicaps and disabilities make no difference. Through e-mail and the other methods of on-line communication, people have become best friends without ever seeing or talking to each other. It is not uncommon for people to turn to the Net for answers; a question posted to on-line communities—mailing lists and conferences—can yield dozens of invaluable tales of experiences and testimonials within hours. On-line communication eliminates all the barriers of physical distance and place.

On the Internet, people can communicate asynchronously and in real time. Asynchronous (taken from Greek word for 'not at the same time') communication means that someone can type in a message and send it off, but the recipient does not have to be around to receive it. This type of communication has some real benefits. You can send messages whenever you want to, they reach their destination quickly and the recipients can read and respond when they want to. Answering machines and voice mail are everyday examples of asynchronous communication. Real-time, interactive communication, in contrast, means that as someone is talking— that is, typing—you see it on your screen as it is typed. Real-time audio and video conferencing is starting to become more prevalent on the Internet too.

ALL ABOUT ELECTRONIC MAIL

Electronic mail is the most popular application on the Internet today. It is a very powerful tool that is simple to use and easy to understand. Using e-mail can give you a real feeling for the energy and reach of the Net. It is hard to imagine any other form of communication that can be so intimate and yet so wide reaching, so focused, or so expansive. You can communicate as easily with someone across twelve time zones as with someone in the same building. Your message can be limited to just one person, or it can reach hundreds of people.

How to Send E-Mail?

Postal mail is often called snail mail in comparison to e-mail. E-mail is really fast—it is sent and received in seconds, minutes at the most. Sending e-mail is easy too. All you need is access to the Internet, an e-mail program and the e-mail address of the person with whom you wish to communicate.

Internet Access

The first requirement for e-mail is the Internet access. The Internet connection can be a dial-up connection or it can be through a leased line.

E-Mail Programs

You will need an e-mail program that will run on your own computer. Most large systems and public-access computers offer several e-mail programs. Some commercial Internet service providers will supply programme to load on your computer. A common characteristic of e-mail programmes is that they let you compose and send e-mail and then read and organize the e-mail you receive. There are many different e-mail programmes; the most popular ones are listed below.

Post Office E-Mail Programs

One of the more popular applications uses the Post Office Protocol (POP). In a nutshell, the POP system allows your personal workstation to get its e-mail from a big computer that serves as a post office, delivering the mail when you (or your computer) ask for it. This eliminates the need for your computer to be on all the time, constantly available to receive e-mail. In order to use a POP-based e-mail application, you need Internet access (via dial-up or full-time connectivity) and a POP mail account on a post office computer. All of these applications provide intuitive editors.

It Requires E-Mail Address

In order to send someone e-mail, you need to know the recipient's address. An e-mail address, like a postal mail address, contains all the necessary information needed to deliver a message to someone. Internet e-mail addresses are, in fact, very simple. They consist of a local part and a host part. The username refers to the mailbox, login name, or user id of the recipient on that computer. For example, if your friend Dhiraj logs in on his computer as dhiraj2001, then that is his username. The host part of the address should be recognizable to you—a series of words separated by dots. The local part and host part of an e-mail address are separated by an '@' sign:

username@hostname

The username is the unique name of the user whereas hostname is actually the address of the host computer on which the user is sending the request. Suppose that you know that Sanyam's username is sanyam2001 you could send e-mail to him using his address:

sanyam2001@indiatimes.com.

Now indiatimes.com is the host name. The host name provides the Internet location of the mailbox, usually the name of the computer owned by a company or Internet service.

Now Send It Off

Once you have an e-mail program and know the recipient's e-mail address, you are ready to send a message. Each e-mail program is different, so if you are not familiar with yours, you may have to fumble around a bit or actually read the manual or on-line documentation. You will need to specify that you want to send a message, either by typing send, clicking a send button, or by performing some other computer function. The e-mail program will prompt you for information, asking for the recipient's e-mail address, the key piece of information the program needs to send the message to the recipient. It will also ask for the subject of your message—usually a summary, title, or brief description. The subject is optional, but you should get into the practice of including it. A good subject description makes the person to whom you are sending aware of the nature of your message, whether it is important or whimsical. The program may give you the option of sending a 'carbon copy' (cc) message. If there is someone else you think would be interested in the message, here is a chance to include his or her address. You can send carbon copies to more than one recipient. If you have the disk space, it is a good idea to send a copy to yourself so you will have a record of your outgoing messages. After you have answered all the e-mail program prompts, you can compose your message, using your e-mail program's editor. It is important to make your message easy to read and understand.

Anatomy Of An E-Mail Message

An e-mail message has two basic parts, the 'header' information and the body of the message. These pieces are separated by a blank line. In most cases, you will be interested only in the body, or the actual text, of the message. The headers contain items such as 'Date:', 'cc:', 'From:', and 'Subject:'. Sometimes, there are seemingly arcane lines such as 'Received:' and 'Message-Id' These normally do not concern you, but they are necessary for the e-mail programmes and for debugging purposes. Following is a sample message:

From: upgupta@yahoo.com

Wed 13 Feb 4 11:51:36 IST 2002

Subject: Today's Seminar

To: sanyam2001@indiatimes.com

Cc: nsharma@mailcity.com

Dear San,

For today's seminar, I'd like your help.

Please guide me regarding the topic and its details.

Thanks,

UP Gupta.

Managing The Mails

Receiving e-mail requires less effort than sending it. Incoming messages are stored in your inbox. When you run your e-mail program, it fetches your mail from an on-line mailbox (if there is anything in it), and then usually displays a one-line summary for each message in there. This summary will include information such as the message number, the date the message was sent, the sender and the subject. You can select which message you want to read by selecting it with your mouse.

Everyone loves to get e-mail because it probably gives a tiny thrill to see the message, 'You have new mail,' when you check your electronic mailbox. But because it is so easy to send and receive e-mail, you may find that you cannot keep up with all the messages you receive. You should set up a good routine for sorting your mail, deleting trivial messages and filing the rest by saving them in separate electronic folders sorted by people or topics. If you do not keep up with your e-mail efficiently, your messages will stack up in the inbox as they proliferate and your e-mail programme may slow to a crawl. Your e-mail programme may allow you to sort incoming messages by date, sender, subject, size, or in other ways and these functions can help you dispense of messages quickly.

Limiting Factors Of E-mail Communication

In the IT age, e-mail has become a major communication tool for many people. Communicating via e-mail has many benefits, but there are also instances where this medium is highly inappropriate and can cause significant problems.

The popularity of the Internet is very much associated with its use as an e-mail communication medium. Most of the people use Internet to send and receive e-mails only. It is more true in the case of India where Internet is still a costly affair. The Internet user in India pays around Rs. 24 per hour to the DOT plus Rs. 7 more per hour to the ISP for surfing on the net.

Everyone hates junk mail, but e-mail users hate it even more. Junk mails eats up valuable e-mail space and moreover, bounce out genuine e-mails. Sometimes, junk e-mails are also a source of virus infusion. Bogus and fraud schemes are also sent through junk mails. Our Information

Technology Act, 2000 is silent about Junk mails. In order to stop the junk mails and protect the sanctity of the e-mail service, there is a great need for an appropriate measure to stop this. There should be appropriate provisions in the law to curb this malpractice. Business people are easily tempted to take advantage of the Internet for their business marketing programmes, but they should consider the consequences before broadcasting product material and advertisements. Instead, it is advisable to provide a database or archive with details of product or company offerings that people can peruse when they want to.

E-mail, if not properly used, can be the coldest of the communication tools because it prohibits the voice tone and body language that help soften communications. As a result, an e-mail message can easily be read as rude or offensive, even if that is not the intent.

Cyber pornography is also a big issue for India. India should take necessary steps to prevent invitations to visit pornographic sites being sent through e-mails. These invitations are sent directly to the e-mail users on their e-mail addresses regularly. This is a violation of Section 67 of the Information Technology Act, 2000. Experiments conducted, throughout the world, in the context of pornography have concluded that attempts to block sites is ineffective. The attempt to block access to pornographic sites commonly block access to large numbers of other clean sites. Identifying senders of Internet messages and publishers of web pages, is also seriously difficult. Internet traffic carries little or nothing in the way of attributes of a user, other than his or her net-identification or Internet protocol (IP) address. IP addresses, moreover, are capable of being routed through other IP addresses, masking the point of origin. Each time one address is blocked, another could be used. This is not mere conjecture — the techniques required to mask an IP address are both readily available on the Internet and within the reach of reasonably competent users.

Therefore, if the Internet usage has to grow and IT means have to develop, it is necessary for the Indian government to promote e-mail usage and protect it from being misused.

The Information Superhighway

Albert Gore, the Vice-President of the United States, in the early 1990s when he was a Tennessee Senator popularized the metaphor 'The Information Superhighway' for a wired universe interlinked by networks of computers. Almost anything one can think of is available on the Internet—graphics, software, books, library catalogues, bulletin boards, data, sounds, movies, journals, newsletters, newspapers and magazines. There are many thousands of independent databases, archives and online services available via the Internet. Unfortunately, this electronic information jungle is not as well organised. There is not just one catalogue where you can check to find what is available or where things are located. However, graphical interfaces and user-friendly tools have entered the scene and can help you chart a course through what at first may appear to be a vast and unnavigable information jungle. The Internet allows two-way communication by facilitating services like telephone calls, on-line discussions, video-conferencing, teleshopping, interactive multi-media applications etc. the communication on the information superhighway can be in the form of one-to-one (chat, telephonic conversation, e-mail etc); one-to-many (broadcasting, newsgroups, Web TV, video-conferencing, etc.); or many-to-many (bulletin boards and discussion groups).

Of course, not everything is on-line yet, but the amount and diversity of information available on-line is increasing so rapidly that today you can find quite a bit of what you are looking for. The Internet landscape is constantly changing, and enumerating its resources is next to impossible.

There are too many useful information resources to list. The Internet is a vast storehouse of information resources. There are certain things to keep in mind while accessing information over the Internet. In day-to-day life, there is no guarantee that what we hear or read is one hundred percent true. The same thing applies on the Internet also. However, on the Internet you can obtain information from a variety of sources to crosscheck and form your own opinions.

Security Issues

Security was never a key design parameter of the original Internet. But now security has become a matter of vital importance, as Internet transactions are becoming more strategic in nature and involves information of increasing sensitivity and value. Security is a major issue no matter where you go, what type of computer you use, or whether or not your computer is connected to a network. You might be wondering, 'Can people read my e-mail? Can they login to my computer? Will my computer get a virus?' Now, let us try to answer these questions and take up security issues on the Internet. First of all, you should realize that despite its military origins, the Internet is not a classified network. The ARPANET was a network research experiment, so there was a lot of collaboration, with information being transferred between machines and researchers. Today, the Internet is a massive collection of thousands of networks all tied together. And because there is still a lot of research being conducted, it is still considered an open and sharing network. Sensitive information is stored on computers on the Internet and is, therefore, vulnerable to attack from intruders. Any computer directly connected to any network is potentially at risk if proper precautions are not taken.

Hackers Can Break In

Actually, a more accurate term for these computer hackers is 'cracker'. Hacker in the computer world is a term of respect. Hackers are basically nuts about computers and like to learn systems inside and out. Real hackers do not try to break into other systems to exploit holes and using someone else's information. Most break-ins are accomplished by incredible patience and brute force. There is not anything magical about those who do it. Password-breaking recipes, giving step-by-step instructions on how to break into certain systems, have even been published over the network.

What Can You Do?

As a user of the Internet, you cannot do much about fixing security problems if the computer you are using to access the Net is not your own. There is, however, something very important that you can and must do. You can stop an intruder in his or her tracks simply by being responsible about the passwords you use. Most levels of service on the Internet require some type of authentication to prove it is really you accessing the service. Most of the time, this involves user identification and a password to allow access. Your user id is usually well known (you give it out so people can send e-mail), so the only way you can protect yourself is with a secret password. Your password is the key to the locked door of your account or your electronic mail service.

Most common security problems can be prevented by simply being careful with your password. If you do not know how to change your password, put it at the top of your list of things to learn. Crackers often use on-line dictionaries and programs to guess words by 'brute force.' Never give anyone your password without a valid reason. When you do give it to someone so that he or she can obtain necessary information or perform an action, change the password as soon as he or she is done. If you get an account on another system, such as a public database or bulletin board, do not use the same password that you use on your local system. You have no way of knowing where it is stored or how private passwords on other systems are. Do not write your password down and leave the paper in an obvious place, such as in the desk drawer next to your computer. Some computers tell you upon login when you were last seen on that account. You should check to make sure it agrees with when you were really last logged in to that computer.

User IDs and Passwords by themselves do not provide any real assurance that a user is who they state they are because passwords can be stolen without notice and used from any location on the Internet. User IDs and Passwords travel over the Internet making them more susceptible to attack. Digital certificates, in conjunction with local passwords (and optionally additional authentication factors such as smart cards or biometrics) provide a stronger level of assurance of whom you are dealing with. An added bonus to using digital certificates is the ability to use digital signatures for binding users to transactions.

Making Of A Password

An easily guessed password is one of the most common causes of security problems. Most of us do not think much about the passwords that we use. When asked to enter a password, either to log on to the company network or to access your Web based e-mail account, the password that we choose is usually something easy to remember, but it is also easy to crack. Not only that, it is usually easy to guess. The password is, usually, the first initial and then the last name of the user or the first name and last initial of the user. Even a better password than that will be easily guessed or cracked. Generally, people use their spouse's name, children's names, or some other word that is easy to guess. Passwords should never be based on your own name. They should also not be easily guessed, such as husband/wife's name, girl/boyfriend's name, the pet's name, your vehicle number, the house where you live, your birthday etc. Passwords also should not be dictionary words. It is not a matter of choice of words; any password made up of only alphabets is very easy to crack. A cracker who really wants to get into a computer system or network uses a software tool called a password cracker. There are many password crackers on the Internet and all of them work basically the same way. The first thing a password cracker program will do is run the target password through its default dictionary. A password-cracking program uses a built in dictionary of thousands of words to break the target password. If the target password is in the default dictionary, it will be cracked in a fraction of a second. So what can passwords be? It is recommended that the word be at least six characters long. This way the password is not a word, but it is easy to remember and hard to guess. It is also recommended to mix some numbers with the letters and throw in some punctuation, but never make your password all numbers. It is a combination of alphabets and numbers that make up a really secure password.

Getting Access To The Internet

Now, that you know what you want to do on the Internet, or at least where you want to go exploring, you will want to get connected. There is not just one place you can go to get access; paths and roads to the Internet are many. If you work for an institution or a company with full-time access through a network connection to the Internet, you have the shortest path of all. All you need to do is sit down at your office terminal or workstation and, using the instructions and Internet applications supplied by your in-house computer gurus, log on and get going. Most Internet connections have been made just like that—as connections between two networks, rather than between two computers. For example, a college's local-area network (LAN) might get access to the Internet by making a connection through a leased phone line to a regional network. Once that connection is made, in most cases, every computer on the local-area network has full-time access— meaning, the Internet is available all the time, day and night. More and more businesses are getting connections and most universities provide access. Fortunately, these days there are more and more ways to get access to the Internet if you are an individual computer user or small business. All you need is a personal computer, a modem, communications software and a phone line.

Modems

Today's modems are complex and offer so many functions and features that the user manuals accompanying them are sometimes hundreds of pages long. For example, most contemporary modems include functions such as support for multiple transmission rates, standard telephone operations, connection negotiation, compression, error correction, facsimile transmission, security and loop-back testing. Modems can also be physically characterized by whether they are internal or external models and whether they are suitable for use with a laptop computer. Modems are computer appliances that convert the digital signal from your computer into an analog sound wave that can be transmitted over telephone lines. A modem at the other end converts the analog signal back into a digital signal that is understood by the computer you are talking to. Exciting advances are being made in the modem technology, with faster speeds and more error-free data transmission. High-speed modems can reduce errors from line noise and even do data compression. As with any computer-related purchase, you should buy the very best modem you can afford. Technology changes fast and one year from now, today's high-speed modem will be as obsolete as that ancient modem, the 300bps acoustic coupler.

If you have already got a slower modem, do not despair just yet. Many individuals are still using 28.8Kbps modems that they have had for several years to access the Internet and other services. All of the access and information systems support them and for the occasional user, the difference in on-line and/or long-distance charges may not be too significant. The higher your modem speed, of course, the less time it takes you to get information. Using a 28.8Kbps modem, you can access electronic mail, Telnet, FTP and the terminal client gopher application. However, the bigger the message or file, the longer it will take to show on your screen or transfer to your computer. If you plan to spend a lot of time on-line and if you need quick, error-free access, go for a high-speed modem with error correction and data compression. Most of the Internet applications incorporate graphics and multimedia and requires a fast modem. 56Kbps modems are common now with the prices falling everyday. The faster your modem, the faster you can access information.

The ideal modem for telecommunications not only communicates at high speeds but also has error correction and data compression features. Error correction protocols help filter out line noise and they ensure an error-free transmission. Most file transfer programs also have a mechanism to ensure accurate file transfers. Data compression, while a useful feature, may not help you much on some bulletin boards and information services that have already compressed their files because your modem cannot compress them any further. Shopping for a modem gets you into a complexity of feature combinations: speed, modulation protocols, data compression and more.

Communication Software

The second required component is software that will enable communication. Communication software, which is installed on your personal computer, sets up the three-way conversation between your computer, the modem and the remote computer or terminal server. Since you are dialing into the Internet, there are many types of communication packages available, enabling three different kinds of connections. These are terminal emulation, offline access and SLIP/PPP. All of these are commonly used and available from a large number of Internet providers. The best choice for you depends on your existing equipment situation and how much you are willing to spend. The different types of connections are explained as below:

(a) Terminal emulation: Terminal emulation is the easiest type of dial-up Internet access. Using your modem and communications software, you can dial into an Internet-connected computer or communications server. Or in other words you will dial-in to your Internet service provider. Each user has an account on the ISP's Internet Services host computer on the Internet. Your computer will use terminal emulation software and not TCP/IP to talk to the Internet host computer, whereas the Internet host computer will use TCP /IP to communicate to the rest of the network. You can get communication software from a number of places. Some modems come bundled with communications software. You can also buy it from any software store. Once connected, everything you do is from the perspective of the remote computer into which you have dialled. When you read e-mail or news, you are using e-mail and news applications that reside on the remote computer. Similarly, remote logins, file transfers and other tools are all executed on the remote computer. Your computer provides only the display.

(b) Offline access: Offline access brings some of the Internet functions, such as electronic mail, USENET news and file transfer, straight to your computer, but lets you work offline. This means that you are not actively dialled-in while you are working, only when the need arises. When that happens, the software makes the connection, performs the required functions, such as transferring e-mail back and forth and then disconnects. Internet Providers or services supply you with special software, called client or agent software. Although, you are not interactively using the Internet, you can still do a lot of useful things, such as download electronic mail and news, reading messages etc. at your convenience on your computer rather than tying up a phone line or running up connection charges. But this way all of the Internet applications are not, particularly remote login, Gopher and Mosaic, available to you. Because you cannot issue commands and receive information interactively when you are not connected. Despite this limited functionality, these client connections are recommended for novice users, because they are more user-friendly.

(c) SLIP/PPP (Full-access dial-up connection): The use of SLIP (Serial Line Internet Protocol) or PPP (Point-to-Point-Protocol) means the user's computer has full Internet connectivity permitting full client/server operation and graphical user interface applications with access to all Internet services. It is a more advanced client connection that uses client networking software and a high-speed modem to actually become a directly connected computer on the

Internet. This happens because of a fast modem and with the help of software that conforms to SLIP or PPP. Either of these, used in conjunction with graphical Internet client applications like Gopher, Internet Explorer, Netscape Navigator and Eudora brings the power and flexibility of the Internet straight to your computer over an ordinary telephone line. SLIP and PPP are different, but each performs essentially the same function—that is, they make your computer a peer computer on the Internet. A SLIP or PPP connection is a way to connect to the Internet. Through modem, you dial into another computer or terminal server that is running SLIP (if your computer is running SLIP) or PPP (if your computer is running PPP) to make this connection. These remote ends are known as SLIP or PPP servers. They help you get set up at the beginning of the connection, but they are invisible after connection. You will also need a unique Internet Protocol (IP) address, because your computer must be identified on the network. Your Internet provider will assign you an IP address, or the remote SLIP/PPP server will assign you a number to use when you make the connection.

When you use this type of connection, you are actually executing Internet applications on your own computer, not on an Internet-connected computer that you have dialled into. For example, if you want to transfer a file-using FTP from a public-access site, you transfer that file straight to your computer instead of working with the terminal-emulation middle link.

The Internet In India

Till date, the Internet services in India are being provided by the public sector undertaking Videsh Sanchar Nigam Ltd. (VSNL). Although in 1991, the Government of India decided to issue licences to private Internet service providers as a part of its globalisation and liberalization programme. VSNL has also provided backbone network in India known as VSNL's Gateway Internet Access Services (GIAS) network. This network will provide all types of Internet services throughout India.

In 1998, the National Task Force on 'Information Technology and Software Development' under the chairmanship of Shri Jaswant Singh, Deputy Chairman, Planning Commission and Chairperson of the Task Force submitted the report to the Prime Minister Atal Bihari Vajpayee. The report has been accepted by the government with a few modifications. This report, called the Information Technology Action Plan, contains 108 recommendations covering both bottle-neck areas and broad promotional measures that are crucial for boosting IT in India. Among the most important recommendations are those that aim at widening the reach of the Internet. Therefore, Internet access nodes will be opened by the Department of Telecom (DOT) and authorized Internet Service Providers (ISP) at all districts. The Internet revolution is now expected to touch all the areas of the country. The monopoly of VSNL on international gateway for Internet will be withdrawn and private organisations will be allowed to provide Internet access. Internet access through authorized cable TV shall be permitted to any service providers. This is a novel recommendation and would make use of the already available infrastructure to reach more than fifteen million households. Computers and Internet shall be made available in every school, polytechnic, college, university and public hospital in the country by the year 2003. Virtual Institutes in different parts of the country shall be set up to achieve excellence in distance education. The Government shall take necessary measures to develop, manufacture and use indigenous technologies in the wireless telecommunication, remote access switch etc., to achieve the national objective of rapid, low-cost expansion of telephone and Internet connectivity in rural and remote areas. Steps will be taken to achieve a massive expansion in the use of the Internet by all the sections of the society, especially in business and education and development of Indian content on the Internet. Similarly, promotional measures shall be taken to encourage technologies that bring IT and Internet to the masses through the vast network of Cable TV houses. The draft set of Cyber Laws prepared by the Cyber Law Committee set up by the Committee of Secretaries, shall be approved by the Government with suitable modifications and will be implemented to curb malpractices and to save the interests of the users.

❐❐❐

15

Managing With Information

Information is any piece of knowledge which serves as a basis for decision making. Information is made up of bits of messages — verbal and/or non-verbal. Information is a knowledgeable representation of data and is indispensable, without which an organisation cannot operate and succeed. An organisation must understand the importance of accurately acquiring information and accurately interpreting it. Every component of the organisational system is an information point as well as an information target. Every component of the organisation must be brought into the information acquisition process as well as the information dissemination process.

Modern business management is nothing more than information management and without this an organisation cannot even operate. At every level, information is required for decision-making. Decision-making is the most pervasive activity in any organisation. Any worker or manager finds himself constantly faced with decision-making challenges. When all the resources are available all the time; we tend to take them for granted. But when the cost increases or the supply and quality of the resource deteriorate only then we recognize its importance. The same is the case with management information. Timely and accurate information is needed to support the decisions that must be made for the accomplishment of an organisation's objectives. But the question is what type of information does a manager need for effective management? A manager must be clear about the objectives of the organisation, its policies, programmes, plans, strengths, weaknesses etc. The type of information required largely depends upon the type of decisions to be made and the understanding about the organisational levels of management. Therefore, the question of type of information can be answered only in broad terms.

Types of Decisions

Decisions are classified according to their importance, frequency and scope. Broadly defined, a manager takes two types of decisions—structured/programmed or unstructured/non-programmed decisions. The information required depends on whether a manager has to make a structured or unstructured decision. A structured decision is always made using pre-defined procedures or rules. A structured/programmed decision is a routine one, that is, made following the completion of a pre-planned series of steps. These steps spell out the information that must be gathered before pre-stated decision rules are applied. They are also known as programmed decision because they are highly structured and can be made by computer programs. Structured decisions can be easily programmed to handle the routine decisions and the people can deal with the exceptions. The information needed to make structured decisions is thus relatively predictable and steps can be taken in advance to supply it in the reports that decision makers receive.

Decisions that require creativity and intuition are unstructured decisions. An unstructured decision is not routine and it does not follow any pre-defined steps. Hence, these decisions cannot be programmed. They involve the situations where it is not possible to specify in advance about the decision. Unstructured decisions are influenced by internal and external factors that affect the final outcome of the decision. Strategic decisions are unstructured decisions. These decisions lack a structure and the information needed to make unstructured decisions is not completely known in advance.

Decision-Making Process

The right information, available at the right time leads to effective decisions which help in achieving organisational goals. All the decisions usually follow the same process. Different authors have given various decision-making models. Let us discuss, how humans take decisions.

Decision-making is a process by which one chooses between two or more alternative course of actions for the purpose of attaining a goal or set of goals. A decision is the conclusion of a decision making process. Herbert A. Simon,[1] Professor of Psychology and Computer Science, Carnegie Mellon University, Pittsburgh, developed a model of decision-making. The model consisted of three steps, intelligence, design, and choice. Simon's decision-making model is based on the concept of 'satisficing', which is that people tend to settle for acceptable, rather than optimal, solutions and to attend to problems sequentially, rather than simultaneously. People tend to utilize existing repertoires rather than develop novel responses to each situation.

Decision making process involves following phases:

- Intelligence phase
- Design phase
- Choice phase

Intelligence phase – In the intelligence phase, the problem is identified and information is collected concerning the problem. This can be a long process, as the decision to be made comes from the information. In this phase, the problem situations and opportunities are identified by monitoring the organisation and its environment for problems and opportunities. The data about the problems or opportunities are gathered. For example, a finance and investment company monitors the share prices, whenever the prices are changed, the decisions whether to buy or to sell the stocks are taken. The data gathered after identification may be internal or external. Internal data are available within the organisation itself. External data involve the data collected from outside environment such as inflation, economic parameters, political news and government policies.

1. Herbert A. Simon, *The New Science of Management Decision*, Harper and Brothers, New York, 1960.

Design phase – The design phase develops several possible solutions for the problem. This phase involves finding, developing and evaluating possible courses of actions. Various alternatives are explored through building models and making appropriate calculations to predict the consequences that would arise from the particular alternatives. The mathematical model for the problem is formulated, tested and validated. It is essential to develop the criteria or the standards to compare the alternative courses of actions generated by the specified model.

Choice phase – Finally, the choice phase chooses the solution. In this phase, the selection of proper course of action from the alternatives is done. This includes search, evaluation and finding the appropriate solution to the model. Finally, a best or satisfactory decision is sought and selected, some final verification is undertaken.

In addition to the three stages identified by Simon, a post-decision stage of monitoring and evaluation should be included to follow-up the outcome of a decision. This phase is termed as implementation phase which includes actual implementation of the decision and monitoring the performance of the decision.

Another model we can discuss here is for Group-decision making. Group support systems help groups make decisions. A group makes a better decision, than even the best person in the group. They provide technical support to the group to aid in their decision-making. They aid in the brainstorming process; this improves all input and, therefore, the ultimate decision. This can be divided into a three-part process. Part one is the sharing of information and dialogue to shape the body of knowledge relevant to the current decision. Part two is a brief thinking or gestation time. This is for contemplation and thinking in depth. Group members can be sent away to think about the problem for some time say 10 minutes (important decision may require more time). Part three is a sharing of any further ideas and insights through communication, discussing the pros and cons of each alternative and finally making a decision.

The method of decision making in an individual is as varied as there are individuals making them. There are two types of decision-makers the normative or rational and the administrative model. The rational decision-maker uses probability and is unbiased. This type of decision cannot always be used; only if the problem is easy to define and the parameters can all be quantified. The administrative model may be used for decisions that are not so defined. Satisficing may be the only available means to pick the solution. To satisfice is to pick the best alternative of all available solutions. It may have both positive and negative aspects, but it is the best at hand.

Decision-Making: A Tough Challenge

Decision-making has never been easy but it has become especially challenging for today's managers. Decision-making in today's business world has become a very complex job.

Today, a decision must satisfy a number of often conflicting criteria representing the interests of different groups like creditors, shareholders, regulatory agencies etc. Factors such as customer's preferences, goodwill, employee morale, corruption and government policy etc. are difficult to measure but they often determine decision alternatives. Moreover, every decision brings with it uncertainty and chances of failure.

Decisions have not only short-term impact but they also sometimes involve long-term implications. The complexity of a decision is greatly increased when technical experts such as lawyers, tax advisers, accountants, technicians and production experts etc. are consulted before making a decision. This is usually a very time-consuming process.

These days, every important and major decision is taken in groups. But when there are people with differing backgrounds, perceptions, expectations, values etc., the decision-making process will be marked by disagreement over what is right or wrong and ethical or unethical. But for a decision, these have to be neutralised or synchronised.

Organisational Levels

The objective of 'organising' is to make human cooperation effective and the reason for levels of organisation is the limitations of the span of management. In other words, organisation levels exist because there is a limit to the number of persons a manager can supervise effectively. Moreover, the information a manager needs also depends upon the organisational level of the manager's job. In the small organisations, there are few managerial levels and the managers tend to be 'all-rounder.' In other words, they are knowledgeable about most of the organisation's functions. But as organisations grow in size, people with specialised knowledge are hired and additional managerial levels are created. Information that is satisfactory for generalists is often not acceptable when supplied to specialists. It thus, becomes necessary to supply different types of information to people at different levels.

Top management people must have in-depth understanding of the organisation's activities. Their responsibility is to take major strategic decisions and to make major policies and guidelines for the smooth functioning of the organisation. They take major decisions such as introduction of a new product, new market exploration, new plant authorisations and so on. For this, they need the type of information that will support these long-range strategic plans and decisions. These decisions have very long-term implications on the functioning of the organisation. Moreover, these decisions, once taken cannot be reversed easily without incurring huge losses.

Middle management people are responsible for making the tactical decisions. A tactical decision is concerned with the allocation of resources and establishing the control standards required to implement the top management's decisions. These decisions have a medium term impact on the functioning of the organisation.

Lower management people make the routine and operational decisions. For example, issuing stock, recording sales transactions, pay roll processing etc. These decisions have a very short-term impact on the functioning of the organisation.

As we go up higher in the organisational ladder, the decisions also become more unstructured. Lower-level management people requires access to the information systems that process transactions, produce monthly or fortnightly reports etc. But higher-level managers often require that information which is not routine and which cannot be easily anticipated in advance. They then build decision models that support them in the decision-making process.

ROLE OF INFORMATION TECHNOLOGY

Both the information and information technology have a role to play in the attainment of organisational goals as can be illustrated below:

(a) Information Technology provides us abilities to process and transmits data very efficiently. This also enables us to automate the data dependent tasks and the related physical processes.

(b) The information on the other hand allows the organisations to improve the performance by better control and coordinated decision-making. The information also provides capability to provide or sell value added services.

The synthesis of these two capabilities, therefore, opens new opportunities and an array of new means and ends. To illustrate, the corporate strategy of gaining competitive advantage in the market can be supported by technological applications developed by the organisation. At the same time, technological applications can be developed so as to gain strategic advantage. Thus, the strategic plans and information technology become mutually reinforcing team of ends and means.

The analysis of technological changes is necessary for formulating strategic goals and this analysis should be made use to identify:

(a) Ways in which changes in technology can affect strategic decisions.

(b) The innovation process which can transform abstract capabilities into tradable goods and services using technology.

(c) Attitudinal shift necessary in the organisational thinking process so that the technology is adopted as an instrument of development process by all the members of the organisation.

The first step in strategic planning is to define the nature of business clearly in the current context. The role of research and development is determined by the level of competition in the industry in which the organisation competes. The organisation may adopt a defensive strategy or proactive strategy depending on its relative position at the time of formulating the strategy. In the defensive strategy, the organisation may for instance focus on maintaining the marketability of its existing products and services; improve its organisation process to reduce cost and increase operating efficiency. This strategy might be adopted when the organisation is facing difficult situation. Whereas if the organisation has already safeguarded its position in the current level of competition and is comfortable with its existing position, it may adopt a proactive strategy to market new products, to gain competitive advantage or even diversify its activities.

The IT can be applied strategically in four different ways as follows:

- In improving productivity and performance
- In finding new ways of managing and organising
- In gaining competitive advantage
- In developing new businesses.

The role of IT would therefore depend on organisation's strategic decisions. While deciding strategic role for IT, it is necessary to distinguish between the roles of Information and Information Technology, as these two are separate resources with their own capabilities. The capabilities of information are more abstract and also strategically more important in nature.

As the information is an important resource supported by information technology, the management of information systems becomes an important management function and consists of the following three important components:

(a) Information Technology which provides capability of organising the information efficiently.

(b) Information System which decides the essential attributes of the information sought to be organised using the information technology. The planning for information system is a strategic exercise which evaluates present information system, identifies its weakness and strengths, identifies the threats to existing systems and looks forward to the opportunities from the IT. The resource allocation to IT and information system can be decided only after such an exercise.

(c) Information Management which decides the process of organising the data and information, controls the access to the information of the organisation and decides the usage of the information for business strategy.

All these three aspects are required for the information to be used in the best possible manner.

Communication And Information

Communication is possible only when there is free exchange of information; it is not mere sending or receiving of messages (information) from sender to receiver. Rather it requires right kind of information in the right proportion, in the right place, at a right time and with a feedback information loop to ensure proper communication. Human relations exist and grow only with a right balance of communication and information. It is also important to note that more information does not necessarily mean better communication. With the technological advancements we now have so much information that managing with it presents a challenge for executives and managers. Advancements in the technology have had a phenomenal effect on communication. To assist decision-making, computers can process and produce great quantities of information. Our proficiency at generating information has exceeded our abilities to find, review and understand it. It is believed that an average employee (in a big corporate house) receives about two hundered communications a day. That means a lot of paper work, discussions, e-mails etc. This is Information overload. Information overload can jeopardize timely, effective communications upon which productivity, morale and customer satisfaction depends. Moreover, in this information overload is the overload of non-essential communications. Information overload is the inability to extract needed knowledge from an immense quantity of information. It can result in the loss or distortion of information.

Wurman[2] explains that information overload can occur when an employee:

- Does not understand available information.
- Feels overwhelmed by the amount of information to be understood.
- Does not know if certain information exists.
- Does not know where to find information.
- Knows where to find information, but does not have the key to access it.

---

2. Richard Saul Wurman, *Information Anxiety*, New York, Doubleday, 1989.

All of the above responses to overload have negative consequences for communication and for job performance. It is better to design information systems and communication networks that minimize information overload than simply relying on individuals in the organisation to cope with the overload. When considering the value of providing a piece of information, the following should be the qualities of the information to be provided to management:

Qualities Of The Information

- Information must be relevant, that is, it must relate to task for what it is intended. Relevant information is pertaining to the problems, decisions and responsibilities of the recipient and it is economically justified.
- Information must be complete in all respects that is, it is sufficient to support the decision-making process without critical omissions.
- Information should be available whenever it is needed.
- Information must be reliable and accurate. Remember: incorrect information is worse than no information.
- Information should reduce uncertainly about a situation.
- Information should be timely. Delayed information may sometimes be of no value. Information should also be up-to-date. It should include all data available at the time of processing.
- Information must have surprise content that is, it must tell us something we do not already know or strongly suspect.
- Information must be in the form suitable for intended task. Information must cause us to take an action, otherwise that would not have been taken. Peter F. Drucker in his popular book *'Managing A Time of Great Change'* defines essentials of information as "Information effective in action, Information focused on results."

Data vs. Information

'Data' is the plural of the word 'datum'. The dictionary meaning of 'datum' is "any fact assumed to be a matter of direct observation." For the discipline of information systems, data is any symbol, sign or measure which is in a form which can be directly captured by a person or a machine. Data are groups of characters recognised as having the lowest level meaning. They are raw facts and opinions. When one records facts or figures, it becomes data. Data is processed and analysed to generate information that is meaningful and knowledgeable.

The most common manner in which data can have value and thereby become information, is by making a difference to a decision. A decision is a choice among alternative courses of action. Information has more meaning than data in that it is useful in present decision situation. In a simple term, one can define information as the processed form of data or in other words, 'Information' is data that has value. Informational value depends upon context. Until it is placed in an appropriate context, data is not information and once it ceases to be in that context it ceases to be information.

There is another term 'Knowledge.' The word knowledge can be defined as a body of facts and principles accumulated by mankind in the course of time; or the matrix of impressions within which an individual situates newly acquired information.

Knowledge has the highest level of meaning because it represents information that can be potentially useful in future decision situations. There is still difficulty in distinguishing data from information or knowledge, however, because a certain data element may be information to a user at one time and knowledge to the same user at a different time or place.

Finally, we must again recognize that the term 'information' is frequently used, even in the information systems discipline, in senses different from the formal definitions discussed above. In particular, 'information' and 'data' are often used interchangeably.

Types Of Information

We can categorize the information on the basis of the purpose for which the information is utilized. Depending upon the different types of decisions made by the management, information is supplied to them as per decision needs. Broadly, we can categorise information as following:

Strategic Information

Strategic Information is the information needed for long range and strategic decisions. Strategic decisions are taken by the top management people. Strategic information is required for planning and policy formulation of the business. Strategic information includes information concerned with new technologies, market availability, raw-material costs, new product developments, manpower planning and competitors etc.

Tactical Information

Tactical Information is needed to take medium range decisions and usually the time period it covers is around one year. Tactical information includes sales analyses and forecasts, financial projections, production resource requirements and the annual financial statements. Usually the data for this type of information is generally based on current activities and transactions. This requires immediate generation and processing of data. Tactical decisions require information from several sources, both internal and external, before making decisions.

Operational Information

Operational information is required for routine operations of a business organisation. This information applies to very short-term period which may vary from an hour to a few days. It includes information about current stocks-in-hand, outstanding purchase orders, inventory re-order level, and customers' outstanding orders etc. Almost all the operational information is generated internally. Operational information is derived from current activity data.

Information System

Information System is a particular discipline or branch of learning which is concerned with the application of information to organisational needs. The scope of information system includes manual, computer-based and other forms of automated procedures and applications of information technology generally.

Any system designed to provide Information with above-discussed qualities to the managers in an organisation for decision-making is called an 'Information System.' But before formalising the word 'Information System', we need to understand the meaning of the term 'System' in more detail and then look into the 'Management Information System' which is an important subset of the overall Information System in an organisation.

Systems Concept And Information Systems

The word 'System' is a common term that we use in daily life. Literally speaking, a system is a set of components that interact to accomplish some purpose or in other words, a system is a set of inter-related components or objects that work together for the overall objective of the whole.

The term system is taken from the word *'Systema'* which means an organised relationship among its components. The system can be defined as orderly grouping of interdependent components linked together according to plan to achieve a specific objective or goal. Therefore, a system is designed to achieve one or more objectives. The components/parts of a system refers to sub-system. A 'sub-system' is a system which is an element of a larger system. The large system is called a super system or supra system.

Although the word system is used in many diverse areas, all systems have some common properties — They have elements, environments and communication between their elements and with the environment. A system is designed to achieve a pre-defined objective. Also, interrelation and interdependence must exist amongst the components.

So, broadly we can define a system as an organised collection of people, machines, procedures, documents, data or any other entities such that they interact with each other as well as with the environment to reach a pre-defined goal.

Following are the major characteristics/components of a system:

Organisation: It defines the order and structure within the system. It also defines the authority and responsibility relationship, procedures and arrangement of components, sub-systems, flow of communication etc.

Communication/Interaction: It refers to the manner in which each component functions with other components of the system.

Integration: All the components of system or sub-systems are integrated together to achieve pre-defined goal of the whole system. The whole is greater than the sum of its parts. The parts are integrated into a different, more complex and generally more competent thing by virtue of their relationship to each other in pursuit of a common goal, in a common environment.

Environment: Anything outside of the system with which the system must interact in order to fulfill its goals is its environment.

Objective: In the absence of an objective there can be no system. All the components of a system try to achieve its pre-defined objectives.

Interdependence: All the parts of a system are dependent on one another. These sub-systems are properly co-ordinated and linked together according to a plan. Output of one sub-system is taken as input to another sub-system. This interdependence is of a great importance for the proper functioning of the system.

Constraints: While a system is characterized positively by wholeness and integration, it is dependent upon its component parts for optimum functioning; any internal limitations placed on the system by its component parts are constraints. Limitations placed on the system by its environment, including the supra-system to which it belongs (and the sub-systems of which it may be composed) may also be considered to be constraints.

Feedback: Feedback or self-regulation is the way a system attempts to keep a steady state in response to its environment: it acts, it affects its environment, it gets response back, it reacts to the response and so forth.

Definition Of An Information System

Information system is the study of information production, flows and use within organisations. Information system makes extensive use of information technology means. But it is very important to appreciate that its scope encompasses systems in their entirety, including manual activities, the interface between manual and automated components of systems, design aspects of IT means and economic, legal, organisational, behavioural and social aspects of systems.

Information systems overlaps with both the computer science and business management disciplines; for example, software engineering and database management and some aspects of application software development overlap with computer science and systems analysis and organisational behaviour overlap with the business-related disciplines.

The information system of an organisation may be defined as a system that serves to provide information within the organisation when and where it is needed at any managerial level. An information system is a set of people, procedures and resources that interact to satisfy the information processing needs of an organisation. During the processing the data is collected, stored, transformed and distributed in an organisation. Such a system must take the information received and store, retrieve, transform, process and communicate it using the computer system or some other means. It is not necessary that information system cannot function in the absence of computers. An information system is a logically interrelated set of business processes that accomplish organisational goals.

Components Of An Information System

Broadly, an information system includes five major components — people, data, hardware, software and procedures.

People – This includes end users and system specialists. End users are people who use an information system. System specialists are those people who develop and operate an information system. System analysts, programmers, computer operators, maintenance engineers etc. are all system specialists.

Data – Data is the raw material for any information system; it is the data which is to be processed. Data is the representation of thousands of facts and figures. This data is processed by the information system to produce information. The data which is processed and stored by the information systems may have various forms such as numbers, alphabets and other characters, text, charts, images, figures, audio and video clips, database etc. Data may be entered into information systems or generated by information systems themselves.

Hardware – Includes all physical devices and materials used in an information system. This includes computers, media, input-output devices, communication devices etc. The selection of hardware components depends on the information system's requirements such as number of users, response time and locations of users.

Software – Software component includes various programs. It can be of two basic types — system software and application software. System software includes operating systems, translators, software development tools and utilities. Application software is basically intended for end users. Application software helps users to solve day-to-day problems easily and quickly. Like hardware components, choice for the software component also depends on the information systems' requirements.

Procedures – Procedures are operating instructions for the people who use the information system. These procedures help in smooth operations of the information system. Instructions about how to check the system security and integrity, recovery from the failure, proper documentation of programs help in better management of the information systems.

TYPES OF INFORMATION SYSTEM

The role of Information Systems has developed during the years. The original conception was of automation of existing manual and pre-computer mechanical processes. This was quickly succeeded by the rationalization and integration of systems. In both of these forms, information system was regarded primarily as an operational support tool and secondarily as a service to management.

Within an organisation set up, depending on the level of management the information systems perform various activities and play certain roles. Information systems support top management in setting long-term goals, policies and achieving strategic competitive advantage. For middle management, information systems help in taking tactical decisions. For lower level management, an information system processes daily transactions.

Management Information System

There are different notions of what constitutes a Management Information System (MIS). Some people say that it is an information system which has access to detailed information regarding the functioning of the entire organisation. For some, it is a transaction or accounting system which provides transaction's summary. And many a times it is referred to as a computer-based information processing system. But more useful definitions of MIS are those which are concerned with providing timely information for management decision making, rather than the over emphasizing the role of technology or computers employed in collecting and disseminating the information. Here, we can discuss the definition given by Davis and Olson[3] :

A Management Information System, as the term is generally understood, is an integrated, user-machine system for providing information to support operations, management, and decision-making functions in an organisation. The system utilises computer hardware and software; manual procedures; models for analysis, planning, control and decision-making; and a database.

---

3. Gordon B. Davis and Margrethe H. Olson, *Management Information Systems*, McGraw-Hill, Inc., 1985.

This definition gives a complete picture of a Management Information System. It is clear from the definition that a management information system is :

- An integrated user-machine system
- The function of which is providing information
- To support the operations, management and decision-making functions
- In an organisation
- The system utilises
- Computer hardware and software
- Manual procedures
- Models for analysis, planning, control and decision-making,
- A database

Transaction Processing System

Transaction processing system (TPS) process the data generated from day-to-day business transactions. Transactions refer to the events that occur during the business routine. The data related to transactions are collected and processed. Transaction processing involves capturing, processing, updation of the data and production of results. Transaction processing systems process data in two basic ways:

1. Batch processing and
2. Real-time (On-line) processing.

In batch processing, transactions are accumulated over a period of time and then collectively processed in the batch. For example, if sales transactions are entered into accounts at the end of the day. In on-line transaction processing, the data should be processed immediately to produce the results and all updations should be made instantly. For example, in an airline reservation system a booking transaction should immediately reflect the change in central database.

Decision Support System

Decision support systems (DSS) are interactive computer-based systems, which help decision makers utilize data and models to solve unstructured problems. Decision support systems couple the intellectual resources of individuals with the capabilities of the computer to improve the quality of decisions. It is a computer-based support system for management decision makers who deal with semi-structured and unstructured problems.

A decision support systems is an information system whose primary purpose is to provide knowledge workers with information on which to base informed decisions. A decision support system provides facilities for verification of information integrity and for discovery of discrepancies in received information. Statistical methods and rule-based systems provide some tools for the analysis and pre-processing of data used for generation and evaluation of alternative decisions.

A decision support system is a computer-based system consisting of three interacting components:

(1) *A language system* — a mechanism to provide communication between the user and other components of the DSS,

(2) *A knowledge system* — the repository of problem domain knowledge embodied is DSS either as data or procedures, and

(3) *A problem processing system* — the link between the other two components, containing one or more of the general problem-handling capabilities required for decision-making.

So, a Decision Support System is:

- An information system
- Which is used by managers
- In making decisions
- And to support, not to replace people
- Used when the decision is semi-structured or unstructured
- Incorporate a database of some sort
- It also incorporate models

Expert Systems

The computer systems which store knowledge and experience of the experts and make them available to the users, popularly known as expert systems are commercially available. The parameters of arriving at an analytical decision are programmed so that the computer system can respond to the given data as an expert would respond. These systems are not yet common place and as such not a substitute for human decisions. However, they help the user to speed up the decision making process.

Artificial Neural Systems

The computer systems are gradually being evolved to emulate the human thinking process so that they can be used more effectively where simple human judgment is necessary. Computer systems which emulate human learning process by past experience called artificial neural systems, are being developed in different parts of the world. These systems are trained to analyse the patterns such as nature of transaction or image of object. These trends and patterns are later compared with the actual input pattern so as to reconstruct the entire picture or nature of transaction. These systems are expected to identify irregularities or a most suitable set of decisions based on experience. These systems are expected to speed up decision-making and spare the time of experts for better and innovative activities to be performed.

Strategic Information System

Recently an area has developed within the Information System's discipline which is generally referred to as 'Strategic Information Systems' or SIS. It is concerned with systems whose importance to the organisation extends beyond merely assisting it to perform its existing functions efficiently. A strategic information system is instrumental in the organisation's achievement of its competitive or other strategic objectives.

Strategic information system is concerned with systems which contribute significantly to the achievement of an organisation's overall objectives. In this IT age, it is found that, in some cases, information technology had been critical to the implementation of an organisation's strategy. The dominant sense in which the term is used is that a strategic information system (SIS) is an information system which supports an organisation in fulfilling its business goals.

Typically, a SIS is not necessarily a particular information system, but rather the combination of those parts of an organisation's cluster of information systems which provide information into its strategic planning processes. The functions involved include the gathering, maintenance and analysis of data concerning internal resources, and intelligence about competitors, suppliers, customers, government and other relevant organisations.

❑❑❑

16

DEVELOPMENT OF SYSTEMS

The system approach is a way of looking at how the elements of the world are organised and managed, so that pattern of interactions through which entities in it seek their goals, maintain their equilibrium and relate in meaningful ways with one another and their environment become clear. The approach states that the world is intrinsically organised in hierarchical systems and that communication, the exchange of responses and information, is essential to all living things. The form of any system will be the result of a particular system's goals, components and environment; but the principles of operation will be the same for any system.

The starting point for building a new system in an organisation, is the anticipation of future benefits by improving the operations of the old system. Next is the refinement of that idea into a specific statement of what the proposed system should accomplish, how the automation should help and what parts of the system will be automated. Analysts and designers decide how to create computer programmes that accomplish the functions on specific hardware. The technical staff either writes the programmes or buys them. The organisation acquires whatever hardware is needed. The programmes are tested to ensure the correct functions are performed in the correct manner. A team implements the new system in the organisation through a process involving user training and conversion from the previous system to new system. System then goes into operation and is modified as necessary for further improvements in business systems.

PHASES OF DEVELOPMENT OF SYSTEMS

Immaterial to the fact that the programmers, the users or an outside vendor develops the software, this general process can be summarised in terms of sequential stages or phases. The methodology of developing system is popularly called System Development Life Cycle. The following are the phases that follow a linear cycle in the process of system development life cycle:

(1) Problem Definition

Defining the problems in detail is the most important phase in the system development process. It defines the user requirements, or what the user expects the system to do and thus sets the direction for the whole project. As user has requested to change, improve or enhance an existing system, the system should be clearly understood and studied. Then, the analyst should decide whether the request is valid and feasible. The success of the system mostly depends upon how accurately a problem is defined and investigated along with the choice of solutions. When the problem is completely identified, defined and evaluated then analyst should think about the solutions. After completing the definition scope of the project, its objectives, constraints and resources available can be decided. The project proposal is submitted. After the approval of the project proposal, detail study of the system is carried out. This phase also sets the project bounds, which define what parts of the system can be changed by the project and what parts are to remain the same. The resources to be made available to the project are also specified in this phase. The output of this phase defines the user requirements. It consists of the project goal, its bounds and the terms of reference for the project. Resource limitations are also often specified at this time to indicate the funds, personnel and time available for the project.

(2) Feasibility Study

Whether the system is practically feasible — it is judged under feasibility study. A feasibility study is a test of new system's workability, fund requirements, technological know-how, impact on organisation and ability to meet user's requirements etc. In a feasibility study, the problem is studied in-depth and all the aspects of the problem are determined.

In other words, it helps in defining the scope of the system. The existing system is investigated which may be completely or partly manual. Costs are compared with anticipated benefits. A written proposal is prepared after feasibility study. The proposal should contain detailed specification of the problem, major findings and suggestions with conclusion, detailed findings in the form of methods and procedures followed with cost/benefit analysis and recommendations and conclusions which include project scheduling, target dates, etc.

Thus, a feasibility study must evaluate technical, social and economic feasibility.

Technical Feasibility — The proposed system must be evaluated from a technical viewpoint first and if technically feasible, its impact on the organisation and staff must be assessed. If compatible, social and technical systems can be devised, then they must be tested for economic feasibility. This determines whether the problem can be solved with the help of computers and if yes to what extent. If the problem can be solved with the help of computers then it should study the volume of data, trends and frequency of updating should be taken into consideration. Also, it is necessary to consult the users to see if the computerised function satisfies user objectives and can be fitted into current system operation.

Economical Feasibility — Economic feasibility deals with the cost and expenses of the proposed system. The proposed system must justify by cost and benefit criteria to ensure that effort on the project will give the best return at the earliest. The factors that are considered in the economical feasibility are the cost of operations of the existing and proposed system, cost of development of the proposed system and value of benefits of the proposed system.

Operational Feasibility — The need of various people affected by the proposed system must be taken into consideration. This includes cost of education, training, communication, salary changes, job improvement, redundancy payment and hidden costs like those caused by hostility, ignorance and fear. People are inherently resistant to change and computerisation does facilitate change. Computerisation introduces transfers, retraining and change in job status. The cost for all this should be taken into consideration.

(3) Systems Analysis

This phase is a detailed appraisal of the existing system and includes finding out how the system works and what it does. It includes finding out in more detail what the system problems are and what users require of any new or changed system. So system analysis is a detailed study of the various operations performed by a system and their relationship within and outside of the system. System analysis also defines the boundaries of the system. Following this phase, the analyst should be familiar with the detailed operation of the system and what is required of the new system. The tools used in analysis are interviews, observation, questionnaire, etc. Training, experience and common sense are required for collection of the information needed to do the analysis. Information is gathered during this phase with the help of many information-gathering techniques. These include interviewing the users, questionnaires and observation methods etc. Analysts must spend considerable time examining components, such as the various forms used in the system, as well as the operation of existing systems. Data collected in the analysis is based upon available files, decision points and transaction handled by the present system. Analysis determines whether or not a proposed system should be considered. Once analysis is completed, analyst has a complete, clear understanding of what is to be done.

This phase results in a detailed model of the system, which describes the system functions, data and information flows. The output of this phase includes detailed explanation of the user requirements and changes in the objectives for the new system.

(4) System Design

System design is the most challenging phase of the system life cycle. The system design describes the final system and the process by which it is developed. It refers to the technical specifications (similar to an architect's blueprints) that will be applied in implementing the proposed system. It also includes the construction of programmes and programme testing. Here, format of output is determined. Sample input, output is presented. Also, along with it design of input data and master files is done. Justification of the system, estimate and impact of the system on to an organisation are documented. Tools which are used in these are flow charts, report layouts, etc. Implementation plan is also decided upon. Method of data capture is also elaborated in this.

System design usually proceeds in two steps: Conceptual design and Detailed design.

Conceptual Design

During this phase, the conceptual solutions proposed by the feasibility study are looked at in more detail. Major new functions are proposed and change to existing functions defined. Important inputs and outputs are also defined and performance requirements are specified. Thus, in case of computerising the function, we may consider such decisions as whether to place the actual ordering on the computer or to have manual ordering and only use the computer for dissemination of information. At the conclusion of conceptual design, we may know what we need in order to build the system. This may include the size of the computer and the software needed to put the system together. It will also state which software can be purchased off-the-shelf and which requires new programmes to be developed. The design may also suggest whether the computer should be rented or purchased and whether programmes are to be developed using internal programmers or external software development agencies.

Detailed Design

It is only when a conceptual design is chosen that detailed design starts. During the detailed design, the database and programme modules are designed and detailed user procedures are documented. The interaction between the system users and computers is also defined. These interfaces define exactly what the user will be expected to do to use the system. Thus, the output of this phase includes a proposed equipment configuration together with specifications for the database and computer programmes. The user-manual is also prepared during this phase.

The main outputs of the design phase are input design, output design, database design and processing design. All the above should be documented. This should be presented to the management along with main features of design, the objectives, cost and benefit expected. Operational procedures and documentation should be completed. Security and audit procedures must be developed. It is the most creative phase in the system life cycle.

(5) System Development And Implementation

This is the phase in which computer-based system is constructed from the specifications prepared in the design phase. Hardware is acquired and installed during this phase. All necessary procedures, manuals, software specifications and other documentation are completed. This is analogous to the actual construction of a house from the architect's blueprints prepared in the design phase.

Implementation also covers user training, site preparation and file conversion. During the final testing, user acceptance is tested followed by user training. The user is trained and the complete system is tested for operational readiness. System testing checks the readiness and accuracy of the system to access, update and retrieve data from new files. The programmes become available, test data are read into the computer and processed against the files provided for testing. Most conversions, a parallel run is conducted where new system run simultaneously with the old system. The new system is installed, replacing the old one. Users are properly trained before they are put into the actual operation. At the end of this phase, users are provided with a working system. This includes the set of working programmes and an initialised database. In addition, any system documentation describing the programmes is also completed. The implementation phase is analogous to moving into and living in the new house that we have built. Implementation can take one of the following three forms:

- Implementation (in one go) of a computer system to replace a manual system.
- Implementation of a new computer system to replace an existing one or in other words, upgradation of the existing system.
- Implementation of a modified application to replace an existing one.

Main issues in the implementation are conversion, training and change over.

(a) **Conversion:** It means changing from one system to another. The objective is to put the tested system into operation. It involves creating computer compatible files, training the operating staff and installing the system. The conversion phase begins with a review of the project plan, the system test documentation and implementation plan.

Conversion plan is finalised and approved. Files are converted and parallel processing between the existing system and the new system is initiated.

Result of computer runs and operations for the new system are logged on a special form. Assuming no problem, parallel processing is discontinued. Implementation results are documented. Conversion completes here.

File conversion involves capturing data and creating a computer file from existing files. Once it is determined the next step is to specify the data to be converted. The files to be copied must be identified by name. This is the only way by which the accuracy of the copying will be verified.

(b) User training: The two factors are taken into consideration: user capabilities and nature of the system installed. User must be informed of how the whole system works, objectives of the system along with documentation, files and procedures. User must be instructed how to perform their new tasks. Training sessions must provide user the specific skills required in their new job. The sessions for this should be short and regular containing the practical. The tools which are useful in the user training are manuals which provide detailed information for reference, visual tools such as flow charts for better explanation.

(c) Change over: The change over from the old to the new system may take place when the system has been proved to the satisfaction of the system analyst and the other activities have been completed. Users are satisfied with the results of the system tests, training and reference manual.

(6) Evaluation And Maintenance

After installation phase is completed and user is adjusted to the change created by the system, evaluation and maintenance begins. If the new information is inconsistent with the design specifications then the changes have to be incorporated to meet the requirements. The evaluation of the system takes place after the system is implemented. It evaluates the new system to see if it has indeed satisfied the goals set for it. The system is examined to see if the benefits expected of it have been realised. If they have not, a study is made to see why not. Part of this study is the life cycle itself. It is important at this stage to go back to the original goals of the project. Post-evaluation may suggest minor changes to be made to the system. In exceptional cases, where the system is performing badly, post-evaluation may suggest a total redesign of the system.

Maintenance is necessary to eliminate errors in the system during its working life and to tune the system to any variations in its working environment. There are always some errors detected that must be corrected. Changes are made to remove these errors and deficiencies. If a major change to the system is required, a new project may have to be set up to carry out the change. This new project will then follow all the above system development life cycle activities.

Alternative Approaches for Developing Computerised Systems

The following are the three alternative models for obtaining computerised systems:

(1) Ready-Made Packages

Ready-made packages or Off-the-shelf packages are not developed within the organisation; rather they are bought from outside software development agencies. It is the most economical and expeditious approach to obtain a package which serves the basic requirements of the organisation. Although, every business firm is unique in some ways, most of the operations and functions are same in every business. For example, the payroll systems in two trading firms will be almost similar. This leads to the development of such packages that can be used by many business firms and many software development companies see it as a business opportunity to develop and sell these packages for a price. Such ready-made packages often contain a number of sub-modules and are therefore, called 'Application packages.' These come in two forms: a software package designed particularly for a special application e.g. Inventory management, Payroll etc. and the software designed for general business applications, for example, Ledger, Cash book, Trial balance etc.

The decision to buy ready-made software is best suited to the situation where the firm cannot afford the heavy development costs or the staff lack knowledge and experience to develop the package itself. Also, going for a ready-made package is recommended if it suits the complete needs of the company and economical. Today, there are wide ranges of ready-made packages available for almost every business function. A firm can purchase any one of these, which suits the budget and requirements of the company.

Advantages

(1) **Economical:** Ready-made packages are the most economical alternative for automating the system. It is very much difficult, both in terms of money and efforts, to develop the software independently.

(2) **Time saving:** A ready-made package saves the time, as there is no time lag between the development of the package and implementing it.

(3) **No overruns:** There are no chances of cost and schedule overruns because the package is readily available from the vendor.

(4) **Better documentation:** The professional software firms develop the ready-made packages. Therefore, they are usually properly documented and maintained better than in-house software developed.

(5) **Better features:** Ready-made packages are developed, keeping in mind, the entire general needs of a business firm. Therefore, the software vendor provides almost all the features and options a business firm may require.

Disadvantages

With so many advantages, the ready-made approach seems to be the best solution where the money and the time are constraints. But this approach has its limitations also. Let us discuss.

(1) **Not a complete solution:** The ready-made packages provide all the general features but may not necessarily cater to unique and independent problems of the firm. Usually, a ready made software is not possible to change, therefore, firms have to change their working system to support the software.

(2) **Maintenance cost:** The maintenance and upgradation is required from time to time for proper working of the system. The vendor provides maintenance and other servic

support but for a price. Leaving price aside, the business firm is sometimes totally dependent upon the software vendor.

(3) **No competitive advantage:** Using the ready-made packages provides no competitive advantage to the business, because the rival firms can also buy the same package.

(4) **Risks involved:** Sometimes, when the business firm is going for 100 per cent automation through off-the-shelf approach, there is always a risk that the vendor providing the software and other supports may go out of business in the future. This increases the dependability on the vendor and it also creates the problem of maintaining the software in the long run.

(2) In-House Development

Developing a system in-house from scratch is another alternative. The cost of developing the system can far exceed that of a ready-made package. The most popular and convenient method of developing the software 'in-house' is to get the programmes written, tested, installed and maintained by the regular computer staff of the company. The programmers and system developers are employed as regular staff. Being regular staff, they can study and recognise company's needs and problems in detail. They can minutely study the existing manual system. They can directly interview the end users and collect information and data about the required system. It is a costly method and can be afforded by big organisations. The biggest advantage of this approach is that it completely caters to all the software requirements of the company. Moreover, the computer staff does the maintenance and upgradation of the software from time to time.

The other approach is the 'End-user development.' In this approach, end-users of the system rather than the programmers develop programmes and procedures. The common tools for end-user development are spreadsheets, DBMSs, 4GLs, and data analysis software. In other words, the people who are not trained as programmers develop the software. This approach can be followed where the company lacks computer professionals or where the computer people are overloaded with other work and are not available. This way, in the absence of technical staff, only a limited number of processes can be automated. Or, it may work well where the problems can be isolated from each other, and the users can be given the non-programmable and easy part of the problem. In this approach the system remains full of errors and bugs. Also the maintenance and upgradation is a difficult task for the inexperienced users.

The third alternative for in-house developments is following a Joint application development approach. This approach is a combination of the above two approaches that means both programmers and the users make up a team and develop the system. This approach reduces the chances of miscommunication and misunderstandings that often persist despite lengthy user interviews during the development. Moreover, this approach boosts the morale of the employees as they are directly involved in the designing of a new system. This way, employee's resistance, if any, towards the new system or technology can be eliminated.

SOFTWARE DEVELOPMENT TOOLS

Database Technology

The introduction of database systems has enabled the organisation and retrieval of large volume of data with relative ease. The file based database technology such as dBase or any Xbase systems like clipper store the data in files and the relationship between different files is set externally by the user. The Relational database packages like Oracle, Sybase, Informix or DB2 on the other hand store the data in tables for which the relationship is defined at the time of organisation of data. These packages are designed to handle very large volume of data as well as data which can store images and user defined data types. The concept of 'data-warehouse' wherein large corporate data can be stored is becoming increasingly popular mainly due to the capabilities of these database packages. The incoming technology namely the Object Relational Databases would store the data as well as the operations on that data so as to facilitate encapsulation of data and procedures. Details of these, you will find in Module B.

Rapid Application Development (RAD) Tools

The application development environment is undergoing transformation with specialised tools which speed up the application development by automatic generation of code and use of near natural language commands. These tools make use of GUI interface provided by the operating system and help users in the market today. The trend is towards developments and use of software building to design their screens and input formats, menus and output reports. Delphi, Developer 2000, Visual C++, Visual Basic, Visual FoxPro, C#, Java are some of the RAD tools available, blocks like Java applets — which can be called as software Integrated Circuits — which can be used by the developers just as Hardware chips or Integrated Circuits.

Case Tools

The process of system engineering involves steps like planning, analysis of tasks, specific requirements, design of data structures and developing input and output requirements. This requires human ingenuity and skill. The Computer Aided Software Engineering tools (CASE) which are now available, help the designers to have a well defined and systematic approach in their efforts with facility to store the results for modifications and iterations. They also help mapping the users' requirements to machine understandable design in a manner which translates human understandable diagrams to machine understandable design. Many of these tools also have limited capability to generate code which can be subsequently developed into a database design or user interface. As the size of the application software is continuously increasing, it is imperative to use the automatic code generators to speed up the development.

Object Oriented Methodology

The latest trend in software development is towards use of Object Oriented Methodology (OOM) for designing and development of computer systems. Adoption of this methodology is gaining wider acceptance due to lack of flexibility in traditional structured methodology for development. The object oriented methodology is used in almost all the fields of application development such as Information engineering, RAD tools, CASE tools, Neural Networks, parallel computing, visual programming, virtual reality, client server architecture, etc. The analysis and designing using this method is known as Object Oriented Analysis and Designing.

The methodology aims at identifying and classifying programming objects — similar to real world objects—which have data and operations embedded together also known as encapsulation. The objects inherit the properties of the class to which they belong such as similar data structure and operations which is known as inheritance. This methodology enables higher degree of abstractions wherein the objects have set structure and set operations associated with them. The programmer makes use of library of these pre-designed objects without designing them himself. This helps in reusability of the code which improves the efficiency of application development. This technique of application development is known as Object Oriented Programming (OOP) and is now supported by many computer languages like C++, Object Pascal, Smalltalk, etc.

Automation Models

In India, big organisations need to adopt and provide value added services through technology. The automation can be useful only for big organisations having large network of branches within the country or across the globe. Traditionally, three information technology deployment models have emerged:

- Total branch automation (TBA) model in which the branches are automated without any connectivity within them.
- The distributed model provides total branch automation at the branches in stages and provides interconnectivity across selected branches.
- The centralised model centralises transaction processing, while converting branch offices into delivery channels.

These methodologies have their advantages and disadvantages. In a TBA and distributed automation environment, companies have the comfort of easing themselves into automation both in terms of initial capital investment and implementation effort. The advantages of the centralised model of automation include centralised operational control combined with lower operational costs. MIS processes become both timely and complete. Finally, scalability is easily addressed.

A third option in automation that is increasingly finding interest is the application service provider (ASP) option. The ASP option offers large benefits at low costs as it delivers the benefits of a centralised working solution without large upfront investments in IT or specialized skills training. The ASP is responsible for providing the applications, managing the data centre, ensuring uptime and providing upgrades. This streamlines the business processes of the bank and allows it to concentrate on it core operations.

Most of the big organisations now have realised the limitations of TBA and distributed branch automation strategy, mainly absence of meaningful and timely MIS and high cost of operation. These processing models do not facilitate the deployment of Net-based services. When considering the centralised processing model, several important facets need to be considered. These are the critical attributes of the centralised technology architecture.

Increasingly, companies are also looking for solutions that enable online, real time transaction capabilities for anytime and anywhere service to the customer. The technology of the future will need to be Web-centric, use open standards of connectivity and delivery of services/

products to customers through multiple channels. Delivering services/ products via desktops, ATMs, WAP phones and hand-held devices would be a key technology attribute.

Finally, integrating business intelligence capabilities into the automation process will also become increasingly important. More and more, big companies are choosing to implement data warehouses with data consolidated from diverse sources into one easy-to-use reference database for time-critical decision support. The advantages are clear. Companies are able to track and respond to business trends and analyse data according to business dimensions. A business intelligence package allows companies to focus on customer acquisitions, retain profitable accounts, track customer needs, identify cross-selling opportunities and provide customised service. The customer thus gets additional facilities, while this increases the value of the organisation also.

Indian corporate giants today require technology that will quickly enable delivery of new and existing products/services over varied channels, a high degree of customer intimacy and proactivity. They also require system integration services that quickly assemble best of breed components to provide flexible, scalable and globally deployable E-solutions. These solutions need to be open and inter-operable with existing back-office systems and that can be implemented with lower total cost of ownership.

❑❑❑

17

DATA COMMUNICATION

We all know that communication means exchange of information, ideas, thoughts, etc., between two or more persons using some medium. The problem in communication arises when there is a physical distance between the persons causing a barrier in communication. In the ancient times, there was nothing to overcome the long-distance barrier to communication. But today, in this IT age, physical distance is no more a barrier to communication.

Today's communication age began with the telegraph. It was the first instrument to transform information into electrical form and transmit it reliably over long distances. The original telegraph did not use a key and sounder. Instead, it was a device designed to print patterns at a distance. The transmitter had code slugs shaped in hills and valleys. These patterns were printed at a distance by the receiver. The late 1870s and early 1880s were full of inventive breakthroughs and rapid advancements in communication technologies. Fast-shutter motion photography, the first crude motion pictures, the electric light, the telephone, and vast improvements in the telegraph were the developments in those years. Alexander Graham Bell invented the telephone in 1876. With the invention of telephone, a new area of knowledge called 'telecommunication' opened up.

The confluence of computer and telecommunication technology has been the most important and far reaching development in information technology. In the earlier years of twentieth century, the communication technology had made it possible to disseminate the information quickly using telecommunication media like telephone, radio, television, etc. After the advent of computers in the 1950s, the users had to approach the large computer centres and submit their work to the computer for overnight processing and get the output. With advent of personal computers, this concept gradually changed to computers moving to the users desktop and computers doing independent work.

The concept of Data communication emerged as a combination of computer and communication technologies enabling two computers to get interconnected to each other just as two people are connected over the telephone. When two or more independent computers are exchanging information they are considered to be interconnected to each other. This interconnection that is 'login' onto the other computer, submitting the job as well as moving the data files is known as Data Communication or computer network. In a network, the connection to other computer, submitting the job or moving data files etc. is done 'explicitly' by the user and both the computers remain independent entities doing their own processing and the user retains his control over his own computing resources. Thus, a computer network combines the accuracy and speed of the processing by the computer with the speed of communication provided by telecommunication.

A set up wherein a central computer controls the terminals connected to each other is not considered a network of computers as the terminals are dependent on main computer and have no independent processing capability. Similarly, a distributed system with multiple processors can be considered to be a special case of network rather than a full-fledged computer network since here the operating system selects the processor, moves the data files and gets the job executed.

Why Data Communication?

The objective of data communication is to enable different users to connect their computers, share their data as well as submit jobs to other computers, get the results and share all resources for co-operative computing. The resources include tangible resources like hardware or software or intangible resources like views and ideas.

The main reasons behind the need of data communication can be discussed as under:

(A) Sharing Of Resources

The networking of computers enables sharing of hardware, software and other resources of the organisation by different users who may be located over a geographical area.

(i) Hardware : Networked computers can share different hardware components such as hard disks, floppy drives, printers, CD-ROM drives, Tape backup units, fax modems, plotters, scanners or any device that can be connected to the personal computer. Some peripheral devices like fast printers can be directly attached to the network and shared by all the users without needing a personal computer for attachment. This enables optimum utilisation of hardware available in the organisation and reduces the need to purchase multiple numbers for different users thereby reducing the investment in hardware.

(ii) Software : The network of computers enables storage of multiple copies of the programmes and data so that these can be used across the network. It also allows use of software resources in the networked computers thereby optimising the resource utilisation and reducing the investment. Although not all commercial software packages can be used on network and some commercial software packages have legal requirements to share the copies, the networking can technically help in sharing these resources after fulfilling the legal requirements. Further, the software developed within the organisation as well as the data generated within the organisation can be shared within the restrictions imposed by the organisation.

(iii) Sharing of work : The network enables the users to submit jobs to each other for further processing. This enables the automation of workflow wherein the users can add their part of the function to the transactions and pass on the work to next person in the chain for further process addition. In case of complex reports, different parts of the reports can be independently handled by different persons and complete report can be shared on the network. This can be considered to be a major advantage of network.

(B) Cost Reduction

It provides sharing of costly equipments like laser printer etc. and makes better utilisation of resources. There are generally more than one computer in an office and each requiring printing facilities. Instead of having one printer per computer, one printer through network system can be used by all. Better utilization of costly computer is possible by providing many interactive terminals to different users. A computer with large processing power may remain partly utilized because only one person can work in it. When inter-connected, a number of persons can work simultaneously and utilize the full processing power. The network enables sharing resources of small size personal computers and distribution of workload of different computers. This sharing of tasks makes the network of small computers become as effective as the mainframe computers with large storage and processing capacity. The cost of personal computers networked to each other being much lower than the mainframe computers, the total cost of all networked personal computers performing similar task is much lower to the mainframe computers doing similar job. The network, therefore, provides a cost effective solution to mainframe computers.

(C) Availability and Reliability

As the networking of computers allows storage of multiple copies of data and programmes, it is possible to handle accidental failure of the hardware and the software. As all computers in the network retain their individual computing resources, it is possible to restore data, programmes quickly in case of problem with hardware or software. This improves the overall reliability of the system by building redundancy and ensures greater availability of the system in normal circumstances.

(D) Communication Media

The technique of data communication offers an excellent medium of communication for the people so as to exchange their notes and ideas over the computer network. In case of localised network, the mail facility is built into the networking software which enables communication within network users. In case of long distance networks, the cost of network communication is lower as the communication lines need not be exclusively blocked and the lines are used only during actual communication. Most of the networks provide acknowledgement of messages received and since these are sent on telecommunication channels, the messages are sent speedily. This cost effective and reliable communication among people helps exchange of views and ideas can add value to the work done by the individuals by addition of a team's contribution to the work. As sharing of views and ideas improves the overall productivity and effectiveness of the organisation, this can be considered to be most important advantage of the network. This can be further ascertained by exponential rise in the use of Internet to access information and send electronic mail which is fast replacing traditional mail system.

Incidentally, in case of computers even though sitting next to each other, inter-connection is necessary to share the data and other services between them. It is interesting to note that earlier the technological development in telecommunication and computer systems proceeded in a parallel manner, following their own individual paths. But, in 1970s, it was realized that joint collaboration between the two disciplines would benefit each other and that has actually happened, with communication through wires and non-wires and between computers, attaining newer horizons almost every year. This joint movement became most useful after the microcomputers came into use with their superior capabilities at lower cost.

Components Of A Network

The computer-based networks have two main components namely —

(a) The computers are used for data processing, data communication and storage of data and programmes. These Computers are also called Hosts or Data Computing Equipments (DCE).

(b) The communication part used for connecting one computer (host) to other. This part is called 'communication subnet' or simply 'the subnet'.

Communication Subnet

The subnet or communication subnet has two components:

(i) Switching devices: These devices are used for switching data signals from one host to another host. When the signal to be transmitted arrives on incoming lines, the switching devices, like the automatic telephone exchange, select the proper outgoing line and forwards the data signal on these lines. These devices are popularly referred to as Interface Message Processors or IMPs.

(ii) Transmission lines: The lines which carry data signal from one host to another are called transmission lines. These lines are also called as circuits or trunks or channels. The speed as well as efficiency of networking depends upon the speed at which transmission lines can transmit the data. The unshielded twisted pairs, optical fibres; radio links are some of the examples of the transmission lines. The communication subnets are designed for either a broadcast message (broadcast channels) or point-to-point communication between two hosts (point-to-point channels).

Network Communication

The networks are used for either point-to-point communication between two computers or for a broadcast communication from one computer to all computers. Both type of communications use Interface Message Processors or IMPs and Transmission lines.

(i) Point-to-point communication: The point-to-point communication between two computers is used for data transmission, processing and information sharing. Since this adds value to the transaction processed most of the computer networks in banks need point-to-point channels or communication.

This communication is done using point-to-point channels which need numerous cables or leased lines to connect pairs of IMPs (Interface Message Processors). When the computer network provides point-to-point communication by establishing physical or logical connection between two computers such communication is called connection-oriented service.

The communication between two IMPs can be direct or through intermediate IMP or IMPs. Whenever intermediate IMPs are used for transmission, a data signal or a message or a packet is received and stored in entirety till the requisite output line is received and forwarded thereon to the next IMP. This is called Store And Forward Or Packet Switched Subnet. The point-to-point subnet employs different communication topologies such as star, ring, tree, complete mesh, intersecting rings or irregular mesh. The choice of IMP topology depends on whether the network is localised or long distance.

(ii) Broadcast communication: In a broadcast system, all the machines on the network share a single communication channel. The message may be broadcast for all the receivers or for a single receiver only. In case it is broadcast for only one receiver, the address is read by the receiving machines and ignored by those machines for which it is not meant. As for such communication, exclusive connection is not necessary, such service is called a connectionless service.

A special type of broadcasting is 'Multicasting' where the message is meant for a group of receivers. The groups can be organised by devising the addresses such that they form a group. The broadcast could be of three types as a Bus, Radio or Ring broadcast. In a Bus broadcast, at any point of time one machine acts as the master where others act as receivers. The conflict of two machines broadcasting at a given time is resolved having a system at the centre or distributed system at each host.

In the satellite or radio broadcast system, all hosts have an antenna which transmits message to a central transmitter and receives the signal from the transmitter.

In a ring broadcast topology each bit of message travels around the net on its own and conflict of simultaneous transmission is resolved using different techniques.

The broadcast subnet may be either static or dynamic. In a static broadcast, available time is divided among all hosts and a host can broadcast when it is its turn to broadcast. In the dynamic allocation, the allocation is decided either at a central location by receiving and storing all the requests and deciding which one to broadcast next or the allocation can be decided at a distributed location using a well defined algorithm which would avoid clash of two broadcast messages at the same time.

Analog And Digital Communication

Information that is stored within computer systems and transferred over a computer network can be divided into two categories: data and signals. Data are entities that convey meaning within a computer or computer system. If you want to transfer this data from one point to another, either by using a physical wire or by using radio waves, the data has to be converted into a signal. Signals are the electric or electromagnetic encoding of data and are used to transmit data. Like data, signals can be analog or digital. Typically, digital signals convey digital data, and analog signals convey analog data. However, you can use analog signals to convey digital data and digital signals to convey analog data.

Transporting data from host computers to other host computers is the main function of computer networks. Data communication is, therefore the process of transporting data from one point to another over the communication channels. There are two essential requirements of the process of data communication —

(a) Ability of the device to transmit or receive data,

(b) Ability of the device to correctly understand and interpret the data received over the network.

For successful data communication between the computers, it is necessary that the transmitting computer should correctly send the data and check for proper receipt of the data at the other end. Similarly, it is also necessary that the receiving computer should properly receive the data and send the confirmation for proper receipt or failure to properly receive the data back to the transmitting computer. The success of the computer network depends on proper data communication.

The data or signal to be communicated could be either in the form of continuously changing sinusoidal waveform or in pulses of high and low voltages. Normally all natural forms of communication like the human sound waves, light waves or electromagnetic waves are sinusoidal waves and are called analog signals as the signals are continuously changing waveforms. As against this, all modern computers work on digital or binary waveforms. These computer can understand only binary logic i.e. presence or absence of a electrical signal. A voltage level above certain threshold is defined as 'on state as one level' and below that level as 'off state as zero level.'

The analog signals have three different characteristics namely the Amplitude which measures the strength or height of the wave, frequency or number of cycles in one second and relative state or angle of a wave with reference wave. The analog waveforms are more stable waveforms as these are natural and contain minimum energy. Human sensory organs are designed to interpret only analog signals; these signals are used for audio and video communication for the human beings. Although the strength of these signals fall as they travel through the transmission media, such fall is less as compared to digital signals. As the response of such signals to other devices like amplifier depends upon the frequency of the signal, it is often difficult to reproduce the signals in their exact original form. Such signals are also prone to errors from noise and interference. However, such signals can be multiplexed so that more signals can be sent over the same transmission media which is the main advantage analog signals.

The digital waveforms on the other hand are less stable and tend to break down in sinusoidal forms of primary frequency and its multiple frequencies called harmonics. Thus, digital signals can therefore be viewed as a series of main frequency and its harmonics popularly known as 'Fourier Analysis' after the mathematician who gave mathematical expression for such break up. Such signals suffer greater attenuation as compared to analog signals as the waveforms are not natural and have tendency to breakdown in natural form. However, due to its binary nature (on and off state of signals), it is easier to reproduce the digital signals and therefore there are lesser errors from noise and interference. It also requires less expensive equipments for transmission and reception due to simplicity of the original signal. Further, as digital computers can easily understand and interpret these signals, these are better suited for computer-based communication. The latest approach is to break down analog signals like audio signals into numerous digital signals and compose them again into analog form at the other end thereby improving the exactness or fidelity of the signal.

ELEMENTS OF DIGITAL COMMUNICATION

As already discussed above, the digital signalling method is more suitable for computer-based communication. A digital signal is composed of following elements.

Protocol

The term protocol is used to refer to the set of rules that govern the communication between nodes.

Bits

Electrical pulses of ON and OFF state i.e. presence or absence of electrical signal above or below certain threshold voltage are known as 'bits' of electrical signal. In vocal communication, these can correspond to vowels.

Bytes

The combination of a succession of eight bits is called a byte. A byte is a convenient means of representing up to 256 symbols, such as letters, decimal digits and punctuation marks. In written communication these can be compared with an alphabet.

Packet

Larger sets of symbols require larger combinations. At higher levels, groups of bits or bytes are clustered into groups called packets or datagrams. A set of one or more packets is used to represent a message which is directly useful to the receiver. A packet is a basic division of data sent over the network. It normally consists of a few hundred bytes of data and a header. The header contains information about the type of packet, network address etc. The size and format of the packet depend on protocol and frame used.

Frame

The concept of frame is used in Ethernet networks. The streams of bits are organised in a data unit and checksum is computed for each frame. This checksum is used to detect the error in incoming frame. Character count, starting and ending characters, starting ending flags and physical layer coding violation are some of the commonly used techniques for identifying the new frames.

Communication Channels

For communication between two or more computers, a communication channel is required. The communication or transmission channel is a path which carries electric signals generated by one computer to another in such a manner that the latter can receive, decode and use it. All communications media can be divided into two categories: physical or conducted media, such as wires and radiated or wireless media, which use radio waves. Conducted media include twisted pair wire, coaxial cable and fiber optic cable. In wireless transmission, various types of electromagnetic waves, such as radio waves are used to transmit signals. The communication channels that connect nodes may be implemented using any number of technologies. Any node can transmit a message to any other node, along the communications channels via the intermediating nodes.

When designing or updating a computer network, the selection of one type of media over another is an important issue. The principal factors one should consider in this regard are cost, speed, expandability, distance, environment and security.

The different communication channels generally used are as below:

(A) Copper Wire or Twisted-pair Wire

The oldest, simplest and most common type of conducted media is twisted-pair wire. Copper or twisted-pair wires are the wires commonly used in the local telephone system. Two wires forming a pair are twisted together at 6 turns per inch to eliminate electro-magnetic interference, which contribute to noise during communication. It is the cheapest channel and can be used over short-distance without loss of signal level. Generally, a group of wires is bunched together to form a cable.

(B) Co-axial Cable

It consists of a single metal conductor covered around by a layer of insulating material, which is again covered with a fine wire net called screen and finally a jacket of protective insulating material is put on it. The screen is connected to the earth to prevent external electro-magnetic interferences to distort the signals. It is used for both digital and analog transmission. It can be used over fairly long distance. It is much superior but costlier than the twisted-pair cables.

(C) Fibre-optic

Fibre-optic are the hollow cables made with flexible strands of fibreglass which transmits data using light beams. This media has a very high bandwidth but it may be very expensive and slow to the level of local telephone exchanges, particularly for domestic locations in suburbs, provincial cities and towns. Fibre optic cable is capable of transmitting data at over 100 Gbps (100 billion bits per second) over several kilometers. The fibre-glass itself being insulating material, do not radiate energy, provide electro-magnetic immunity and safety with low loss of transmitted data's energy level. These are cables with small diameter and quite light.

(D) Microwave

Data can also be transmitted without using wires with the help of microwaves. Microwaves are used for some transmissions as an alternative to long-haul cable and are valuable in areas where it is difficult or undesirable to lay cable, but it has limited capacity. Microwaves are the electro-magnetic waves with wavelength and frequency varying from 300,000 MHz to 3000 MHz. These are extensively used in video transmission as well as telephone system, in which a broad range of frequencies called UHF (ultra high frequency 300-3000 MHz) and VHF (very high frequency 30-300 MHz) are used; coming in the range called infrared.

(E) Radio Wave

Radio waves are also electro-magnetic waves but with a low frequency range of 3 KHz to 30 MHz. The greatest advantage is that these are reflected by the ionosphere and so can be used to cover longer distances without repeater station. These are extensively used for audio-transmission.

Bandwidth

In a general sense, this term 'Bandwidth' describes information-carrying capacity. It can apply to telephone or network wiring as well as system buses, radio frequency signals and monitors. Bandwidth is most accurately measured in cycles per second, or hertz (Hz), which is the difference between the lowest and highest frequencies transmitted. But it is also common to use bits or bytes per second instead. Bandwidth indicates the difference between the upper and lower frequencies, that is, the range of frequencies of signals that can be transmitted over the channel using electro-magnetic waves without any loss in power-level. Any electro-magnetic wave can be broken down into a number of symmetrical waves called 'pure tones' having different frequencies. Higher the bandwidth, the greater the volume of data that can be transmitted per unit time. Depending on bandwidth, channels are classified as narrow-band, voice-band and broadband types. Narrow-band has a very low bandwidth, in which data can be transmitted at a rate of about 5 to 30 characters per second and these are used in telegraph transmission. The next higher level, called voice-band are used in normal telephone lines with the frequency range of 300 -3400 Hz for voice transmission and their capacity is about 1000 characters per second. The channel with highest bandwidth is called broadband or wide-band channel, which is being increasingly used even in telephone systems; which has a capacity of about 100,000 characters per second. All the three classifications stated above are used in analog transmission, where electro- magnetic waves are used as signals.

In broadband transmission, the signal to be sent is integrated with a special high frequency wave called carrier-wave and this is transmitted, the actual wave being isolated at the receiving end from the carrier-wave.

There is another way of transmitting signals and this is called baseband transmission, in which either the electro-magnetic wave or digital pulses are transmitted without any change in the original form as generated, but this is possible only over a short distance. For long distance transmission, the digital signals are converted to analog waves and transmitted by carrier waves.

In digital data transmission, the speed of transmission, the data-transfer rate is expressed in number of bits per second, which is called bit-rate. There is another unit for denoting the speed of transmission, called baud-rate, which denotes the number of times the electro-magnetic state of a data transmission line changes per second. For example, if the magnitude of the signal value changes from positive to negative once in a second, the baud rate will be one; If the bit-rate of each signal element is equivalent to 1 bit of information, then both baud rate and bit-rate are equal, otherwise not. The relation between the two depends on the coding method used. Quite often, by mistake, these are described as the same.

Serial and Parallel Communication

(a) Serial communication: When different bits of data are sent over a single line serially, it is known as serial communication. Serial communication is slow as compared to parallel communication but is more economical as it requires only one line and free from skew as compared to parallel communication for transporting data over long distances and therefore, used for long distance communication.

(b) Parallel communication: When all the eight bits of a byte are sent simultaneously over different lines and an additional clock bit is sent to the receiver, it is known as parallel communication. The purpose of clock bit is to notify the receiver that all the bits are present on the respective lines. The parallel communication is very fast and is most suitable for short distance communication such as printer or Video Display Unit (VDU). However, it is not suitable for long distance communication because of the cost of having multiple lines required and the mismatch in signal over different lines due to mismatch of speed. Such mismatch in signal arising out of difference in speed over different lines is known as 'skew.'

As you know, a group of bits are used together to enable different codes to be developed to represent various characters and generally, 8-bits are used together which is called a byte. Suppose the codes for capital A is 01000001. Now these 8 bits can be sent in a transmission channel in two ways. We can have 8 wires to transmit the 8 bits simultaneously and so the receiver will know that 'A' has been transmitted. On the other hand, we can use only one wire and send the bits one after another, starting with the MSB (Most Significant Bit) and the receiver will know by the sequence of bits received that 'A' has been sent. This method is called Serial Transmission, with the earlier one being called Parallel Transmission, where all bits forming a character move in parallel. Leaving aside other factors, parallel transmission is much costlier because of the large number of wires required. All long distance transmissions are serial transmission — parallel transmission being used for short distances, such as from the computer to the parallel printer attached to it.

Data Modulation And Demodulation

To send data from one computer to another with broadband transmission, the digital signals have to be converted to appropriate electro-magnetic waves. Along with digital to analog conversion, the original signal (base band) is mixed with a carrier frequency by Amplitude, Phase, or Frequency Modulation. This is done by a device called modulator. At the receiving end, the analog signal is again converted back to digital pulses and separated from the carrier wave by using a demodulator

Digital signals are prone to faster attenuation as compared to analog signals. Also, analog signals can be multiplexed so as to send more than one signal at a time over the same channel. As already discussed the analog signals have three different characteristics namely the amplitude, frequency and phase. These characteristics are changed so as to encrypt the analog signal with digital signals and transmit. The analog waveform used to carry the digital signal or data is called carrier and the process of varying or encoding the analog signal is known as Modulation. The reverse process that separating digital signal from analog signal is called Demodulation.

In 1981, Hayes Micromodem brought the MOdulator/DEModulator (MODEM) to the market for PCs. The modem had been invented at AT&T Bell Labs in 1960 to connect mainframes and minicomputers. Hayes's modem allowed PCs to communicate with each other. The combined device of modulator-demodulator is called a modem in short.

(a) Amplitude modulation: If the amplitude or strength of the carrier analog signal is modified in two steps i.e. high amplitude and low amplitude, it can interpret as one or zero state of the digital signal at the receiving end. This is known as Amplitude Modulation and method of encoding is known as Amplitude Shift Keying.

(b) Frequency modulation: When the frequency of the carrier analog signal is varied or encoded as high frequency or low frequency, the signal can be decoded into digital one or digital zero. This is known as frequency modulation and method of encoding is known as Frequency Shift Keying.

(c) Phase modulation: When the phase of the carrier signal is varied or encoded to represent digital one or digital zero, it is known as phase modulation and method is known as Phase Shift Keying.

SYNCHRONOUS AND ASYNCHRONOUS COMMUNICATION

The serial communication can be done in asynchronous or synchronous mode. The choice of mode depends on the convenience and suitability.

(A) Synchronous Communication

When the data is transmitted from the sender to a receiver, there has to be a definite way for the receiver to know what it has received — there are two ways by which the receiver can properly decode the data received; this is called transmission mode. In one mode, the clock timing signals of the sender are received and perfectly synchronised by the receiver's system and then the data flows from sender to receiver in regular and correct manner. This method can be used for both serial and parallel transmission. In serial transmission the bits are synchronised by the protocols defined by CCITT (Consultative Committee on International Telephone and Telegraph) in X.25 series and in parallel transmission the bytes are synchronised by the protocol like BSC (Binary Synchronous Communication) X3.28 series developed by ANSI (American National Standard Institute). This mode of transmission is called Synchronous Transmission. Under this mode, each block of code transmitted is preceded by a number of special signals called synchronisation signals. The transfer rate is very high, but storage buffers are required in the channels to receive the data transmitted. It does not call for any additional characters to be sent to identify the data.

This is implemented using following three methods:

(i) Guaranteed state change : In this method the clocking information is embedded in the data signal so that there is guaranteed transition in the signal at predefined interval of time. This helps the receiver to adjust its internal clock.

(ii) Separate clock signal :

In this method, a separate clocking lead is used to transmit clock signal from the sender and the receiver. This method is expensive and less efficient but more effective for shorter transmissions.

(iii) Oversampling : In this method, the incoming signal is sampled much faster as compared to data rate to decide whether the transmitter and receiver are synchronised or otherwise.

(B) Asynchronous Communication

In an asynchronous communication, each character is transmitted separately over the line. Each character is preceded by START bit and succeeded by a STOP bit. These START and STOP bits help the sender and the receiver to synchronise the transmission. The signals are sent in irregular time intervals. As there is no clocking signal within or accompanying the data channel to synchronise transmission and reception, it is called Asynchronous. In asynchronous transmission, additional numbers of bits over and above the actual data bits have to be sent for identification and this is called 'overhead'. So, it is not suitable for transmission of large data at regular intervals. Because of its simplicity, it is generally used for small volume of data, the complex process of synchronisation being absent. Another advantage of asynchronous transmission is that it does not require local storage at terminals —it is transmitted as soon as the signal is generated. The transmissions from a mouse or to a printer are all asynchronous transmissions. Because of the overhead, to compute the data transfer rate in characters per second, the bits per second rate is to be divided by the number of bits used to form a character, which includes the overhead bits.

Circuit Elements

Since communication involves two sources, the ideal circuit condition is when both can simultaneously communicate to each other, like we do in our local telephones. When one person is saying something in the mouthpiece, his earpiece of the set is in attendance to receive what the other person would say. This is called full-duplex circuit — providing a simultaneous two-way flow of signals. The other alternative could be, when a single circuit is used, both being not able to talk to each other simultaneously — only one can talk at a time with the other listening. This is called a half-duplex system which is generally followed in International Subscriber Trunk Dialling System (ISTD) etc; — the signal flows in both direction but only one at a time. There is a third choice, when one can only talk and cannot listen — the signal flows in one direction only. A class example would be the loudspeakers blaring at us. This is called a simplex circuit.

Communications Systems

In a communication system, for data transmission, either you can have a number of terminals which are connected to a computer or a system where several computers are interconnected; in some cases these computers having their own terminals. The simplest method of connection between a terminal and a computer is by using a direct link between the two for point-to-point communication. But since the costs of the communication links are quite high, a number of terminals are usually connected to a single line, the computer being at the other end. But in such a case, only one terminal can be in communication with the computer at a time using the link, each being identified by a unique address. To ensure that only one terminal communicates at a time, a system called 'polling' is used. The system of having more than one terminal connected to a line is called multi-point or multi-drop system. Often multiplexing is used with multi-drop system to achieve economy and ease in communication.

Computer Networks

In network terminology, the points of inter-connection between links are called *nodes*, where a number of links denoting different routes converge. The node can be a computer system or a mere junction point, a sort of exchange where different links meet. At a node, a link containing an incoming message is connected to anyone of a number of outgoing links; but only one at a time. This connection of temporary need-based nature is called switching and there are two types of switching systems, called circuit switching and packets switching. In circuit switching, a direct connection is established between the incoming and outgoing link, allowing the message to flow as it is. For example, in our ordinary local telephone system if you are making a phone call from a number to another number, the link is made directly by circuit switching and whatever communication takes place moves from one end to another directly. In packet-switching system, the message is divided into a number of small packets, which form the physical unit of transmission, the total message being a logical unit of transmission. Each packet is transmitted from one node to another whenever the required link is free without establishing actual physical connection between the sender and the receiver. The packets are stored at the nodes till these are transmitted, minimizing transmission costs.

If each node, comprising computer systems, are all connected to each other, then for each n nodes there will be (n-1) connections, the total number of links being n (n-l). However, since connection between say Node 1 and Node 2 is same as that between Node 2 and Node 1, the total number of inter-connections required would be n (n-l)/2 links for full interconnection. To eliminate the need for so many costly links, switching system is used.

Multiplexing

Under the simplest conditions, a medium can carry only one signal at any moment in time. Many a times, however, we want a medium to carry multiple signals at the same time. Therefore, from economic considerations, a large number of low-speed signals can be combined together and then sent across a high-speed transmission channel — at the receiving end the individual signals being again segregated. This technique of transmitting multiple signals over a single medium is called multiplexing. Here, multiplex means many-to-one. Its reverse is demultiplexing. Three basic methods of multiplexing used are called Space Division Multiplexing (SDM), Frequency Division Multiplexing (FDM), and Time Division Multiplexing (TDM).

In Space Division Multiplexing, the individual channels are grouped together to form one channel with a high bandwidth. The twisted-pair wires, co-axial cables, or even fibre-optic cables are bunched together to form a cable of large diameter, carrying a number of different signals. This is extensively used in local telephone systems.

Frequency division multiplexing is the assignment of non-overlapping frequency ranges to each user of a medium. So that multiple users can share a single medium, each user is assigned a channel. A channel is an assigned set of frequencies that is used to transmit the user's signal.

Time division multiplexing directly supports digital signals. In time division multiplexing, sharing of the signal is accomplished by dividing available transmission time on a medium among users—it is almost like time-sharing of computer systems.

Polling

In a multi-drop system, which contains a number of terminals connected to a computer, the technique of finding out which terminal is going to transmit data is called polling. In one method, called roll-call polling, the computer asks each terminal in turn whether it wants to transmit or not and acts accordingly. In the other method, called hub-polling, the computer sends a 'poll-train' to a terminal, which then forwards it to the next, The terminal which has received the poll-train can transmit data to the computer.

Communication Protocol

The rules, regulations and procedures relating to the functioning of a communication system using a network are called Communication Protocols. It is an attempt to ensure that equipments of different manufacturers of different countries can be used without any problem for communication; making them compatible to each other. The protocol generally provides for:

- How to establish connection and end it during data transmission, called a session.
- How the messages are to be framed for onward transmission. Well, when we send a simple letter, we use envelopes to secure it and so is done with the data transmitted.
- How errors are detected and what steps are taken to correct them by re-transmission, but without duplication, etc.

- How to find out which message has been sent by whom and for whom.
- How the transmission continues during a session.

Network Protocols

It is absolutely essential for various devices including computers used in network operations to be compatible to each other, so that effective communication can take place between different systems. In order to make interconnection of different communication and computer systems compatible to each other, the International Standards Organisation (ISO) has developed network protocols, which is called Open System Interconnection (OSI). Under these recommendations, the total communication system including hardware and software have been classified into seven different interdependent layers; each layer having a distinct role to play and providing the levels at which compatibility between different systems can be achieved. It is called a layered protocol. Each layer is dependent on the adjacent layers only and communicates with it. From the user's application point of view, the topmost layer is called the Application Layer and the bottom-most layer is called the Physical Layer. The layers, starting with the bottom most are:

(A) Physical Layer

This is the layer at which direct physical connection between different nodes take place through links — between the source and destination which are the two extreme nodes, there can be many nodes forming the transmission channel. It defines the mechanical and electrical characteristics of the physical equipments like voltage, pin-connections and the media used for transmission. The recommendations provide for serial and parallel transmission, using half-duplex and full-duplex lines for point-to-point and multi-point configurations. In this layer bits of strings are transmitted from one node to the other.

(B) Link Layer

The link layer protocols specify how the node interfaces with the communications channel. They convert the bits that make up packets into signals on channels. Through a physical port, socket, or plug, they transmit a signal onto a channel provided by a medium such as twisted-pair copper wire, co-axial cable, fibre-optic cable, or a digital cellular phone network. This layer does coding of data at the transmission end and its decoding at the receiving end. Here the messages are converted to frames or blocks of data, which are provided with address of source and destination and error-checking procedures; the layer defining the access control mechanism. It is responsible for error-free transmission, for which it may retransmit a frame; also ensuring that duplication does not takes place. It controls the speed of transmission to ensure that the receiver gets the frames at the right speed even though the sender sends it at higher or lower speeds.

(C) Network Layer

The network layer protocols specify how packets are moved around the network. This includes the important questions of how to address the node that is being sought and how to route each packet to that node. It defines the switching mechanism, which is usually packet switching and also defines selection of the best route for transmission. Here, the frames are converted into packets, which are actually transmitted over the network. It controls movement of data from one node to another along the way, from source to destination and *vice versa* and ensures verification of the receipts of the packets sent to the destination. It selects the route along which the packets are to be sent, without congesting the line. It also ensures that packets are sent in proper sequence. When the packets are sent via different routes, it becomes quite complex to ensure that at destination these are available in sequence.

(D) Transport Layer

The transport layer protocols specify whether and how the receipt of complete and accurate messages is to be guaranteed. In addition, if the message is too large to be transmitted all at once, it specifies how the message is to be broken down into segments. This layer provides how connection between the source and the destination will be made and broken, giving an impression that actually the transmitter and the receiver are directly connected to each other, it is known as virtual connection. Suppose you want to access a particular data file from your computer, which is stored in the main computer, then when you use the necessary commands the file becomes available to you. You would feel that you are directly working with the file, but physically it would not be so and this is where the transport layer comes into play. It provides inter-network routes.

(E) Session Layer

This layer manages the resources allowing interactive communication. It ensures that you have proper authority to get the data file which you have requested for and then establishes the set up so that two parties can communicate with each other. It decides the nature of inter-connection like whether it will be half-duplex or full-duplex. If a link breaks down during a session it arranges for alternate transmission route, ensuring that session continues, till the persons using it break it down. At this layer, the applications can use names to communicate with devices.

(F) Application Layer

The application layer protocols handle messages that are to be interchanged with other applications in nodes on the network. They specify such details as the sequence and format of the data-items. It is the layer where dialogue between the sender and receiver takes place after connection has been made. It comprises the various utilities used for various operations under networked conditions.

The Link Layer and the Physical Layer specify the hardware requirements. The topology used for networking and the speeds of data transfer are determined in these layers. The Network Layer, Transport Layer and the Session Layer, which are provided by network software, work in unison to form what is called the subnet level, which control the hardware. They establish and maintain the virtual connection, which is a temporary link between the source and destination. The point-to-point communication services are generally interfaced at the Session Layer, whereas, all application programs of network are interfaced at the Presentation Layer. The Application Layer is where all program execution takes place.

Error Detection And Prevention

Transmitted data—both analog and digital—are susceptible to many types of noise and errors. Copper-based media have traditionally been plagued with many types of interference and noise. Satellite, microwave and radio networks are also prone to interference and cross talk. Even near-perfect fibre-optic cables can introduce errors into a transmission system, though the probability of this happening is less than with the other types of media. Since there are so many forms of noise and errors and since one form of noise or another is virtually given, every data transmission system must include precautions to reduce noise and the possibility of errors. If you can reduce the possibility of noise before it happens, the transmitting station may not have to slow down its transmission stream. With proper error prevention techniques, many types of errors can be reduced. Despite the best attempts at prevention, errors still occur. If an error is detected, it is typical to perform some type of request for retransmission. Error detection techniques themselves can be relatively simple or relatively elaborate. Generally, simple techniques do not provide the same degree of error checking as more elaborate schemes. For example, the simplest error detection technique is simple parity. It adds a single bit to a character of data, but catches the fewest number of errors. At the other end of the spectrum is the most elaborate and most effective technique available today: cyclic redundancy checksum. Although it is more complex and typically adds 16 bits of error detection code to a block of data, it is the most effective error detection technique ever devised.

TYPES OF NETWORKS

The networks are classified in different ways depending upon the distance covered, hardware configuration or functionality.

Local Area Network (LAN)

A LAN or Local Area Network is normally confined to a building or a campus wherein all the computers within an organisation are connected using copper or fibre optic cables. Such networks have to operate within limits of that organisation. In an effective information system, it is necessary to ensure fast and flexible movement of data in an economical manner with low error-rate between independent computing units which are interconnected to form a network. The unique characteristic which identifies a LAN is that the transmitted signal, which is digital, comes within the category of baseband transmission, that is, the signal generated is transmitted in its original form without any alteration and at any moment of time, only one signal can flow in the network. The network service is controlled through time-sharing or time-division multiplexing. Local area networks have several advantages, including: hardware and software sharing, workstation survival during network failure, component and system evolution, heterogeneous mix of hardware and software, and access to other LANs, WANs, and mainframe computers. Disadvantages include complexity, maintenance costs and the network is only as strong as the weakest link. The majority of users expect a local area network to perform the primary function of sharing resources. This often includes the following applications: file serving, database and application serving, print serving, electronic mail, remote links, video transfers, process control and monitoring and distributed processing.

In a LAN system, a particular computer with higher capacity and speed is generally treated as a File Server where the files are stored and which manages the files, handles communication, allocates resources, controls operations, etc; — it has the network operating system installed in it. The other computing units are called Work Stations, with their own operating system of MS DOS or OS/2, where the processing is carried out. Incidentally, LAN forms peer-Level network, where all the computers in it can communicate with each other. This is unlike the terminals of the mainframe or minicomputer, which can only communicate with the host and not among them.

Wide Area Network (WAN)

A WAN or Wide Area Network is usually spread over a long distance and may cover many countries and continents. These networks have to make use of publicly owned communication channels like telephone or leased lines and have no monopoly over communication. WANs also require special hardware. WAN interconnects computers which are geographically far apart, and hence the medium used for the system is provided by the traditional Telecommunication Network built up for the telephone system. Such networks use broadband transmission, where a number of signals can be transmitted simultaneously; Modern telecommunication networks can carry different types of analog and digital signals for voice and data.

Under the WAN system, each computer has to have a modem for converting the digital signals to analog Waves and then integrating it with carrier waves for transmission — the ultimate connection is from computer to computer. The topology for WAN is described as mesh or tree configuration. The transmission takes place using different intermediate nodes along different links. With latest technological developments, the telephone network system is being changed to be fully digital under the protocol developed for Integrated Services Digital Network (ISDN).

The current trend in networking indicates increase in the bandwidth or the rate at which data can be transported over the network. The networks are being used for both audio and video communication as in case of Video conferencing. The bandwidth of local area network is sought to be increased by introduction of fast Ethernet cards capable of transmitting data at 1000 mbps. The developments in fibre optics technology are being directed to reduce the cost and make it available commercially. The high-speed digital communication lines capable of carrying data up to 64Kbps are being used. The capability of communication network is sought to be increased using ATM and Fibre Optic Technology. However, the developments in satellite technology indicate possible global connectivity using cellular telephones and microwave connectivity using laptop computers and cellular telephones. The IT is all set to make the geographical distances to irrelevance in near future.

Intranet and Internet

The latest trend in networking is development of corporate networks (Intranet) which have started changing the concept of work place itself from home to transborder offices. These networks are specific to the corporate which use them and are used for internal communication of that corporate by installing servers which talk to each other and update each other using public networks.

The Internet on the other hand provides network of networks in which different servers located all over the world are connected to each other. This network is widely used by corporate world over to publish information about themselves and their products. The network uses a special protocol called 'Hyper Text Transmission Protocol' or HTTP for connection and communication. The information published uses a Hyper Text Mark Up Language (HTML) which enables link between one part of the text stored on one server to other text stored on other server. The Internet has brought revolution in information distribution and also social communication by making it instantaneous and yet at very much reduced cost.

❑ ❑ ❑

18

Glossary Of Information Technology Terms

ACTIVE - X

ActiveX is a system for embedding controls and the underlying code into any OLE application, most commonly a web browser.

AGP (Accelerated Graphics Port)

A standard for three-dimensional graphics designed by Intel.

ANI (Automatic Number Identification)

A system similar to Caller-ID, used by the telephone exchange.

ANSI (American National Standards Institute)

It is a non-profit organisation operating in the public interest to coordinate U.S. standards.

API (Application Programming Interface)

A set of function calls allowing communication between programs.

ARCHIE

A system for searching FTP site listings.

ARCHIVE

A single large file from which many smaller files can be extracted.

ARPANET (Acronym for Advanced Research Project Administration NETwork)

It was a US defence project designed as a Wide Area Network capable of surviving a nuclear war. The Internet evolved from the ARPAnet.

ASYNCHRONOUS

A mode of data transfer in which the device cannot proceed to the next block of data until it has received positive acknowledgment that the other device received the block correctly.

AUTHENTICATION

Authentication is concerned with using a username/password pair. It refers to any system by which a system attempts to validate that a user is in fact who they claim to be

ACCESS CONTROL

The are the methods to prevent unauthorised usage of a system with the help of passwords, encryption keys etc.

ADSL (Asymmetric Digital Subscriber Line)

A technology for transmitting digital information at a high bandwidth on existing phone lines to homes and businesses.

ALGORITHM

Algorithm is a sequence of logical operations for solving a problem. The term is derived from the name of the mathematician, Mohammed ibn-Musa Al-Khowarizmi, the inventor of Algebra.

AMBER

A plug-in that allows Adobe Acrobat documents to be read within a World Wide Web browser window.

APPLE

Apple is an operating system like windows.

APPLET

A small Java program that can be embedded in an HTML page.

ASCII (American Standard Code for Information Interchange)

It is a system for encoding characters used in English, including numbers, punctuation and other symbols. ASCII is the most common format for text files in computers and on the Internet.

ASP (Application Service Provider)

An organisation that offers access over the Internet and related services to the individuals or enterprises.

ASYNCHRONOUS COMMUNICATION

In telecommunication, signalling within a network or between networks, an asynchronous signal is one that is transmitted at a different clock rate than another signal.

ASYMMETRIC COMMUNICATION

The term asymmetric or asymmetrical or non-symmetrical refers to any system in which the data speed or quantity differs in one direction as compared with the other direction, averaged over time.

BACKBONE

A backbone is a high-speed line or series of connections that forms a major pathway within a network. It is composed of fiber-optic cables or other high-speed transport media.

BANDWIDTH

Bandwidth describes a network capacity. It is measured in bits-per-second.

BASEBAND

Baseband refers to the transmission of signals at their original frequencies.

BOUNCE

When an e-mail does not reach to its recipient, it bounces back to the sender.

BAUD

The term baud refers to the number of times per second a carrier signal changes value. So, the word baud is used in the term 'baud rate', which describes how many bits per second a modem can send or receive.

BIOMETRICS

The security processes associated with personal identification and authentication performed by analysing the parts of the body or its movements. For example, Fingerprints, voice characteristics, dimensions of the hands etc.

BINHEX (BINary HEXadecimal)

A method for converting non-text files (non-ASCII) into ASCII. This is required because e-mail can only handle ASCII.

BIT (Binary Digit)

A bit is a single binary unit, the basis of digital computing. A bit has a value of 1 or 0. Digital communications speeds are usually measured in terms of bits per second.

BLUETOOTH

Bluetooth is a term used in telecommunications industry that describes how mobile phones, computers and personal digital assistants can easily interconnect with each other and with home and business phones and computers using a short-range wireless connection.

BPS (Bits Per Second)

It is a standard measurement of digital transmission speeds. A 56K modem can move about 57,000 bits per second.

BRIDGE

A combined hardware and software device which is used to interconnect LAN.

BROADBAND

One meaning of this term denotes to the provision of a very wide channel, which may have only one user, or may have multiple users with separate time-divided channels. The second is to multiband systems where a number of users may share the wide spectrum, with each having its own frequency band allocation.

BROWSER

A browser is any client software that is used for looking at World Wide Web resources.

BTW (By The Way)

The term is used to say, 'by the way' in an online forum.

BUFFER

An area of memory used for the temporary storage of information in transit between the computer and peripheral devices. Buffers are used to compensate for the different rates at which devices process data.

BYTE

Byte is a series of 8 bits that represent a single character. Disk space is represented in terms of bytes used.

CARRIER SIGNAL

Carrier signal is a signal of a single frequency that can be altered by a second signal that contains data.

CERN (European Center for Nuclear Research)

CERN developed Web protocols as a means for scientific researchers to exchange documents easily.

CGI (Common Gateway Interface)

A means for adding functionality to the World Wide Web through scripting.

CGI-BIN

The most common name of a directory on a web server in which CGI programs are stored.

CLIENT

A software program that is used to contact and obtain data from a Server software program on another computer.

CLIENT PULL

A tool for determining how long an HTML file stays in the client browser window before it is refreshed or replaced.

COMMERCE SERVICE PROVIDERS (CSP)

CSPs are business organisations or web sites that provide e-commerce solutions.

COMMUNICATION

Communication refers to the transfer of information from a sender to a receiver, for the purpose of increasing the receiver's knowledge, enabling him to carry out tasks, or influencing his attitudes and behaviour.

COMMUNICATIONS SOFTWARE

A program that tells a modem how to work.

COOKIE

Cookie on the Internet refers to a piece of information sent by a Web Server to a Web Browser that the Browser software is expected to save and to send back to the Server whenever the browser makes additional requests from the Server.

CPU (Central Processing Unit)

CPU is the brain of a computer. It is the device that processes most information in the computer. In micros, the CPU is the micro-processing chip; in mainframes it may be a number of discrete chips on a circuit card.

CRYPTOGRAPHY

Cryptography is the science of information security. The word is derived from the Greek word 'kryptos', meaning hidden. Cryptography includes techniques such as microdots, merging words with images, and other ways to hide information in storage or transit.

CYBERSPACE

The term was originated by William Gibson in his novel 'Neuromancer'. The term Cyberspace is used to describe the whole range of information resources available through computer networks.

CACHE

Cache memory on the motherboard is extra-fast RAM that keeps a copy of the most recently requested bits from regular RAM.

CD

Compact Disc is a standard for storing information on an optical media.

CID

Caller-ID is a system by which the calling-party number is transmitted to the called party.

CISC (Complex Instruction-Set Computer)

A CPU designed with a thorough set of assembly calls. The systems based on this philosophy have smaller binaries but generally slower execution of each individual instruction.

COMPRESS

To make a file smaller by applying a compression algorithm, usually for the purpose of conserving space or speeding up file transfers.

DAEMON

A harmless Unix program that normally works out of sight of the user.

DECRYPTION

Decoding of message or file, opposite of encryption.

DOCUMENT

A document is a representation of information (in some language, in some medium) that can be stored and retrieved.

DOMAIN NAME

Domain Name is the unique name for each Internet site.

DOWNLOAD

Copying a file from a host system to home computer.

DIAL-UP

A computer connection that is brought up and brought down as needed — a simple version is dialling in to a service provider over a modem as a dumb terminal — SLIP and PPP can also be dial-up connections — also known as a switched connection.

DIGITAL CERTIFICATE

Digital document that verifies a user's identity and prevent impersonations. Digital certificates are issued by a certificate authority.

DIGITAL MONEY

Digital money or Electronic Cash or E-cash terms are used interchangeably, and they refer to any of the various methods that allow a person to purchase goods or services by transmitting a number from one computer to another. The numbers are issued by a bank and represent sums of real money. Digital cash is anonymous and reusable. Unlike credit card transactions, the merchant does not know the identity of the shopper.

DIGITAL SIGNATURE

It is a cryptographic transformation of the message, which enables authenticating the origin and integrity of the message and protects it from fabrications.

DISINTERMEDIATION

Disintermediation is the process of bypassing retail channels or mail order houses and selling directly to the customer.

DRIVER

A driver is a program that lets hardware peripheral communicate with the computer.

DSL (Digital Subscriber Line)

DSL is a technology for bringing high-bandwidth information to homes and small businesses over telephone lines. A DSL line can carry both data and voice signals and the data part of the line is continuously connected.

DTP

Electronic desktop publishing using publishing/layout software.

DUMB TERMINAL

When a computer runs a terminal emulation program while connected to another computer.

DUPLEX COMMUNICATION

Duplex circuits can transmit and receive data simultaneously such as a phone line.

E-MAIL (Electronic Mail)

E-mail is a tool of electronic communication through which the text messages are sent from one computer to another. Non-text binary files can also be sent. E-mail can also be sent automatically to a large number of addresses.

ENCRYPTION

Encryption is the application of a special algorithm to the data so as to make it incomprehensible to those without the key. It is opposite of decryption.

ELECTRONIC CHEQUES

Customers pay for merchandise by writing an electronic check that is transmitted electronically by e-mail, fax or phone. The cheque is a message that contains all of the information that is found on an ordinary cheque, but it is signed digitally, or indorsed. The digital signature is encoded by encrypting with the customer's secret key. Upon receipt, the merchant or payee may further indorse by encoding with a private key. When the cheque is processed, the resulting message is encoded with the bank's secret key, thus providing proof of payment.

ELECTRONIC COMMERCE

Electronic Commerce or E-Com or Emmerce or EC terms are used interchangeably, and they all mean the same thing — the paperless exchange of routine business information using Electronic Data Interchange (EDI), e-mail, electronic bulletin boards, fax transmissions and Electronic Funds Transfer. It refers to Internet shopping, on-line stock and bond transactions, the downloading, and selling of merchandise and business-to-business transactions.

ELECTRONIC WALLET

Electronic Wallet provides the facility of storing credit card numbers on a hard drive in an encrypted form.

ETHERNET

Founded by Xerox in 1976, Ethernet is a media for LAN communication. Ethernet LANs are moderately fast, reliable and flexible.

EXTRANET

An extranet is an extension of a corporate intranet. It connects the internal network of one company with the intranets of its customers and suppliers. This makes it possible to create e-commerce applications that link all aspects of a business relationship, from ordering to payment.

FAQ (Frequently Asked Questions)

These are the text files that contains and answer the most common questions on a particular subject.

FDDI (Fiber Distributed Data Interface)

A fiber-optic cabling standard for LANs and WANs, FDDI carries up to 100 Megabits per second.

56K LINE

56K line is a leased line capable of transferring 56,000 bps.

FIBER OPTICS

The branch of optical technology that deals with the transmission of light or images across short or long distances, through transparent fibers.

FREQUENCY

The number of times a repeated event occurs during a given time period. Frequency is often measured in units of cycles per second.

FINGER

An Internet software tool for locating people on other Internet sites.

FIREWALL

Firewall is a technology used for protecting Internet-connected enterprise networks from break-ins by unauthorized outsiders.

FREEWARE

Software developed by individuals or small companies that costs nothing to use.

FTP (File Transfer Protocol)

FTP is the most common method for copying files over the Internet. FTP is a way to login to another Internet site for the purposes of retrieving and/or sending files.

GATEWAY

A gateway is a network point that acts as an entrance to another network.

GIF (Graphics Interchange Format)

A format for image files, used for images containing large areas of the same colour.

GIGABYTE

A Gigabyte is a billion bytes or a thousand megabytes. Even PCs now often have ten- or twenty-gigabyte hard drives. Some servers have mass storage measured in terabytes.

GOPHER

Gopher is an Internet-browsing client that was especially popular before the advent of the World Wide Web. It was invented at the University of Minnesota in 1993.

GUI (Graphical User Interface)

A graphical user interface provides its user a more or less graphical or picture-based way to interact with technology. A GUI is usually a more ergonomic satisfying or user-friendly interface to a computer system.

HARDWARE

Hardware is the physical aspect of computers and other IT devices. Hardware is a collective term. It includes all the physical components such as cables, connectors, power supply units, and peripheral devices such as the keyboard, mouse, audio speakers and printers.

HARD DISK/HARD DISK DRIVE

A hard disk is part of a computer, often called a disk drive or hard drive or hard disk drive, that stores and provides quick access to large amounts of data on an electro-magnetically charged surface.

HOMEPAGE

Homepage is the web page that the browser is set to use when it starts up.

HOST

Any computer on a network that is a repository for services available to other computers on the network.

HTML (Hypertext Markup Language)

The coding language used to create Hypertext documents for use on the World Wide Web. HTML files end in the file extension .html or .htm.

HTTP (Hypertext Transport Protocol)

HTTP is the protocol for moving hypertext files across the Internet.

HTTPD (Hypertext Transfer Protocol Daemon)

A computer program which manages the transfer of hyper-text and multimedia documents over the Internet.

HUB

A hub is a place of convergence where data arrives from one or more directions and is forwarded out in one or more other directions.

HYPERTEXT

Hypertext is any text that contains links to other documents.

ICONS

Icons are pictographic representations.

IMAP (Internet Message Access Protocol)

IMAP is the main protocol used by e-mail clients in communicating with e-mail servers.

IMMERCE

Immerce is the new term being used for commerce that is transacted totally over the Internet.

INSTRUCTIONAL DESIGN

It is the process by which information is systematically mapped, categorized, and organised to facilitate the transmission of information or skills to people.

INTERNET

The network of networks. It is a vast collection of inter-connected networks that are connected using the TCP/IP protocols and that evolved from the ARPANET of the late 1960s. It is the largest Wide Area Network in the world.

INTRANET

A private network inside a company or organisation that uses the same kinds of software that is used by the public Internet, but that is only for internal use.

IP (Internet Protocol)

A method or protocol by which data is sent from one computer to another on the Internet. Each computer (known as a host) on the Internet has at least one IP address that uniquely identifies it from all other computers on the Internet.

IP ADDRESS

The unique network address used by TCP/IP.

ISDN (Integrated Services Digital Network)

A technology for moving more data over existing regular phone lines. Data users generally enjoy a transfer rate of 56,000 bits per second, though it is possible to use both the data and voice channels for data and increase transfer rates. ISDN hardware is still a limiting factor for home users, due to its relatively high cost.

ISO (International Organisation for Standardization)

It is an organisation based in Geneva that publishes standards in industry and technology. It was founded in 1947 and it is a worldwide federation of national standards bodies from some 100 countries, one from each country.

ISP (Internet Service Provider)

A company that allows home and corporate users to connect to the Internet. Smaller ISPs buy bandwidth from larger ISPs.

JAVA

Java script is a programming language that is mostly used in web pages, usually to add features that make the web page more interactive. It was invented by Sun Microsystems.

JDK (Java Development Kit)

A software development package from Sun Microsystems that implements the basic set of tools needed to write, test and debug Java applications and applets.

JPEG (Joint Photographic Experts Group)

JPEG is a standard for photographic image compression.

JAVASCRIPT

An implementation of the Java programming language that allows non-programmers to build Java-based applications easily.

KERMIT

Kermit is a terminal program and file transfer protocol which can be used to download files from a remote system to your home computer.

KERNEL

The Kernel is the set of functions that make up the operating system, used to provide an application interface between programs and the underlying virtual and physical devices.

KILOBYTE

A thousand bytes, but specifically 1,024 bytes.

LASER

An acronym for Light Amplification by Stimulated Emission of Radiation. The light waves in a laser move in exactly the same way as each other and are all the same frequency. This results in a powerful beam of light that can produce intense heat when focused at close range.

LATTICE

The regular pattern of points in a crystal that atoms, molecules, or ions vibrate around in a crystal.

LAN (Local Area Network)

A computer network limited to the immediate area, usually the same building or floor of a building. LANs are linked together in larger networks as Wide Area Networks (WANs).

LEASED LINE

A special-purpose telephone line that is used exclusively for high-speed digital transmission. Leased lines are necessary for linking larger networks to the Internet.

LINUX

A freeware version of Unix, Linux is becoming popular as a powerful, low-cost operating system for operating servers.

LOGIN

To 'log in' is to gain access to a protected computer. It is the account name used to gain access to a computer system. It is not a secret like a Password.

LOG OFF

Disconnect from a host system.

LYNX

An early text-only World Wide Web browser.

MAILING LIST

A Mailing List or Maillist is an automated e-mail group mailing list. A mailing list is an automated system that allows people to send e-mail to one address and the message is copied and sent to all of the other subscribers to the maillist.

MASER (Microwave Amplification by Stimulated Emission of Radiation)

A device that can produce coherent electromagnetic radiation in the microwave frequency band. It is used in atomic clocks and to amplify weak radio signals. Masers which operate at optical frequencies are called lasers.

MEGABIT

A million bits. Transmission speed over local area networks (LANs) is often measured in terms of Megabits per second (Mbps).

MEGABYTE

A million bytes. A thousand (1,024, to be exact) kilobytes.

MERCHANT BROKERS

Merchant Brokers specialize in obtaining credit card accounts for on-line businesses. Brokers charge a setup fee and lease or sell the software and hardware as needed.

MIME (Multipurpose Internet Mail Extensions)

A standard for defining the types of files attached to standard Internet mail messages. The MIME standard is used in many situations where one computer program needs to communicate with another program about what kind of file is being sent.

MODEM (Modulator/demodulator)

A modem is a device that allows users to connect to other users over telephone lines. Since standard phone lines carry only analog signals, a modem is needed to convert between digital information and analog sound.

MODEM POOL

A group of modems provided by an ISP or a company. Dial-up connections are established through the modem pool.

MODULE

Individual unit of information or instruction. A module is a uniquely characterised self-contained representation of a conceptual information unit, which is aimed at communicating that information.

MOSAIC

Mosaic was developed at the National Center for Supercomputing Applications (NCSA), at the Univeristy of Urbana-Champange in Illinois, USA. Mosaic was the first graphical World Wide Web browser.

MPEG (Motion Pictures Experts Group)

A popular standard for digital video compression.

MULTIPLEXER

A unit or technology that allows several users or processors to share the same resource.

NIC (Network Information Center)

An office that assigns domain names on the Internet.

NODE

Any single computer connected to a network.

NT

Windows NT is the Microsoft Windows personal computer operating system designed for users and businesses needing advanced capability. It has two variants: Microsoft NT Workstation and Microsoft NT Server.

NETIQUETTE

A set of etiquettes for not annoying others on the Internet.

NETIZEN

A citizen of the Internet, or someone who uses networked resources.

NETSCAPE

A WWW Browser and the name of a company i.e. Netscape Navigator.

NETWORK

A collection of two or more computers connected together, sharing hardware or software, is a network.

NEWBIE

A person who is new to the Internet.

NEWSGROUP

The name for discussion groups on USENET.

NNTP (Network News Transport Protocol)

The protocol used by client and server software to carry USENET postings back and forth over a TCP/IP network.

OB (Out-Of-Band)

When information sent is outside of the normal communications stream.

OFFLINE

When a computer is not connected to a host system or the Internet, it is offline.

OLE (Object Linking and Embedding)

OLE is Microsoft's proprietary mechanism for allowing documents and applications to access data and sub-routines from within other applications.

ONLINE

When a computer is connected to the Internet.

ONLINE SERVICE

A closed, pay-to-use system for e-mail, chat groups, newsgroups, and the like.

OO (Object Oriented)

Any programming language or system which is based on the concept of grouping related routines and data structures together in objects.

OPEN SOURCE SOFTWARE

Open Source Software is software for which the underlying programming code is available to the users so that they may read it, modify it, and make new versions.

OPERATING SYSTEM

An operating system is the program that manages all the other programs in a computer. The other programs are called applications or application programs.

OPTICS

The science that deals with the properties and phenomena of both visible and invisible light and with vision.

OSCILLATOR

A device that generates a periodic variation of electric current of a particular frequency in an electronic circuit.

PACKET SWITCHING

The method used to move data around on the Internet. Data is broken up into packets before being transmitted over the Internet.

PASSWORD

A code used to gain access to a locked system.

PDF (Portable Document Format)

The file format used by Adobe Acrobat.

PHOTONS

The quantum of electromagnetic energy, a discrete particle having zero mass and no electric charge.

PERL

A UNIX-based scripting language that is often used on the World Wide Web.

PGP (Pretty Good Privacy)

An open data-encryption standard written by Phil Zimmermann.

PING

A program that can trace the route a message takes from one site to another site.

PKI (Public Key Infrastructure)

A method that enables users of the Internet to securely and privately exchange data and money through the use of a public and a private cryptographic key pair that is obtained and shared through a trusted authority.

PLATFORM COMPATIBILITY

The term is used to describe software that can be used on more than one kind of computer.

PLUG-IN

Usually a small piece of software that adds features to a larger piece of software.

POP (Post Office Protocol)

Post Office Protocol refers to a way that e-mail client software gets mail from a mail server.

PORT

A physical connection to a computer through which data flows.

PORTAL

It is a marketing term to describe a Web site that is intended to be the first place people see when using the Web.

POSTING

A message sent to a newsgroup.

PPP (Point to Point Protocol)

The most common protocol used to connect home computers to the Internet over regular phone lines.

PROTOCOL

In information technology, a protocol is the special set of rules that different end points, in a telecommunication connection, use when they communicate.

PROXY SERVER

A Proxy Server is a middle link between a Client and the actual Server that a Client is trying to use.

PSTN (Public Switched Telephone Network)

The regular traditional telephone system.

QI (Query Interface)

The QI is a database system that can be accessed to retrieve and edit entries in the server.

QUANTUM

Discrete unit of electromagnetic energy such as that produced by an electronic transition in an atom.

QUINE

A program that generates a copy of its own source text as it completes output. The term is derived from the logician Willard van Orman Quine.

QWERTY

The Standard English language keyboard layout.

ROUTER

A router is a device or software that determines the next network point to which a packet should be forwarded toward its destination.

RELOAD

It is a web browser term. It refreshes the current page being viewed.

SCREEN SHOT

An individual computer screen captured and printed or saved as a graphic to be inserted in user documentation (also called screen dump).

SDSL (Symmetric Digital Subscriber Line)

A version of DSL where the upload speeds and download speeds are the same.

SEARCH ENGINE

A special software/hardware implementation that allows users to search the Internet for information based on keywords and other search criteria.

SERIAL PORT

A data pathway that is usually used to connect modems and mice.

SECURITY CERTIFICATE

A chunk of information that is used by the SSL (Secure Socket Layer) protocol to establish a secure connection.

SERVER

A computer or a software that provides a specific kind of service to client software running on other computers.

SHAREWARE

Shareware is software that is freely available on the Internet. It is usually developed by a small company or an individual, that is distributed via the Internet, online services, and CD-ROMs, and which costs very little to use.

S-HTTP (Secure Hypertext Transmission Protocol)

A standard used for transferring secure documents over the World Wide Web.

SIMPLEX

Simplex communication means that communication can only flow in one direction and never flow back the other way.

SIMPLIFIED ENGLISH

An English with reduced vocabulary i.e. 800 plus words.

SLIP (Serial Line Internet Protocol)

A non-standard method of electronically connecting to the Internet via a modem and a regular dial-up telephone line.

SMART CARD

A smart card is a plastic card with an embedded microchip that can be loaded with data, used for telephone calling, electronic cash payments and other applications.

SMDS (Switched Multi-megabit Data Service)

A standard for very high-speed data transfer.

SMS (Short Message Service)

A service for sending messages of up to 160 characters to mobile phones.

SMTP (Simple Mail Transfer Protocol)

The predominant transport protocol for Internet e-mail. Many enterprise e-mail systems use other protocols that must be translated into SMTP by gateways when being sent over the Internet.

SNMP (Simple Network Management Protocol)

A set of standards for communication with devices connected to a TCP/IP network. Examples of these devices include routers, hubs and switches.

SPAM

The term Spam is used for distributing unwanted, unsolicited information to the Usenet newsgroups or mailing lists.

SPECTROSCOPY

The study of the characteristic frequencies of atoms or molecules by observing the radiation they emit or absorb.

SSL (Secure Socket Layer)

A protocol designed by Netscape Communications to enable encrypted and authenticated communications across the Internet.

START PAGE

The first screen a user sees when he or she starts the Internet browser.

SQL (Structured Query Language)

A specialized language for sending queries to databases.

SWITCH

A switch is a network device that selects a path or circuit for sending a unit of data to its next destination.

SYMMETRIC COMMUNICATION

The term symmetric or symmetrical refers to any system in which data speed or quantity is the same in both directions, averaged over time.

SYNCHRONOUS COMMUNICATION

Signalling within a network or between networks, synchronous signals are those that occur at the same clock rate and all clocks are based on a single reference clock.

SYSOP (System Operator)

Individual responsible for the physical operations of a computer system or network resource.

T-1

A leased-line data connection with a maximum capacity of 1,544,000 bits-per-second.

TCP/IP (Transmission Control Protocol/Internet Protocol)

The suite of protocols under which all the computers on the Internet communicate with each other. It can also be used as a communications protocol in a private network (either an intranet or an extranet).

TECHNOLOGY

The sum total of knowledge of ways of doing things, it includes inventions, techniques and the vast store of organised knowledge of how to do things.

TELE-CONFERENCING

A telephone conversation or video-conference between two or more Internet-connected workstations.

TELEPHONE BILLING SYSTEMS

A very new approach, telephone transactions allow the customer to purchase an item or service and the amount will be billed to his or her telephone bill.

TELNET

A program that connects the user to other computers on the Internet.

TERABYTE

A trillion bytes or 1000 gigabytes.

TERMINAL

A device that allows a computer to send commands to a computer somewhere else.

TERMINAL SERVER

A piece of hardware that allows dial-up connections to enter a network.

TEXT SWELL

The increase in word count from one language to another language in the written communication of a specific idea/concept.

THALLIUM

A soft, malleable, rare, bluish-white metallic element; used in the manufacture of alloys and in the form of its salts, in rodent and ant poison.

TOPOLOGY

The topology describes pictorially the configuration or conceptual arrangement of a network, including its nodes and connecting lines.

TRANSPARENT

The term describes the transmission of data to be smooth and problem-free.

TRANSISTOR

A semiconductor device that amplifies, oscillates, or switches the flow of current between two terminals by varying the current or voltage between one of the terminals and a third.

T-3

A leased-line data connection with a maximum capacity of 44,736,000 per second. This connection is extremely expensive to maintain and is used for only very big installations.

UNIX

Unix is an operating system that originated at Bell Labs in 1969 as an interactive time-sharing system. Unix is designed to be used by many people at the same time (it is multi-user) and has TCP/IP built-in. It is the most common operating system for servers on the Internet. The Unix environment and the client/server program model were important elements in the development of the Internet and the reshaping of computing as centred in networks rather than in individual computers. Unix has evolved as a kind of large freeware product, with many extensions and new ideas provided in a variety of versions of Unix by different companies, universities and individuals.

UPLOAD

Copy a file from your computer to a host system.

USB (Universal Serial Bus)

It is an interface between a computer and add-on devices (such as audio players, joysticks, keyboards, telephones, scanners and printers).

USL (Uniform Resource Locator)

The address of any document or other resource on the Internet.

USENET

A worldwide network of discussion groups.

UUCP (Unix-to-Unix Copy Protocol)

An old protocol for sending e-mail between different Unix machines via regularly scheduled modem and network connections.

UUENCODE (Unix to Unix Encoding)

A method for encoding binary information into ASCII data or text so that they can be sent across the Internet.

UDP (User Datagram Protocol)

One of the protocols of TCP/IP family used for data transfer.

VAR (Value Added Reseller)

Reseller who offers equipment or system as a part of their own services.

VoIP (Voice over Internet Protocol)

The system of transferring voice data in digital form in discrete packets rather than in the traditional circuit-committed protocols of the public switched telephone network (PSTN).

VPN (Virtual Private Network)

It refers to a network in which some of the parts are connected using the public Internet, but the data sent across the Internet is encrypted, so the entire network is 'virtually' private. A VPN is a private network that makes use of the public telecommunication infrastructure, maintaining privacy through the use of a tunnelling protocol and security procedures. Using a virtual private network involves encrypting data before sending it through the public network and decrypting it at the receiving end.

VERONICA (Very Easy Rodent Oriented Net-wide Index to Computerized Archives)

Developed at the University of Nevada, Veronica was a constantly updated database of the names of almost every menu item on thousands of Gopher servers. It has now become obsolete by web-based search engines.

VRML (Virtual Reality Modeling Language)

A standard for platform-free three-dimensional (3D) description. _It is primarily used for web sites.

V. 90

The new 56k analog modem standard as defined by the Veronica.

VIRTUAL

Virtual items have no direct corresponding physical equivalent, for example most computers have one or more physical hard drives, on which can be defined a number of virtual storage areas called partitions.

VAN-JACOBSON COMPRESSION

A form of IP header compression used for SLIP connections.

VLSM (Variable Length Subnet Masks)

VLSM are a mechanism for providing subnets of different sizes within a single IP block.

WAN (Wide Area Network)

A Wide Area Network is a network connecting several physically distant locations, as opposed to a LAN. A wide area network may be privately owned or rented, but the term usually connotes the inclusion of public (shared user) networks. An intermediate form of network in terms of geography is a metropolitan area network (MAN). The Internet is an example of a worldwide WAN.

WAIS (Wide Area Information Server)

It is a software that builds searchable databases from various types of Internet resources.

WAP (Wireless Application Protocol)

A specification for a set of communication protocol to standardize the way that wireless devices, such as cellular telephones and radio transceivers can be used for Internet access.

WCDMA (Wideband Code-Division Multiple Access)

It is a third-generation mobile wireless technology offering much higher data speeds to mobile and portable wireless devices than commonly offered in today's market.

WINDOWS, 16-BIT (3.1)

The predominant desktop operating environment. Quickly replaced by the next generation of Windows, NT and 95, 98, these are called '16-bit' because the software communicated to the processor in 16-bit words.

WINDOWS, 32-BIT (NT, 95, 98)

The most popular operating systems from Microsoft. NT is predominantly used for servers, while 95, 98 are mainly for workstations.

WINSOCK

A protocol for implementing TCP/IP on Windows computers.

WIRELESS NETWORK

A method using infrared, ultra-violet or radio waves of connecting computers into a network.

WWW (World Wide Web)

Frequently used when referring to 'The Internet', the term WWW refers to the collection of resources across the Internet that is accessed using World Wide Web browsers. It was invented by Dr. Tim Berners-Lee, at the European Center for Nuclear Research (CERN), who wrote the first hyper text transfer protocol daemon (HTTPD) and the first hyper text markup language (HTML) browser, as a way to allow nuclear physicists to exchange working papers over the computer networks.

XML (Extensible Markup Language)

A widely used system for defining data formats.

X-MODEM

A file transfer protocol used for transferring binary files. Slower than Z-modem.

X-WINDOWS

A network-based GUI designed for Unix systems.

YELLOW BOOK

The international standard defining the physical properties of a CD-ROM disk.

Y-MODEM

A file transfer protocol based on X-Modem, to add batch transmission and variable block size.

Z-MODEM

The default protocol commonly used with windows when sending binary files.

❏❏❏